Schools a

Persistent Abs

Other Pergamon titles of interest

Troubled Children: Troubled Systems
S. J. APTER

Learning and Language in the Classroom
P. CHILVER & G. GOULD

Disadvantaged Eleven Year Olds
T. COX & M. JONES

Unwillingly to School, 3rd edition
J. H. KAHN *et al.*

The Early Window, 2nd edition
R. M. LIEBERT *et al.*

Schools and Persistent Absentees

By

DAVID GALLOWAY

PERGAMON PRESS

OXFORD · NEW YORK · TORONTO · SYDNEY · PARIS · FRANKFURT

U.K.	Pergamon Press Ltd., Headington Hill Hall, Oxford OX3 0BW, England
U.S.A.	Pergamon Press Inc., Maxwell House, Fairview Park, Elmsford, New York 10523, U.S.A.
CANADA	Pergamon Press Canada Ltd., Suite 104, 150 Consumers Rd., Willowdale, Ontario M2J 1P9, Canada
AUSTRALIA	Pergamon Press (Aust.) Pty. Ltd., P.O. Box 544, Potts Point, N.S.W. 2011, Australia
FRANCE	Pergamon Press SARL, 24 rue des Ecoles, 75240 Paris, Cedex 05, France
FEDERAL REPUBLIC OF GERMANY	Pergamon Press GmbH, Hammerweg 6, D-6242 Kronberg-Taunus, Federal Republic of Germany

First edition 1985

Library of Congress Cataloging in Publication Data

Galloway, David.
Schools and persistent absentees.
Bibliography: p.
1. School attendance—England—Sheffield (South Yorkshire). 2. Problem children—Education—England—Sheffield (Yorkshire). 3. Juvenile delinquency—England—Sheffield (Yorkshire). 4. Educational surveys—England—Sheffield (Yorkshire). 5. School attendance—Law and legislation—England—Sheffield (Yorkshire) I. Title.
LC145.G7G34   1985   371.93   84–14913

British Library Cataloguing in Publication Data
Galloway, David
Schools and persistent absentees.
1. School attendance—Great Britain
I. Title
371.2′95′0941   BL3081

ISBN 0–08–030834–1 Hard cover
ISBN 0–08–030833–3 Flexicover

Printed in Great Britain by A. Wheaton & Co. Ltd., Exeter

Preface

The origins of this book lie in a working party established ten years ago in Sheffield Education Department to consider the adequacy of existing provision for problem children. The working party consisted of teachers, senior officers of the l.e.a., educational psychologists and educational welfare officers. As a psychologist I was concerned about two groups of children who were being referred to me and my colleagues in considerable numbers. One group consisted of disruptive pupils who had been, or were in danger of being, suspended from school. Subsequent work with this group is described elsewhere (Galloway *et al.*, 1982). The second group consisted of absentees from school.

It quickly became clear that many people, both inside and outside the working party, had strong views about unauthorised absence from school. It was equally clear that they disagreed: (i) on the size of the problem (ii) on its causes, and (iii) on the most effective responses from schools and from the l.e.a.'s support service. These differences in opinion paved the way for a city-wide survey of all pupils who had missed over half of their school education in the first half of the Autumn term.

This pilot project attracted the interest of H.M.I., and led to the survey being repeated in the following three years. In addition we began a study of persistent poor attenders and their families. This study was completed in 1978–1979 with the help of a grant from the Department of Education and Science. The grant also enabled us to extend our work into schools, and to carry out a series of studies on the usefulness, or rather the lack of usefulness, of legal action in connection with school attendance.

The research in Sheffield is referred to throughout the book, along with a large number of other studies on school attendance. The organisation of chapters into fairly discrete topics is, I hope, logical. It does, however, have the possible disadvantage of referring in several different places to the same group of studies. I have therefore included as an appendix a summary prepared for the D.E.S. on completion of the research programme. I should add that since this summary was written, more detailed analyses have been carried out on some of the results. With hindsight, moreover, my views on some of the implications of the research have changed, or developed, in the last three years. I hope, nevertheless, that this summary illustrates the overall structure of the research and of the principal conclusions.

The pedigree of the research probably makes clear that the principle of free and compulsory education was not considered problematic. I accept unreservedly that education is replete with examples of innovations which have further disadvantaged the very groups they were ostensibly designed to help. I also accept that many schools cater inadequately for a substantial minority of their pupils. I do not, however, accept that there is anything inherent in a system of free and compulsory education which makes schools unable to arouse interest and enthusiasm in this minority.

Accepting the principle of compulsory school attendance implies no preconceived beliefs about the reasons for absenteeism. It soon became clear that the problem was greatest in the last two years of compulsory education. It also became clear that many absentees came from multiply disadvantaged families. It is as naïve to conclude that schools are to blame for the increase in absenteeism amongst fourteen- to sixteen-year-olds as to conclude that family background is to blame at any age. Parental attitudes and family background have obvious possible relevance to school attendance. If parents consider regular attendance unimportant, we should not be too astonished if pupils stay away. Just as obviously, experiences at school have a potential influence on attendance. Bored and/or disaffected pupils have little incentive to attend regularly. Studying school attendance without investigating family *and* school background is inevitably one-sided and misleading.

Unfortunately, l.e.a. responses tend to focus on the family background rather than on the school's own influence over its pupils' attendance. As I show in Chapters 6 and 7, neither "clinical" treatment from psychologists and psychiatrists nor legal action have more than a peripheral value in improving overall attendance levels. This does not imply that treatment is unnecessary. For some children it is necessary and beneficial. Treatment, however, has a good prognosis for no more than a tiny minority of all absentees. Legal action is generally ineffective, and in any case is a time consuming, expensive process which can only be used in rare cases.

The most important point, though, is that problems at school need to be tackled at school. In asking educational welfare officers, psychologists or the courts to tackle their problems for them teachers are missing solutions which are both potentially more effective and closer to hand. If this book helps teachers become more sympathetic towards the pupils who reject what they have to offer by staying away I shall be fairly satisfied. If it promotes constructive critical discussion of teaching and pastoral practices which encourage, or inhibit, regular atttendance, I shall be delighted.

David Galloway
February, 1984

Acknowledgements

The research on school attendance in Sheffield l.e.a. described in this book was carried out with the help of a grant to the University of Sheffield from the Department of Education and Science. The encouragement and support of the Department's officers and inspectors is gratefully acknowledged. Without the active encouragement of Mr. Michael Harrison, Chief Education Officer, and Mr. John Mann, former Deputy Education Officer, the research could not have taken place. I am also grateful to many other officers in Sheffield l.e.a., particularly Dr. W. R. Kneen, Second Deputy (Schools), Mr. Brian Wilcox, Chief Adviser, Mr. R. W. Patton, M.B.E., former Chief Educational Welfare Officer, and Mr. H. Torry, former Acting Chief Educational Welfare Officer. The research had its origins in work of the l.e.a.'s Psychological Service under the guidance of Mr. David Loxley, Principal Psychologist, who, with his colleagues supported the project in all its stages. I am grateful to the City Treasurer's Department, and in particular to Mr. Graham Dawson of the Computer Software Section for computer programming. Without the ability and energy of two research officers, Tina Ball and Rosalind Seyd, the research would inevitably have covered less ground. Professor John Roach of the Division of Education, University of Sheffield, gave invaluable help as Chairman of the advisory committee. I also acknowledge helpful advice on statistical analysis from Professor R. Loynes. Dr. Richard Lansdown, Top Grade Psychologist in the Hospital for Sick Children, Great Ormond Street, London, and Dr. Peter Ashworth, Principal Lecturer, Sheffield City Polytechnic also provided helpful guidance throughout the project. I am grateful to Dr. John Pratt, research officer in the School Attendance and Legal Action Research Project at Sheffield, for making available pre-publication copies of two of his papers. Mrs. Helen James showed great patience and skill in deciphering and typing the manuscript. Finally, I am grateful to the necessarily anonymous schools, teachers, pupils and parents whose cooperation made the research possible.

Disclaimers

The views expressed in this book should not necessarily be taken as those of the Sheffield l.e.a., the Department of Education and Science or the University of Sheffield. In quoting from interviews and observations in schools all names, nicknames and other identifying characteristics have been altered. The intention is to report as accurately as possible what was said, while preserving the anonymity of informants and of schools.

Contents

1 INTRODUCTION   1
Historical background. Reasons for concern. Legal responsibilities.
Summary and conclusions.

2 UNAUTHORISED ABSENCE   9
How many absentees are unauthorised? Age, social class and
geographical area. Patterns of absence. Persistent absence. The
Sheffield Studies. Summary and Conclusions.

3 SEMI-DESCRIPTIVE CATEGORIES   20
Introduction. Definition of terms. Truancy. School refusal. Other
categories of absence. How many children in each category?
Comments on usefulness of the categories. Conclusions: Social and
psychological objections

4 SCHOOL AND COMMUNITY INFLUENCES   38
Introduction. Community influences. Sociological perspectives.
The school's influence on attendance. School attendance,
delinquency and disruptive behaviour. Conclusions.

5 PERSISTENT ABSENTEES AND THEIR FAMILIES   54
Questions arising from earlier studies. Planning the study.
Interviews with parents. Interviews with children. Subsequent
absence. The meaning of poor attendance for the pupils and their
families. Comment.

6 PARTIAL SOLUTIONS? I. CLINICAL
TREATMENTS   76
Introduction. Treatment of school refusal. Truancy and other
reasons for absence. Community based approaches to
management. Treatment needs: truants and other absentees.
Comment.

7 PARTIAL SOLUTIONS? II. ADMINISTRATIVE
   AND LEGAL SANCTIONS   95
   Introduction. Preliminary, ostensibly preventive action: a growth
   area. Investigation by committee: local councillors. Prosecution in
   the magistrates' court. Care proceedings in the juvenile court.
   How does the l.e.a. decide who to prosecute? Subsequent
   attendance. The Leeds juvenile court procedures. Conclusions.

8 USING RESOURCES: ANALYSING
   AND PLANNING   122
   Overview. Towards a critique of existing services. The level of
   analysis. Wider pressures. Conclusions: Multi-faceted nature of
   persistent absence.

9 WIDER IMPLICATIONS FOR TEACHERS   139
   Introduction. The aims of schooling. The curriculum. Special
   educational needs. Pastoral care. Overview.

10 CONCLUSION: BACK TO THE SCHOOL?   157
    Introduction. Support services. Legal action. The half way house
    fallacy. A coordinated approach based on the school. Concluding
    comments.

Bibliography   168

Appendix. Summary of Completed Research Programme   176

Index   191

CHAPTER 1

Introduction

HISTORICAL BACKGROUND

Free and compulsory education came to England and Wales following the Elementary Education Acts of 1870 and 1876, though not always on a full-time basis. The Education Act of 1918 finally abolished half-time schooling, and made elementary education entirely free and compulsory until the end of the term after the child's fourteenth birthday. Nevertheless, in most parts of the country the problem of illegal absence dates from 1876.

Poor attendance was a problem to teachers and parents well before school attendance became compulsory (Pallister, 1969). Urban schools in the 1850s suffered from an extremely high turn-over of pupils, many staying less than four months. Teachers today in schools serving socially disadvantaged areas with a rapidly shifting population, would have a sense of *déjà vu*. Rural schools in the 1850s had lower turn-over, but even worse attendance. Many reasons were given for poor attendance, but by far the most common was the parents' low opinion of what education had to offer. Except at a very few schools, children had no wish to attend, and were often kept at home for trifling reasons. More than a hundred years before Reynolds and Murgatroyd (1977) rediscovered the influence of a school's rules, policies and general climate on its pupils' attendance, Pallister notes that: "enthusiasm for education varied with the standards of the schools, good schools quickly obtaining the support of parents, and similarly bad schools, at least in the eyes of parents, quickly losing support".

Making education compulsory reduced the problem, but did not solve it. Attendance at London Board schools improved from 66 per cent of pupils on roll in 1872 to 89 per cent in 1906 (Rubenstein, 1969). There has been no subsequent improvement. Hill (1971) reported an average attendance rate of 89 per cent at Inner London Education Authority schools in 1970.

A similar pattern was evident in Sheffield (Sheffield Education Committee, 1907; 1938). Table 1.1 shows the percentage attendance up to 1900 at elementary schools, and at primary and special schools combined up to 1938.

1

Table 1.1 *Attendance rates at elementary schools in Sheffield from 1873–1900, and at primary and special schools from 1904–1938*

Year	Average number on register	Percentage average attendance
1873	35,053	65
1880	50,319	68.5
1890	57,625	80
1900	66,957	82.5
1904	76,375	87.4
1910	76,162	88.2
1920	86,196	85.8
1930	77,584	90.1
1938	62,955	89.6

It is clear that attendance rates varied little between 1904 and 1938, except in 1920 when lower average attendance followed the social upheaval of the First World War. To summarise, there is little evidence that attendance rates over the last ten to fifteen years differ very much from those earlier in the century.

The evidence could be seen either as encouraging or depressing depending on one's point of view. Two extra years have been added to the period of compulsory education. Absence rates in these years are higher than in any other age-group. Yet overall attendance rates have not deteriorated. On the other hand, the improved standards of child health since the early part of the century do not seem to be reflected in the results of attendance surveys.

A further problem in interpreting the evidence, is that it comes from attendance registers. These are not always accurate, and cannot account for the "hidden truancy" which occurs when pupils miss lessons after registering. Further, attendance registers necessarily record the pupils *present*. The absentees will include pupils who have legitimate reason for being away. Numerous attempts have been made in the last thirty years to assess the prevalence of unauthorised absence, frequently with conflicting results. These are discussed in Chapter 2. We have no way of knowing whether a higher proportion of today's absentees are absent without a good reason than was the case at the beginning of the century.

REASONS FOR CONCERN

Poor school attendance arouses strong feelings in teachers, parents, members of the educational support services, educational administrators, politicians and—not least—pupils. These strong feelings are expressed in different, and often contradictory ways, depending on the individual's own perspective.

Conflicting Explanations

Psychiatrists and many psychologists regard poor attendance as a symptom of disturbance in the child or in the family. The disturbance may result from temperamental vulnerability, or from disturbed family relationships. The assumption is that the child and/or the family should be offered treatment. Whether treatment aims to secure an early return to school, or sees return to school as secondary to resolution of underlying conflicts, will depend on the therapist's own bias. The point is simply that many poor attenders are thought to need professional assessment and treatment.

On the other hand, absenteeism may be regarded from a sociological perspective. Here the emphasis is not on the individual child or family, but rather on the individual's reaction to pressures in society or at school. Thus Gutfreund (1975) considers the alienation of some pupils from the competitive ethos of schools to be a cause of truancy. At a more concrete level, work described in Chapter 4 has started to identify some of the social and administrative characteristics within secondary schools which seem to be associated with high or low attendance rates.

It follows from this overview that some people may see poor attendance as a legitimate, even healthy response to an impersonal or inappropriate education system. Others may see it as a symptom of psychiatric disturbance in the child, or the family. Others still, see it as an indication of neglect on the part of parents, or anti-social behaviour on the part of absent pupils. Probably the most prevalent view among teachers is that, while a minority of absentees may require psychiatric treatment, the majority reflect an indifferent or irresponsible attitude towards education on the part of parents, child or both. In such cases, teachers and administrators are likely to consider legal action. It is probably not unfair to say that these conflicting perceptions of poor attendance owe less to a comprehensive analysis of the evidence than to the background and priorities of the professional people concerned. We shall return to this question in later chapters, and re-examine each view in the light of the evidence.

The Economics of Poor Attendance

It would be impossible to place an accurate figure on the cost of poor school attendance in cash terms. In 1979 the average annual cost per pupil of secondary education, was calculated at £715. In the case of poor attenders, this money is hardly being used effectively. Moreover, sporadic attendance of some pupils may have a harmful effect on the majority who attend regularly. This can happen if the teacher has to spend time helping the absentees catch up on the work they have missed.

Checking on the legitimacy of absence notes can be a time-consuming responsibility for class teachers. Investigating more prolonged cases and liaising with the various educational and social work support services, is an even more time consuming one for teachers with "middle management" responsibilities such as year tutors. Typing lists of absentees and sending letters of inquiry to parents who have not already explained their child's absence to staff, is a tedious chore for busy office staff. This time and energy cannot easily be measured, but it must detract from other educational activities.

The support and treatment services are becoming increasingly expensive. Almost every l.e.a. has an educational welfare service (often known as the educational social work service). The development of this service and the current activities of educational welfare officers, are discussed in Chapter 6. The relevant point at this stage is that their principal responsibility has always been to investigate and act on cases of poor school attendance. The salary paid to e.w.o.s varies between l.e.a.s, but there is an increasing trend for them to be paid on the national scale for social workers. Moreover, the Certificate of Qualification in Social Work is a recognised qualification in both professions.

Members of three other professions spend a substantial amount of time working with poor attenders. Both educational psychologists and child psychiatrists are frequently asked to provide a diagnostic and treatment service. Social workers in local authority social services departments often have to prepare a report on family circumstances before school attendance may be used as evidence in juvenile court proceedings. At the hearing, Magistrates can make a "care order", requiring an expensive residential place, or a "supervision order" requiring a social worker to provide long-term supervision. The possible legal procedures are dealt with in Chapter 7. The point to bear in mind here, is that the cost to society of investigating and acting on cases of poor attendance is not confined to the cost of the educational welfare service.

Effects on Educational Progress

It is often assumed that pupils who are persistently absent from school become educationally retarded because of their absence. An alternative explanation is that some pupils may absent themselves because of their educational retardation. Several studies report truants as being less successful in tests of attainment and general intelligence than regular attenders (Tyerman, 1958; May, 1975; Carroll, 1977a). May's study provides slight support for the view that truants were performing badly before they started truanting, though the evidence was inconclusive, and it does not follow that their absence was caused by educational retardation. Carroll supports May's view, on the grounds that poor attenders were significantly more likely to be in a low stream than good attenders.

Longitudinal studies have helped to answer this "chicken and egg" question. Douglas and Ross (1965) compared composite scores on intelligence, reading, vocabulary and maths tests, with attendance in the previous four years. In general, they found a positive relationship between average scores and attendance, but this did not hold for a group of upper middle class children. Children in this group with an average of eight week's absence per year, did not have lower test scores than those obtained by the best attenders. As part of the National Child Development Study, Fogelman and Richardson (1974) recorded the attendance of eleven-year-olds born in one week of March 1958. They also found a significant association between attendance and attainment. When they took social class into account, however, the relationship only reached significance for children whose fathers were in manual occupations.

These results suggest that children in more affluent homes have experiences *at home* which assist their progress at school. The home life of working-class children does not appear, on this evidence, to be as effective in compensating for poor school attendance. Another possibility, though, is that middle-class children are under more pressure from home to "catch up" on return to school.

More recently Fogelman (1978) extended analysis of the National Child Development Study to the age of sixteen. He found that poor attenders at age seven were not educationally retarded at sixteen compared with their peers, *provided* they had been attending regularly at fifteen. On the other hand, continued poor attendance at fifteen *was* related to poor educational attainments. This tends to suggest: (i) that children who miss a considerable amount of schooling at an early age can catch up through subsequent regular attendance, and hence (ii) that the poor attainments of the pupils who continued to attend badly were causally related to their absence.

Teachers and parents may feel encouraged by the evidence that poor attenders are likely to recover lost ground, provided they attend more regularly in the future. Yet teachers may also have reservations about spending time with a backward reader who has not been attending school regularly. However much they may sympathise with the child concerned, they may feel greater sympathy for the child with learning difficulties who has always attended regularly. They may also feel pessimistic, with some justification, about the chances of regular attendance in the future.

LEGAL RESPONSIBILITIES

Poor school attendance is a problem to society, to teachers and to parents. What are the legal obligations on parents, teachers and the l.e.a.?

The 1944 Education Act

The legal requirements regarding school attendance are laid down in the 1944 Education Act and subsequent amendments. Parents are required by Section 36 to ensure that their children receive education "suitable to their age, ability and aptitude" between the ages of five and sixteen. In practice, most parents do this by registering their child at a school maintained or aided by the l.e.a. The l.e.a.'s obligation is simply to provide schools at which children may be registered. In the case of a handicapped child, the l.e.a. may not have a suitable school. The chief education officer must then seek a place at a school in another l.e.a., or at an independent school.

Once a child is registered at a school, it is his parents who have a responsibility under Section 39 of the Act to ensure regular attendance. This remains the case even if the "child" happens to be a sixteen-year-old married daughter who has not yet reached the legal school leaving age. It also remains the case if a parent delivers the child to school, but the child leaves by another door as soon as the parent's back is turned. The Act acknowledges three principal reasons for absence: (i) "sickness or any unavoidable cause", (ii) "religious observance", and (iii) "the l.e.a.'s failure to provide suitable travel arrangements if the child lives more than three miles from school".

The l.e.a. is empowered under Section 40 to prosecute parents who fail to meet their responsibilities. The child may not, strictly speaking, be prosecuted in the Juvenile Court for non-attendance. Under Section 1 of the 1969 Children and Young Person's Act, however, non-attendance is one of the grounds for "care proceedings", although the magistrates must also satisfy themselves that the child is in need of care and control before making an order. The l.e.a. may bring him before the Juvenile Court for care proceedings on its own initiative, but it may also be instructed to do so by the magistrates when a parent is charged under Section 40.

Areas of Uncertainty

Although the legal position is clear in theory, it is far from clear in practice. Some doctors refuse, as a matter of principle, to issue certificates saying a child is medically unfit to attend school. Their reasons appear to be a combination of reluctance to involve themselves in a possible conflict between parents and the l.e.a., and lack of time to spend distinguishing genuine illness from possible malingering. Without clear medical direction, the point at which a child becomes fit to return to school after illness is a matter for some debate. In the infrequent cases where there is disagreement, an officer of the l.e.a. must satisfy himself that the general practitioner has no objection on medical grounds, to the child's return to school.

Another grey area is exclusion or suspension from school. Section 54 of the 1944 Education Act empowers a medical officer of the local authority to exclude a child "infested with vermin or in a foul condition". Barker (1944) notes that the proviso about "sickness or any other unavoidable cause" in Section 39 "seems to open a door rather wide". A child expelled from school would presumably be regarded as absent with leave until his name was removed from the school register. Technically, it could then become the parent's responsibility to register him at another school, though in practice the l.e.a. would have to accept that responsibility.

The situation is not, however, quite so simple. A child excluded from school for refusal to accept some aspect of the school's rules or regulations, is not legitimately absent, unless the school has indicated a refusal to allow him to return. The point is, that teachers are *in loco parentis*; hence, they are empowered, like parents, to make reasonable regulations for the safety and discipline of their pupils.

A pupil who fails to accept these regulations is considered to be acting unreasonably, and his parents may be prosecuted under Section 40 for not ensuring his continued education. This became clear when a parent was successfully prosecuted for not causing his child to attend school, even though the child had been excluded for not wearing the correct uniform (Spiers vs. Warrington Corporation, 1954).

SUMMARY AND CONCLUSIONS

Irregular school attendance was a problem before education became free and compulsory, and it has continued to be one since. Although the figures can be interpreted in different ways, there is little evidence that school attendance rates have changed noticeably throughout the twentieth century. Many sociologists see failure to attend school as an expression of resentment by pupils at what they consider to be the school system's failure to meet their needs. Many psychiatrists see it as a symptom of personality problems or family stress. Most teachers accept that some poor attenders require treatment, but regard the majority as irresponsible in their failure to accept what the school is offering.

Whichever view one takes, it is clear that investigating poor school attendance requires an enormous amount of professional time. It is thus expensive in cash terms. In addition, the evidence suggests, not surprisingly, that long-term absence contributes to educational retardation. This creates problems for the children and adolescents concerned, which may not be solved by reaching school leaving age. It also presents obvious problems for teachers, who cannot easily adapt their lessons to cater for pupils who attend irregularly.

Responsibility for school attendance rests firmly with the parents. The l.e.a. may have some difficulty in proving in Court that a child has been illegally absent. The main area of doubt is whether the child has been ill. Although average attendance rates are not seriously disputed, we must remember that these are based simply on attendance registers. Many of the absentees may be absent legitimately. The important question is, how many?

CHAPTER 2

Unauthorised Absence

HOW MANY ABSENTEES ARE UNAUTHORISED?

Illness

Although attendance registers have consistently yielded overall attendance rates around 90 per cent, Table 2.1 shows surprisingly little agreement on how many of the absent children are ill. Bransby (1951) reported that 3.3 per cent of non-attendance was due to non-medical reasons. Similarly the Plowden Report (D.E.S. 1967) attributed 4 per cent of all absences to non-medical reasons. In contrast, the National Association of Chief Education Welfare Officers (1974) thought that 60 per cent of absence was due to non-medical causes, and hence, by implication, unjustified. This is broadly consistent with Harbison and Caven's (1977) Northern Ireland study where 46.5 per cent of pupils who had missed over 25 per cent of possible attendances were thought by education welfare officers to have been physically ill. These figures for illness, however, are high compared with those of Reynolds and Murgatroyd (1974) who considered 75 per cent of absences to be *unjustified*.

Thus the estimates for non-medical reasons for absence range from 3.3 per cent to 75 per cent. This variation does not seem to be attributable to different definitions of truancy, though not all studies have followed the same practice in including other legitimate reasons for absence, for example holidays, in the "non-medical" category. An interesting point which is obvious from Table 2.1 is that teachers have a marked tendency to attribute a higher proportion of absences to medical reasons than education welfare officers. It would be wrong to read too much into these results, since they are based on surveys of different age groups and in different parts of the United Kingdom. Moreover, the estimates reported by education welfare officers could simply be an artifact caused by the fact that teachers *only* ask them to investigate cases of non-medical absence. To summarise the evidence: (i) it is possible that teachers take a more charitable view of the reasons for absence than education

Table 2.1. *Number of Absences Attributed to Non-medical Reasons*

Author and date of publication	Per cent absence attributed to non-medical and/or unjustified reasons	Informants
Bransby (1951)	3.3	Teachers
D.E.S. (1967) (Plowden Report)	4.0	Teachers
Shepherd *et al.* (1971)	20	Teachers
Mitchell (1972)	30	Teachers
N.A.C.E.W.O. (1974)	60	E.w.o.s
D.E.S. (1974)	22.7	Teachers
Reynolds and Murgatroyd (1974)	75	Pupils
Harbison and Caven (1975)	46.5	E.w.o.s

welfare officers; (ii) it is certain that there is little consistent evidence on the prevalence of *justified* absence.

Reports by Teachers, Parents and Pupils

One way of assessing the prevalence of unauthorised absence is to ask whether the absent child has been ill. A slightly different approach, involves asking whether pupils have been absent from school without a good reason. The question can be asked of teachers, parents and pupils themselves. The answers do not necessarily tell us what proportion of all recorded absences are unauthorised. They do, however, give some interesting information about the number of pupils who may occasionally miss school without an adequate reason. Here, too, the replies depend not only on how the question is asked, but also of whom it is asked.

In their second follow-up at the age of eleven, the National Child Development Study (Fogelman and Richardson, 1974) estimated truancy rates from teachers' returns on Stott's (1971) Bristol Social Adjustment Guide. Only 1.2 per cent of their sample had truanted or been suspected of truanting. Of these, nearly 75 per cent were boys.

When the pupils were followed up at the age of sixteen a different picture emerged (Fogelman, 1976). On Rutter's (1967) teachers' questionnaire, truancy applied "somewhat" to 12 per cent of pupils and "certainly" applied to 8 per cent. When parents completed a different version of the questionnaire (Rutter *et al.*, 1970) 10 per cent were said to have truanted occasionally, but only 3 per cent at least once a week. A possible reason for the higher truancy rates reported by teachers is that 12 per cent of parents admitted they had "found it necessary to keep the child off school in order to help at home".

Teachers may have regarded this as truancy even though parents and pupils did not. The different ways of defining truancy frequently lead to confusion. We deal with this point more fully in Chapter 3.

A further complication in results from the National Child Development Study, is that 52 per cent of the sixteen-year-olds themselves, replied "yes" to the question: "have you stayed away from school at all this year, when you should have been there?" This surprisingly high rate of unauthorised absence was not contradicted in another self-report study by Mawby (1977). Eleven- to fifteen-year-old pupils in two Sheffield secondary schools, were asked the question: "have you ever, in the last twelve months, deliberately not gone to school although you were well enough to do so and had no other good reason for not going?". The results showed that 46 per cent of boys and 50 per cent of girls admitted unauthorised absence. Mawby referred to all these absences as truancy, though it is clear that he was using the term to include all unauthorised absentees, irrespective of the reason for their absence.

AGE, SOCIAL CLASS AND GEOGRAPHICAL AREA

Age

There is ample evidence that unauthorised absentee rates are higher in the final years of compulsory education than at any other time. We have already noted the high truancy rates amongst sixteen-year-olds compared with eleven-year-olds in the National Child Development Study. In Scotland, Mitchell (1972), too, found a consistent trend for absence rates to increase with age, although the overall attendance rate fell below 90 per cent in only one of the seven secondary schools she studied. In a study of over 6000 Buckinghamshire children, Shepherd *et al.* (1971) reported parents and teachers as agreeing on the higher prevalence of truancy in older boys, though the differences only became marked in adolescence.

A national survey by the Department of Educational Science (1974) recorded attendance of all pupils in England and Wales on one day in January. Just under 10 per cent of pupils were absent, and the schools knew of no legitimate reason for 23 per cent of the absentees. These unauthorised absentees represented just over 2 per cent of the total on roll. Yet in the final year of compulsory education, 5 per cent of the total on roll were regarded as unauthorised absentees, and a total of 15 per cent were absent. In other words, absence *and* unauthorised absence were highest in the final year.

Home and Community Influences

Several studies have reported an association between school attendance and social class. Fogelman and Richardson (1974) showed that only 6 per cent of pupils missing more than 15 per cent of attendances came from social class I on the Registrar General's classification, while 20 per cent came from social class V. With absence rates of less than 5 per cent these tendencies were reversed. Mitchell's (1972) study in central Scotland, found that poor attenders frequently came from families where the father was an unskilled or semi-skilled worker. The same tendency was found in Aberdeen (May, 1975) where it was even more evident in the case of absentees regarded by their teachers as truants. Earlier, Mitchell and Shepherd (1967) showed that boys who disliked school were significantly more likely to come from non-manual homes.

Within any one social class, absentees are more likely to come from the more disadvantaged homes. Tibbenham (1977) showed that overcrowding in all social class groupings was more common in the families of absentees. This supports May's (1975) evidence, that 38 per cent of truants lived in families with five or more children, compared with 26 per cent of absentees whose teachers did not regard them as truants. In the same study, May also showed that truants were more likely to be illegitimate, and that their fathers were more likely to be unemployed. Mitchell (1972) also found family size to be largest in the case of pupils absent entirely for non-medical reasons.

We shall deal in the next chapter with evidence about the family backgrounds of clinically defined school refusers, and also of truants, defined as absentees without parental knowledge or consent. There is general agreement, however, that these two groups constitute a relatively small proportion of all unauthorised absentees. Two points emerge from the relatively scanty evidence about the backgrounds of the majority of absentees.

First, although absentees are more likely to come from disadvantaged backgrounds, only a minority of children from such backgrounds become absentees. Wedge and Prosser (1973) for example, showed that only one child in fifty from socially disadvantaged families, missed more than three months' schooling. Second, the reported correlations between absenteeism and disadvantage do not imply a causal connection. Whether or not any particular child is absent from school, probably depends not on his family size, income, or social class, but on other factors within his home, school or community.

Geographical Area

Most post-war studies based on attendance registers have reported an average attendance around 90 per cent. There is a small but reasonably consistent tendency for lower rates to be reported from large industrial towns and higher rates from mixed areas or from national samples. The National Association of Chief Education Welfare Officers (1974) based their study on four counties and twelve county boroughs. The average 93 per cent attendance compares with 90 per cent in a nation-wide study (D.E.S. 1974) and 89 per cent in the Inner London Education Authority (Hill, 1971).

An exception to the general finding of average attendance rates around 90 per cent is Wales, which has consistently had lower rates. The National Child Development study, for example, showed Wales to have a higher proportion of pupils missing more than 15 per cent of attendances than Scotland or any of the nine regions of England (Fogelman and Richardson, 1974). Similarly, Reynolds and Murgatroyd (1977) reported average attendance rates over seven years at nine small secondary modern schools ranging from 77 to 89 per cent.

The reasons for the relatively poor Welsh attendance rates are not certain. One possibility is that teachers and parents may place a higher prority on criteria such as public examination results, compared with their counterparts elsewhere. If so, this could lead to the relative neglect of non-academic pupils, who might then develop anti-authority attitudes.

PATTERNS OF ABSENCE

Several studies have shown attendance to be higher at the beginning of the week than the end (Sandon, 1938; Trigg, 1975; Jackson, 1978). Jackson's study was of interest in demonstrating in the fourth year of a large comprehensive school, a cumulative tendency for attendances to deteriorate towards the end of the day, the week, the term and the year. Except when afternoons were compared with mornings, all the differences were statistically significant.

Unlike Jackson, Sandon (1961) found absence rates highest in January and February, though he did not take into account the possibility that attendance at some secondary schools is affected by teachers not encouraging attendance of older pupils in the last four weeks of the summer term, when public examinations have finished. Sandon's suggestion that weather may affect attendance was supported by Karweit (1973), who found that absenteeism increased on rainy days.

A possibility which has so far received little investigation, is that there may be a link between high absence rates and: (i) certain subjects in the curriculum, and/or (ii) the lessons of certain teachers. "Hidden truancy" occurs when pupils absent themselves after the attendance register has been completed. Anecdotal evidence from teachers, suggests that this is a substantial problem at some schools. A closer look at the pattern of such absences might reveal problems in the pupils' perceptions of certain teachers or certain curriculum areas.

PERSISTENT ABSENCE

An average attendance rate of 90 per cent does not, of course, imply that only 10 per cent of pupils were absent. The National Association of Chief Education Welfare Officers (1974) found that over 22 per cent of pupils had been absent at some stage in the week, even though the overall attendance was 93 per cent. Should we talk of an absence rate of 22 per cent, or an attendance rate of 93 per cent?

A similar point was made by an anonymous writer who quoted attendance rates at two schools in his authority (Anon, 1973). Each school had almost the same average attendance (88.4 per cent and 88.5 per cent). At the first, 54 per cent of pupils had a recorded absence, while at the second, only 11 per cent had any recorded absence.

We have already seen how attendance can vary according to the time of the day, the week, the term and year. It follows, as Baum (1979) points out, that an attendance rate based on a single day, or even a single month, may be extremely misleading. Yet even when they are based on a full year, they still fail to identify the number of persistent absentees.

The distinction between persistent and occasional absence is important, both from an educational and from an administrative view point. Even if, as May (1975) believes, poor attendance is partially a reaction to poor educational attainments, the educational problem is likely to become even more acute as a result of persistent absence. Persistently poor attenders are more likely than occasional absentees to be referred to the educational and social work support services. One reason for this, is that they require an administrative decision from the l.e.a. The decision concerns the form of action needed to encourage return to school on a regular basis. The choice is widely believed to be between prosecuting the parents, taking care proceedings on behalf of the child, and working directly with parents and/or the child. None of these are necessarily incompatible with a fourth possibility, namely attracting pupils back to school by creating a more satisfying and stimulating environment.

Unfortunately, there has been remarkably little work on persistent absence from school. Eaton and Houghton (1974) agreed with Tyerman (1968) that the "hard core" of persistent absentees missed an average of 20 per cent of possible attendances. In Northern Ireland, Harbison and Caven (1977) reported that 7.8 per cent of the compulsory school age population missed over 25 per cent of possible attendances in the spring term, 1977. In keeping with other studies, they found an increase with age in the secondary school years, with a peak in the final year of compulsory education.

This was also the case in a pilot project carried out by Galloway (1976a) in Sheffield. This study adopted an even more rigorous criterion for persistent absence. Only pupils who had missed more than half their possible attendances in the first seven weeks of the 1973 Autumn term were included. Even so, 872 pupils were identified as persistent unauthorised absentees. In primary schools, an average of 0.4 per cent of pupils were persistently absent, but by the final year of compulsory education this had risen to 4.4 per cent. Altogether, 2.1 per cent of secondary school pupils were identified as persistent unauthorised absentees.

The pilot project in Sheffield raised several questions. It seemed that very severe school attendance problems were nothing like as rare as some administrators and head-teachers had believed. It was immediately clear that only a small minority of the pupils involved were being seen by the support services. Particularly in the last two years of compulsory education, when persistent absentee rates rose dramatically, little could be done for—or about—the majority of cases. There were major variations between schools. At some, well over 10 per cent of final year pupils were persistently absent; at others, less than 1 per cent.

There was no evidence that school attendance problems in Sheffield had become more acute in the years leading up to the survey. The results were nevertheless criticised for two reasons. First, it was argued that the seven week survey period was too short. A flu epidemic affected some schools at the time and could have increased absentee rates. Education welfare officers might incorrectly have regarded some of these pupils as unauthorised absentees. Second, 1973 was the year in which the minimum school leaving age was raised to sixteen. The high fifth year absentee rate could simply reflect some pupils' disapproval of this innovation. As the raised school leaving age became more widely accepted, there would, in theory, be less of a peak in the final year.

We therefore decided to carry out similar surveys in 1974, 1975 and 1976 (Galloway, 1982a). The broad aims were to gather information about the prevalence and reasons for persistent absence from school. We hoped to show whether absentee rates in the fifth year of secondary schooling were in fact declining as the raising of the school leaving age became more widely accepted. A related aim was to investigate the possibility of trends within schools, or across the city as a whole. For example, were there some schools in some areas in which the problem was apparently getting worse, while in others teachers were recording fewer pupils as persistent absentees?

THE SHEFFIELD STUDIES

In the course of the Spring or Summer terms of 1975, 1976 and 1977, the chief education welfare officer asked head teachers to provide the name, sex and age of all children who had missed at least 50 per cent of attendances in the previous Autumn term. Hence, the survey period was from September to

December each year. This was necessary for administrative reasons, but probably resulted in an underestimate of the number of persistent absentees over the year as a whole. The reason, as indicated earlier, is that the Autumn term is the first term in the school year, and attendance frequently deteriorates as the year progresses.

Having received a list of persistent absentees, the education welfare officer for each school stated whether more than half of each pupil's absences were due to illness or some other legitimate reason. If not, he stated which of eight categories accounted for the highest proportion of absences. These explanations for absence are described in Chapter 3. This chapter is concerned only with the number of children regarded as unauthorised absentees.

Prevalence

Fig. 2.1 shows the percentage of persistent unauthorised absentees in each age-group in 1974, 1975 and 1976 as a per cent of the total number of pupils on roll. Except for an apparent rise in twelve-year-olds at primary schools, discussed below, absentee rates remained stable throughout the primary school years at .4 to .5 per cent. In contrast, there was an increase in each year of secondary education, with particularly sharp rises in each of the two final years of compulsory schooling. There were no important variations from year to year.

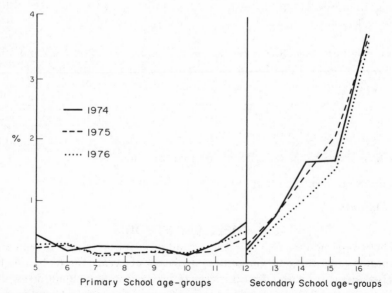

Fig. 2.1. Number of persistent unauthorised absentees, shown as a percentage of the total on roll in each age group.

These results confirm the evidence from the pilot study. They also make it quite clear that poor attendance in final year pupils was not a transitory problem associated with the raising of the school leaving age in 1973. The problem was as acute in the fourth year after the raising of the minimum leaving age to sixteen, as it was in the first. Conflicting explanations can be put forward for the sharp increases in unauthorised absenteeism throughout the secondary school years. One possibility is that the pupils concerned feel that the school curriculum is irrelevant to their needs. They may also resent aspects of the school's regime. Another possibility is that family responsibilities are more likely to keep some older pupils away from school. A fifteen- or sixteen-year-old can look after younger siblings, or even a sick parent; a six- or seven-year-old cannot. A third possibility, is that counter attractions in the local community, or from the peer group, become more powerful for older pupils. "Space invaders" may attract more fifteen- and sixteen-year-olds than younger pupils. Fifteen- and sixteen-year-olds may have friends who have left school, have no job, and welcome company during the day. We return in later chapters to these possibilities.

Transfer from Primary to Secondary School

In Sheffield, roughly 50 per cent of children enter secondary schools from junior schools, at the age of eleven. The other 50 per cent enter secondary schools from middle schools at the age of twelve. Table 2.1 shows that the proportion of eleven- to twelve-year-old absentees attending secondary schools, was lower than the proportion attending middle schools. Superficially, this result suggests that transfer to a secondary school at eleven may protect some pupils from persistent absence. However, that is almost certainly not the case. Persistent absence is strongly associated with low parental income. Low incomes were significantly more frequent in the families of middle school pupils than in those of junior schools. The clear implication is that the higher rates of absence in eleven- to twelve-year-olds at middle schools is attributable to family rather than to school factors.

Sex Differences

There were minimal differences in the numbers of boy and girl absentees in the primary school years. Throughout the secondary years, there was a slight, but consistent tendency for more girls to be recorded as persistent unauthorised absentees. However, we shall see in Chapter 3 that very few girls were thought to be absent without their parents' knowledge or consent.

Prevalence in Families

Many teachers and education welfare officers believe that absenteeism runs in families. If one child in the family is persistently absent, the same is likely to apply to the others. As it is known that poor attenders often come from large families, we might therefore expect that many families would be represented by more than one child. In fact, only 10 per cent of families involved in each of the three surveys had more than one child recorded as unjustifiably absent for more than half the term. On the surface, this does not support the view that absenteeism runs in families. On the other hand, the results also show that absenteeism becomes much more prevalent amongst older pupils. The surveys could not show whether the siblings of these pupils were, or would become, persistent absentees in their final two years of compulsory education.

SUMMARY AND CONCLUSIONS

There is extensive disagreement about the proportion of absent pupils who are away from school without an adequate explanation. The estimates have ranged from 3 to 75 per cent. The figures are not, strictly speaking, comparable, since they were collected for different age groups of children, by different professional groups, using different methods. Nevertheless, it does seem that pupils themselves admit to a great deal more unauthorised absence than is generally recognised by their teachers.

It is clear from several studies, that unauthorised absence becomes more common in adolescence. In all age groups, large families living in socially disadvantaged circumstances are at particular risk. Urban areas tend to have slightly higher absentee rates than the national average. Wales is the only part of the United Kingdom, however, where the average attendance has consistently been well below 90 per cent.

Average attendance rates do not reveal the number of pupils who are persistently absent. These are an important group, who make serious demands on the time of teachers and members of the support services. In extreme cases, the l.e.a. may consider legal action. The three Sheffield surveys showed that persistent unauthorised absentee rates remained stable in the primary school years at around .4 per cent, but increased at secondary schools, with a particularly sharp rise in each of the final two years of compulsory schooling. In some schools, over 10 per cent of final year pupils were persistently absent. The problem was as acute four years after the raising of the school leaving age to sixteen, as it was in the first year following the change.

It is little use, however, knowing how many pupils are absent without adequate reason, unless we also know *why* they are absent. We have already mentioned that the majority are not absent without their parent's knowledge or consent. We have also noted, that clinically diagnosed school refusers account for few unauthorised absentees. We now need to look at some of the evidence on the reasons for unauthorised absence.

CHAPTER 3

Semi-descriptive Categories

INTRODUCTION

Psychologists and psychiatrists have devoted an enormous amount of time and energy to distinguishing between groups of poor attenders and describing the personal, family and social characteristics of each group. Hersov (1977), for example, notes three broad categories: (i) truants; (ii) school refusers or school phobics; (iii) children whose parents withhold them from school.

There are legitimate reasons for attempting to distinguish between groups of poor attenders. For example, it has been found that some groups of children classified as school refusers respond well to clinic-based treatments offered by psychiatrists and psychologists. This point is discussed further in Chapter 6. It is clearly desirable that teachers should recognise that children fail to attend school for a variety of reasons. It is equally desirable that they should have some idea of the sort of intervention that may be helpful in different cases.

The most widely used categories nevertheless have important limitations. They seem to have led teachers and clinicians to focus principally on characteristics of the children and their families. Moreover, they have concentrated mainly on "abnormal" characteristics, seeing a problem in terms of individual or family psychopathology. As a result, researchers have tended to overlook two important areas. One is the relevance of stressful experiences at school as an explanation of poor attendance. The second is the significance, and hence the possible legitimacy, of the child's and parents' perceptions regarding the poor attendance. Viewed from their perspective, poor attendance might perhaps be seen not as a symptom of deviance and/or abnormal psychopathology, but as a rational, even necessary, course of action.

Scope of the Chapter

This chapter will describe the terminology used for different groups of poor attenders. It will then review the research on truancy and on school refusal, before describing surveys in Sheffield and in Northern Ireland which used a more extensive set of categories. Finally, we shall consider serious limitations in the various categories, and the questions which arise from their use.

DEFINITION OF TERMS

Truancy and School Refusal

There appears to be no legal definition of truancy. The 1944 Education Act makes no reference to the term. The Little Oxford dictionary defines a truant as: "a child who absents himself from school without leave". This is not as clear as it appears: does permission rest with the teachers or the parents? Since responsibility for attendance rests with parents, one may legitimately conclude that a child who is absent with their leave is not, strictly speaking, truanting.

Unfortunately, the term truancy has been used in different ways by different writers. Consequently, conclusions about one group of "truants" do not necessarily apply to another. Reynolds and Murgatroyd (1977) use truancy to describe all absentees, irrespective of reason. Less sweepingly, May (1975) distinguishes poor attenders who are truants from those who are not on the basis of teachers' statements. More specifically still, Tyerman (1968) reserves the term for children who are unlawfully absent on their own initiative without their parents' permission. This last definition is the one used throughout this book when referring to truancy. Truancy thus defined is generally regarded by psychiatrists. as only one aspect of a more extensive pattern of delinquent or anti-social behaviour.

Defining school phobia or school refusal is even more difficult than defining truancy. While truancy generally involves absence from school *or* home during school hours, school refusal is seen as the major manifestation of a "neurotic" disorder characterised by reluctance to leave home. Problems arise because different authors prefer different terms. Psychoanalysts tend to prefer school phobia, since this reflects the classical psychoanalytic belief that phobias arise by externalising frightening internal conflicts, and projecting them on to a neutral object, such as school, which is then avoided. Davidson (1960) and Chazan (1962) refer to school phobia, while Hersov (1960a and 1960b) prefers school refusal. Evans (1966) uses "school avoidance" but also refers to school phobia. Cooper (1966a) confusingly uses the term school refusal to include both truancy and school phobia.

Different writers conceptualise the condition in different ways, and do not always agree about its sharp distinction from truancy. The term school refusal is used throughout this book, except when referring explicitly to the work of a writer who prefers school phobia or some other term. The reason for preferring school refusal is simply that school phobia is misleading since the problem is not always a straight-forward phobia of school (and the psycho-analytic view of phobias is not widely accepted).

Withholding by Parents

Parents may withhold their children from school unlawfully for many reasons. Horn (1977) cites employment on the local farms as the prime cause of poor attendance in Oxfordshire in the 1890s. The School Board could—and did—exercise its powers to take parents to court, but was reluctant to prosecute the children's employers; some of its own members were the worst offenders. Double standards have continued to bedevil the use of legal sanctions in cases of poor attendance. More prosaic reasons for withholding a child are lack of suitable clothing, needing the child to help look after a younger sibling, or needing the child to do the shopping when the parent is ill.

Statements that a child is "withheld" distinguish him from a school refuser in not ascribing any quasi-medical condition to the child himself or to his family. There is also an implication that the *parent* is withholding the child; much of the literature on school refusal implies that the child is refusing to attend, in spite of his parents' attempts, at least at a conscious level, to persuade him.

TRUANCY

The Children and their Families

Tyerman (1958) compared 23 persistent truants selected by education welfare officers with controls selected from two child guidance centres in the same areas. There were, in fact, 40 children in Tyerman's original sample, but the remainder were either only occasionally truanting, or were at home with their parents' knowledge. The children were matched for age, sex and township. He found that the truants were significantly more likely than the controls: (i) to have parents who exerted control principally by corporal punishment; (ii) to live in unclean and over-crowded homes with more than three children in the family; (iii) to be inadequately clothed; (iv) to lack a strong emotional tie with a responsible adult of good standards; (v) to have fathers who were unskilled workers and both parents taking little interest in their welfare; (vi) to be withheld from school unlawfully on occasion; (vii) to experience a faulty parent–child relationship. Looking at factors within the child he found that truants tended to have few friends, to be of below average intelligence, and to be retarded educationally. The last observation was consistent with Burt's earlier suggestion (1925) that truants tend to be backward. It is worth noting, however, that it is not legitimate to draw any *causal* connection between truancy and the characteristics noted by Tyerman. What he does seem to be showing is that truancy is associated with multiple disadvantage in the Welsh town under study.

The average age in Tyerman's full sample of 40 children was eleven. This is consistent with later studies (Hersov, 1960a; Cooper, 1966b). It does not seem from these studies that family position is particularly significant, nor that there are any particularly frequent precipitating factors.

Tyerman's study has been widely quoted, so it is worth considering criticisms of it. His emphasis on child and family variables at the expense of precipitating factors within the school has led to some severe criticism. Reynolds and Murgatroyd (1977), for example, complain that he "seems to feel justified in scapegoating parents and exonerating teachers, perhaps because this is convenient to a model of truanting which sees the parents as the cause of the problem".

This, perhaps, is criticism of Tyerman for not doing something which he never set out to do though it is certainly true that he does not pay similar attention to school and community influences. More serious is the problem facing any study which compares a clinic population with an arbitrarily selected non-clinic population. The problem is that we do not know how far social, family and attitudinal characteristics influence referral. It may be that referral agencies consciously select children who do *not* have the characteristics of Tyerman's persistent truants, on the reasonable grounds that they are thought unlikely to keep clinic appointments.

This problem is to some extent overcome in Hersov's (1960a) comparison between a group of 50 truants, 50 school refusers and 50 child psychiatric department out-patients, since both groups of poor attenders had also been referred to the same department. Hersov's study sought to test the view that persistent absentees are split between the two principal diagnostic categories commonly used in child psychiatry (Rutter, 1965): (i) those whose behaviour is one facet of a "neurotic" disorder involving emotional disturbance or withdrawn introverted behaviour and (ii) those whose attitude and behaviour indicate a "conduct" disorder involving aggressive and/or anti-social behaviour.

The truants in Hersov's study did show many of the problems associated with "conduct disorder". Over three quarters had appeared before the Juvenile Court (a point dealt with in more detail in Chapter 4 when dealing with the connection between absence and delinquency). Between a third and a half had a history of enuresis, tension habits, "aggressive manifestations", persistent lying and wandering from home. Turning to factors in the child's environment, Hersov confirmed Tyerman's observations regarding inconsistent home discipline, but also noted a high incidence of absence of one or both parents in the first five years of life, and of fathers subsequently. Like Tyerman, he found his truants tended to have poor social adjustment, a poor standard of work, and to have a low average I.Q. Cooper (1966b), however, found that truants were working up to standard for their intelligence, though their I.Q. tended to be lower than that of their peers.

School Influences

The school's probable influence on overall attendance levels is dealt with in Chapter 4. We are here concerned with causal or precipitating factors in the relationship between schools and the small proportion of absentees who fit the limited definition of truants used by most psychologists and psychiatrists.

Tyerman (1958) reported that nine of his 23 persistent truants stated fear of a teacher as the reason for their truancy. Other common fears were bullying or caning. Tyerman seemed to discount these fears on the grounds that truants' excuses should probably not be accepted at face value. This conclusion was criticised by Reynolds and Murgatroyd (1977) but Hersov (1960a) devoted similarly little attention to school factors.

Cooper (1966b) found schools noticeably less sympathetic to truants than to school refusers. Truants were regarded as offenders. They were somewhat more likely than "normal" controls from the same class to have experienced frequent changes of school. Only $12\frac{1}{2}$ per cent were in classes considered to be run on informal lines.

The lack of systematic attempts to examine causal or precipitating factors in the school represents a notable gap in the literature on truancy. This has not, however, prevented discussion of the subject. In an early article, Dayton (1926) opposed the current eugenicist lobby by arguing that mental deficiency is seldom a cause of truancy. He considered school factors a great deal more important. Claiming that truants usually dislike their teachers, he argued that this could be "due to teachers' vindictive attitude towards past offences". Large classes geared to the needs of the normal child, academic difficulties resulting from improper grading, and detention after school were all given as possible explanations.

More recently D. Jones (1974) goes further than Dayton in attributing responsibility for truancy to schools: "it seems not so much that school means nothing to them, but that they sense in school a lack of respect and sympathy for them". Jones also acknowledges the possible influence of powerful sub-cultures within the school which require truancy as a token of non-conformity with the "enemy". This would seem to be inconsistent with Tyerman's and Herov's picture of the truant as a somewhat socially isolated child, but is in agreement with the notion of "secondary deviance" in the school setting, put forward by Hargreaves *et al.* (1975). This point is considered further in Chapter 4.

SCHOOL REFUSAL

The Children and their Families

As indicated earlier, school refusal is regarded in the psychiatric literature as the main symptom in a neurotic disorder, usually reflecting disturbed family relationships. Following Broadwin's (1932) description of two school refusing children with obsessional fears about harm befalling their mother, the aetiology, current symptomology and treatment of school refusal have attracted extensive discussion.

In a detailed review Hersov (1977) considers that school refusal should not be regarded as "a true clinical entity with a uniform aetiology, psychopathology, course, prognosis and treatment, but rather a collection of symptoms or a syndrome occurring against the background of a variety of psychiatric disorders". Later in the same article, Hersov states that the clinician has to decide what causes the school refusal, and cites as possibilities separation anxiety, a phobic manifestation, an aspect of depressive illness, a psychotic disorder or a personality disorder. The problem can occur at any age, though acute onset is more often seen in younger children (Hersov, 1977). There is a tendency for the children to be the oldest or youngest in the family or an only child (Chazan, 1962). Common precipitating factors are a change of school or class, death or disturbance in the family, and illness (Hersov, 1977).

While there is broad consensus in the psychiatric literature on the overall clinical picture, there is considerable disagreement on points of detail. Johnson *et al.* (1941) were the first authors to use the school phobia label for Broadwin's (1932) "exceptional" cases of truancy. They described a mixture of hysterical, phobic and obsessional symptoms, and related these to an unusually dependent mother–child relationship. Subsequent attention to this relationship led to an emphasis on separation or anxiety as a frequent characteristic of school refusal (Estes *et al.*, 1956; Eisenberg, 1958; Waldfogel *et al.*, 1957). Separation anxiety is not, however, a necessary condition for a diagnosis of school refusal. In his study of 50 school refusers referred to a hospital child psychiatry department, Hersov (1960a, 1960b) found fear of separation from home reported in only seventeen cases, and Berg (1970) found differences in dependency on parents between adolescents who did not show acute onset and those who did.

There has been similar disagreement on the significance of depressive reactions in school refusal. Davidson (1960) found signs of depression in 23 out of 30 cases, but in the same year in the same city Hersov (1960a) reported it in only 10 out of 50 cases. This inconsistency may simply reflect differences in diagnostic practice. Davidson's children were withdrawn and unable to take part in social activities; it is not clear that they would have been regarded as depressed if the criterion for diagnosis had been inability to experience pleasure or to accept the possibility of recovery and successful return to school (Gittleman-Klein and Klein, 1971).

Other traits reported in many of the children are eating problems, sleep disturbance, tension habits such as nail-biting, aggression towards other members of the family (Hersov, 1960a), emotional immaturity and dependency, timidity and nervousness (Chazan, 1962), fastidiousness, and anxiety to respond to authority (Cooper, 1960b). In addition, a "somatic disguise" is said to be characteristic of school refusers (Eisenberg, 1958). The child is ill, but no organic cause is evident; the overt physical symptom reflects a covert refusal to attend school, or simply to leave home.

Family relationships in cases of school refusal have attracted attention, especially from writers with a psychoanalytic orientation. Developing the early suggestions of a faulty mother–child relationship (Broadwin, 1932; Johnson *et al.*, 1941), Davidson (1960) and Kahn and Nursten (1968) claimed that the mothers gave their children conflicting messages; at first it seemed they were trying to send their children to school, but gradually it became clear that they were themselves maintaining the problem.

Hersov (1960b) attempted a more detailed analysis, and identified three main groups of relationships: (i) "an over-indulgent mother and inadequate, passive father, dominated at home by a wilful, stubborn and demanding child who is often timid and inhibited in social situations away from home"; (ii) "a severe, controlling and demanding mother who manages her children without much assistance from her passive husband; the child is most often timid and fearful away from home, and passive and obedient at home, but may become stubborn and rebellious at puberty"; (iii) "a firm, controlling father who plays a large part in home management and an over-indulgent mother closely bound to and dominated by a wilful, stubborn and demanding child, who is alert, friendly and outgoing away from home".

Intellectual and educational assessment has generally shown a majority of school refusers to be of high average intelligence or above when compared with other clinic populations (Hersov, 1960a; Chazan, 1962; Cooper, 1966b). This conclusion has, however, been questioned in America by Hampe *et al.* (1973) on the grounds that school refusers themselves constitute a clinic—and hence biased—population. Different studies have yielded conflicting results on the educational attainments of school refusers. Chazan (1962) reported that more than half the children in his study were experiencing great difficulty with their school work. In contrast, only 8 per cent of Hersov's (1960a) school refusers showed a poor standard of school work, and both Cooper (1966b) and Leventhal and Sills (1964) obtained similar results.

School Influences

Studies of the school's possible influence in the development of school refusal are conspicuous mainly for their absence. Carroll (1977b) accepts the prevailing view in the psychiatric literature that school refusal should be included amongst medical reasons for absence. One result of this has been to focus attention on psychopathology in the child and his family at the expense of causal or precipitating factors within the school. Likely reasons for the dearth of research on school influences are:

(1) the small number of children diagnosed as school refusers, with the associated wide scatter of schools;
(2) the professional training and bias of the psychiatrists and psychologists who make the diagnosis, which may incline them to emphasise child rather than school variables.

In one of the few studies of possible school influences, Cooper (1966b) found that neither size of school nor streaming policy within the school could reliably be said to differentiate school refusers from truants. On the other hand, the percentage of unstreamed classes was higher than the overall percentage in the area under study. A quarter of the sample children were on the register of classes considered to be run on informal lines, and a similar proportion attended schools which administered corporal punishment. As noted above, teachers were a great deal more sympathetic towards the school refusers than towards the truants. On the other hand, only 60 per cent of heads were willing to consider changing a child's class or allowing him not to attend certain lessons. It is not known how often a change was actually arranged, nor whether it helped.

Chazan (1962) reported that 22 out of 33 school phobics stated difficulties at school as possible precipitating factors. The most common of these were dislike of punishment or being shouted at in class, and fear of other children. The latter is, of course, consistent with the observations about difficulty in social relationships with other children. Eight children attending grammar schools showed anxiety associated with failure to adjust to new demands; four of these came from homes with no grammar school tradition and felt a sense of social inferiority.

OTHER CATEGORIES OF ABSENCE

Extended Illness

Although illness is one of the legitimate reasons for absence from school, it is often impossible to state with confidence whether a child's absence is attributable to illness. The point at which a slight cold turns into an upper respiratory tract infection requiring treatment is one which few doctors would be happy to define with confidence. This is reflected not only in the general concern in the medical profession about over-prescription, but also in doctors' refusal in some areas to issue medical certificates to children as proof of justified absence. Similarly, a recuperating child's fitness to attend school may depend on such indeterminate factors as the weather, the length of journey, whether he has to wait at the bus stop or can be taken to school by car, how warmly clothed he is, whether his school will make provision for him to remain inside at play-time and so on.

An even more difficult point to quantify is the effect of a child's attitude towards school—or towards separation from home—on his physical health. The "somatic disguise" in school refusal has already been mentioned. Yet for every diagnosed school refuser presenting in this way, it is likely that there are many children whose absence with minor complaints is prolonged by limited emotional resilience or by experience of stressful circumstances at home or at school.

Parental Withholding

As stated earlier, psychiatric diagnosis distinguishes between truancy, school refusal and parental withholding. The last is used for all cases of poor attendance which do not fit the clinician's model. Two points should be made about it:

(1) In practice psychiatrists seem to use this category very seldom indeed. This may indicate a high level of diagnostic reliability amongst referring agencies; alternatively, it may indicate a bias on the part of psychiatrists or psychologists against an assessment likely to result in punitive action against the child's parents; a related possibility is that "diagnosis" of parental withholding implicitly negates the professional's role in treatment; there is no assumption of abnormal psychopathology either in the child or his parents.

(2) The term parental withholding is an over-simplification. Children may remain at home with their parents' knowledge and consent for many different reasons. They may be kept at home to help look after younger siblings or a sick parent; they may be expected to help their parents with the housework or the shopping; they may remain at home because their parents have simply given up trying to persuade them to attend school.

Yet even these reasons over-simplify the position. In a longitudinal study of children's development Moore (1966) found that 80 per cent of ordinary children experienced difficulties at some stage in adjusting to their infants' school. The most frequent problem was over-dependence, with associated reluctance to go to school. In most cases, this is presumably dealt with satisfactorily by a mixture of firmness and sympathy. A physically or mentally sick parent, however, may lack the resources to cope with what is essentially a quite normal problem. When this happens, prolonged absence may result. To refer to this simply as parental withholding would be misleading, yet neither is it clear that the label of school refusal would be appropriate.

HOW MANY CHILDREN IN EACH CATEGORY

Although truancy is generally regarded as more common than school refusal (e.g. Tyerman, 1968), there has been little systematic research. The studies described in Chapter 2, for example, investigated overall attendance rates, without attempting to calculate the numbers of school refusers, truants or children whose parents keep them at home. One reason for this may be that teachers are often not aware of the circumstances behind each child's absence, and few studies have sought information from the educational welfare service, the branch of l.e.a.s which is responsible for investigating and acting on cases of poor attendance.

Sheffield Surveys

The surveys of persistent absence carried out in Sheffield in 1975, 1976 and 1977 involved all educational welfare officers in an attempt to assess the prevalence of eight categories of absence (Galloway, 1982a). The categories were selected in discussion with senior members of the service, and reflected their assessment of the most frequent reasons for absence. When the school staff had identified all pupils who had missed at least 50 per cent of attendances in the Autumn term, the form was passed to the school's education welfare officer. The e.w.o. was asked simply to state which category accounted for the greatest proportion of absence.

The "mainly illness" category applied when the e.w.o. thought that more than half the absences had been due to illness. "Some illness, but other factors also present" applied when a child was thought to have missed over two weeks because of illness, but less than six weeks (in a twelve week term). The possibility of attributing non-medical absences of children in the "some illness" group to one of the other categories was reluctantly dismissed as impractical. We felt that an e.w.o. might often suspect strongly that some absences were due to other factors, but not feel sufficiently confident to state which other category applied.

Absence with parents' knowledge was distributed between two categories: (i) pupils who were absent with their parents' knowledge, consent and approval; (ii) pupils whose parents knew about their absence, disapproved of it in theory, but were unable or unwilling to insist on return to school against the child's wishes. Deliberately, this overlapped with the "school phobia" category, while lacking the clinical connotations of school refusal or school phobia. The term school phobia was used in the surveys as it was more familiar to e.w.o.s than school refusal. There was no indication in the accompanying notes that the condition should have been recognised by a psychologist or psychiatrist. Instead they focused attention on the child's refusal to leave home, and severe relationship difficulties within the home.

It was recognised that there would be a good deal of overlap between the categories. Senior e.w.o.s thought their colleagues would be able to state which one accounted for the greatest proportion of absence. They doubted, however, whether it would be feasible to quantify the proportion of absence attributable to different categories.

Results

Figures 3.1 and 3.2 show the percentage of boys and girls in primary and secondary schools respectively whose absences were attributed to each category. Although persistent absentee rates increased very sharply in the secondary school years, it is clear from Figs 3.1 and 3.2 that the absences of secondary pupils were less often attributed to illness than those of primary pupils. Analysis of the results for each year separately showed that illness was seen either as a partial or as the principal explanation for between 84 and 72 per cent of the primary age absentees. For primary school absentees, illness accounted wholly or in part for between 34 per cent and 44 per cent, depending on the year in question.

Both for primary and for secondary pupils, the two categories of absence with parents' knowledge accounted for the largest proportion of unauthorised absence. Excluding the "mainly ill" group from the analysis, these two categories combined accounted for 59 per cent of primary school absentees and 51 per cent of secondary absentees, averaged over the three years. Truancy accounted for a negligible number of the primary school pupils, but was considered a good deal more common amongst the older children, being regarded as the principal explanation for 16 per cent of secondary pupils over the three years, excluding the "mainly ill" group.

The most notable sex difference in statistical analysis was that truancy was significantly more often considered the principal explanation for the absences of boys than of girls. This is consistent with the results of other studies: girls' attendance rates are similar to those of boys, but samples of truants, defined

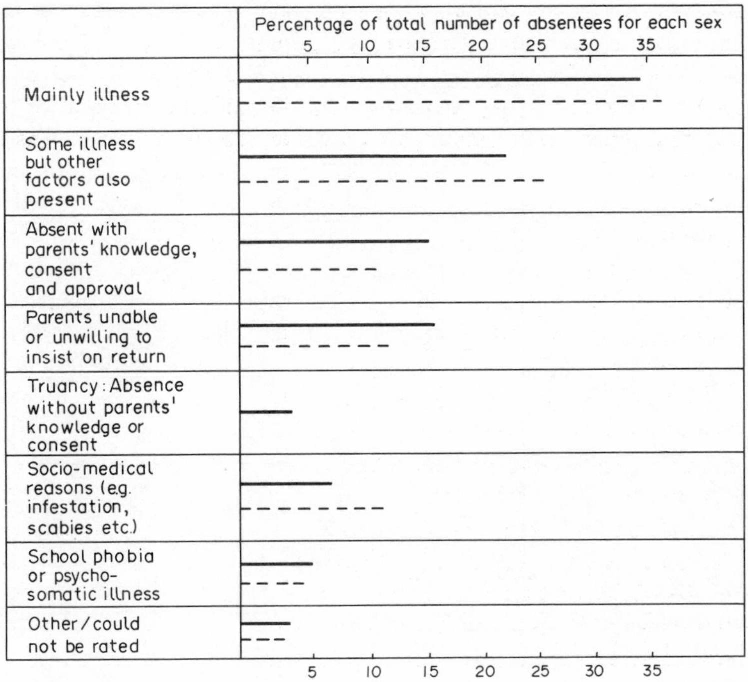

Fig. 3.1. Categories of absence for persistent absentees aged 5–11 in three annual surveys, assessed by Educational Welfare Officers: Boys ——— ; Girls – – – –. From Galloway (1982a).

strictly as absentees without parental knowledge or consent, contain a disproportionate number of boys..

The low percentage of children placed in the school phobia or psychosomatic illness categories raises interesting questions, particularly when compared with the proportion in the two categories of absence with parents' knowledge. There was evidence from informal comment that many e.w.o.s were only willing to use this category if the "diagnosis" had formally been confirmed by a psychologist or psychiatrist. Yet there was also evidence from informal comment that they would only refer a child to an educational psychologist, or seek referral to a psychiatrist, if they thought the family was likely to co-operate by keeping appointments. There are two implications: (i) that estimates of the prevalence of school refusal based on children referred to specialist agencies may be misleading; in particular, children from socially disadvantaged homes may be substantially under-represented, (ii) that many of the children considered to be at home with their parents' knowledge may have many of the characteristics associated in the clinical literature with school refusal.

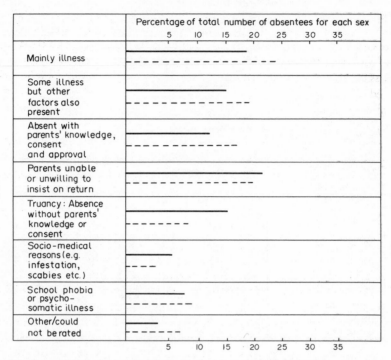

Fig. 3.1. Categories of absence for persistent absentees aged 12–16 in three annual surveys, assessed by Educational Welfare Officers: Boys ——— ; Girls – – – –. From Galloway (1982a).

COMMENTS ON USEFULNESS OF THE CATEGORIES

The title of this chapter implies considerable scepticism about the usefulness of the categories which have been used to distinguish groups of poor attenders. In this section we consider first the supposedly "clinical" nature of school refusal and the usefulness of the distinction between truancy and school refusal. We then discuss the categories used in the Sheffield surveys, arguing that although they may perhaps constitute a rather modest improvement on the distinction between truancy and school refusal, they raise questions both about the children concerned, about their schools and about l.e.a. policy.

The "Clinical" Nature of School Refusal

School refusal is generally seen as a quasi-medical problem. In some cases, for example when the "somatic disguise" is suspected, medical oversight is undoubtedly necessary. Whether it is legitimate to select one numerically small group of absentees for psychiatric treatment is more open to debate. As we have seen, Moore's (1966) study showed that 80 per cent of ordinary children had difficulties in adjusting to infants' school. It is possible that only those with the most severe disturbance are eventually referred to psychologists as possible school refusers. Another possibility, though, is that some teachers and educational welfare officers differ not only in their success in managing the problem themselves, but also in their willingness to refer to psychologists or psychiatrists.

A more fundamental objection to the medical aura surrounding school refusal is that it has unjustifiably concentrated specialist resources on a small, and perhaps arbitrarily selected group of absentees. Before accepting that this is an appropriate use of resources, more information is needed about the management of other, numerically larger groups of absentees.

Validity of Distinction between Truancy and School Refusal

Although the bulk of the psychiatric literature makes a clear distinction between truancy and school refusal, its validity has been questioned (Tyerman, 1968). The argument is not about the existence of poor attenders who have the characteristics described in the literature. Disagreement centres on the question whether these are discrete diagnostic categories, or merely opposite poles on the same continuum. The distinction is of more than academic importance. School refusal seems to have a good prognosis, whatever treatment is used. In contrast, truancy has a bad prognosis, both short term and long term.

If the outlook for professional intervention in cases of school refusal is good, l.e.a.'s may reasonably ask how widely they should extend their selection criteria. Is it, for example, impossible for a child whose parents deposit him at school on their way to work—leaving the house locked—to be a school refuser? He may show all the "neurotic" symptoms associated with school refusal, yet he is not at home; moreover, he is absent without his parents' consent and probably without their knowledge.

A similar problem can be seen in the assessment of absentees living in areas with a high incidence of delinquency and other indices of social malaise. The implications of a court conviction differ from area to area, indicating gross non-conformity to prevailing norms in one district and relative conformity in another. Viewed in this light the distinction between truancy and school refusal loses some of its clarity. Moreover, it is insufficient to say the distinction remains valid, but that some children in each category have "mixed disorder" indicating a combination of neurotic disorder and conduct disorder. If the overlap is great enough, the distinction itself is suspect.

Referral Biases and Sampling Difficulties

The effects of possible differences in referral policy have already been mentioned. The fact that almost all absentees referred to psychiatrists are regarded as truants or school refusers could simply result from diagnostic policy. A more important point, however, is that virtually all the clinical literature on both truants and school refusers is drawn from samples that may be biased by referral practices. With the exception of some rather limited information from longitudinal studies information is derived from pupils who have been selected for advice or treatment from a psychologist or psychiatrist.

Uses of the Categories

Before considering the uses, and limitations of the categories it is important to know something about their reliability and their validity. Reliability, essentially, is concerned with the question whether educational welfare officers use the same criteria when deciding which of the seven categories offer the best description of a child's absences. Validity is concerned with the accuracy of their judgements. Thus it is logically possible for two e.w.o.s or two psychiatrists, to attribute a child's absence to truancy on the basis of hearsay evidence, when in fact the real cause is illness. Such a judgement would be technically reliable, but invalid.

Another question concerns the consistency of each e.w.o.s judgement over a period of time. If many officers allocate a child to a different category on a second occasion, whether or not they have additional information, the reliability of their judgements will be suspect.

In fact evidence on the reliability of information used in research on poor school attendance is conspicuously lacking. In most of the work carried out by psychologists and psychiatrists we can rely only on the "clinical judgement" of the people concerned. Similarly, in May's (1975) study in Aberdeen we have to rely on the teachers' judgements as to whether a poor attender was a truant or not. We have no information on the chances of two teachers independently making the same judgement.

In the Sheffield studies Galloway (1980a) showed that errors in identifying persistent poor attenders from attendance registers could not be discounted, but were not sufficient to throw doubt on any of the basic results. Although a conventional reliability check was impractical there was strong indirect evidence that e.w.o.s were *not* reliable, in the technical sense, in allocating pupils to categories. The analysis showed highly significant differences between selected schools in the proportion of absentees allocated to each category, even though the schools served similar areas. Moreover, there were also highly significant differences within eight out of ten schools with high absentee rates in the number of pupils allocated to each category over the three years of the study; yet in most cases the total number of absentees did not vary significantly from year to year.

The implication is that e.w.o.s probably cannot distinguish reliably between the categories when considering which one best fits a particular individual. Two obvious questions are: Is this surprising? and: Does it matter?

At one level it is not at all surprising. It was recognised from the outset that there would be considerable overlap between the categories. This problem must have been heightened both by changes in personnel throughout the three years of the study, and possibly also by changes in the sort of children schools were referring to their e.w.o.s at a time when the service was undergoing several changes. Perhaps a more important point is that research in other professions suggests that a satisfactory level of inter-rater agreement *can* be achieved, but only when categories are tightly defined and relate to observed behaviour (e.g. Rutter and Graham, 1968). The nature of the surveys made it impossible to base the categories on observed behaviour, and informal attempts to define each one more tightly produced more questions than they answered.

Whether the low reliability matters depends on the uses to which the categories are put. One reasonable use may be to provide a *general* picture of the situation across the whole city. The *general* picture across the city remained similar throughout the three years, even though there were some variations from year to year within particular categories.

The general picture showed consistently: (i) that the majority of unauthorised absentees were at home with their parents' knowledge and often with their consent; (ii) that truancy accounted for a much smaller proportion of other pupils; (iii) that less than half of all persistent absenteeism was attributed to illness; (iv) that other possible explanations accounted for relatively few pupils. Viewed in this way, the categories may perhaps be seen as a modest improvement on the traditional distinction between truants, school refusers and pupils withheld by their parents. That judgement, however, must be considered in the light of the next two sections.

Administrative Uses

The crucial point here is that the categories were based on discussions with senior members of the educational welfare service. Hence, they reflected an informal classification system which these e.w.o.s expected that their colleagues might use when investigating the reasons for a child's non-attendance. It would be extremely difficult in practice for e.w.o.s *not* to use these categories, or similar ones, when justifying a decision to take legal action against the parents or the child.

Hence, there is an important sense in which the categories may be said to have high validity. This may be called "administrative validity", and implies simply that e.w.o.s' assessments are assumed to be valid when the l.e.a. makes the administrative decision to take—or not to take—formal action in connection with the child's poor attendance. The l.e.a. takes formal action in connection with a relatively small proportion of all unjustified absentees (see Chapter 7). Thus, there is a process of selection in which the e.w.o.s decide which parents or pupils they can work with successfully on an informal basis, and which they should recommend for more formal action. This is, of course, inevitable; all it implies is that the l.e.a. makes its decisions on the basis of advice from the officers responsible for investigating and acting upon cases of poor school attendance.

In practice the evidence on which the advice is based is most unlikely to be challenged in the Magistrates Court, since the bench is concerned primarily with whether or not an offence has been committed, and this is almost invariably established from the record of the school's attendance register. In the Juvenile Court the fact of illegal absence is unlikely to be challenged, though in Sheffield the implicit inference that the child is in need of care or control can be subjected to independent scrutiny by a social worker from the local social services department. This happens because a social worker (or occasionally a probation officer) is asked to investigate the circumstances and report to the court on the child's needs, even when the case is brought by the l.e.a.

The concept of administrative validity, then, implies simply that the assessments of e.w.o.s are accepted by the l.e.a. and the courts as valid, at least to the extent of basing decisions on them. The evidence presented above about their poor reliability—and hence probable low validity in the scientific sense— could charitably be viewed in the context of most other decisions about social policy. The nature of the processes involved in legal action over poor attendance is probably no more subjective than that of the processes involved in, for example, the decision to seek a place of safety order on the grounds of parental neglect. Whether that constitutes a justification for legal action is another matter altogether.

CONCLUSIONS: SOCIAL AND PSYCHOLOGICAL OBJECTIONS

The categories may be defended or attacked on administrative grounds. There is no doubt, though, that they may legitimately be criticised for social and psychological reasons. Essentially, the problem is that they all relate to family or child variables, and hence implicitly make certain questionable assumptions about the nature of persistent absenteeism. A good example is the category: "parents unable or unwilling to insist on return". From an administrative and legal point of view, this is relatively straightforward, and the l.e.a. has a clear right to initiate proceedings against a parent or pupil. It may be, however, that the parents are unwilling to insist on return because they feel—rightly or wrongly—that their child has been bullied at school.

It would be quite easy to draw up another list of categories which are all school-based. Examples are: bullied at school; afraid of punishment/ridicule; difficulty in social relationships with other children; personality clash with particular teachers; crippling sense of educational failure, and so on. Taken in isolation, there is no reason, on the evidence presented so far, to believe that these would be any more or less valid than the categories which were in fact used.

There is in fact evidence that educational variables may be of considerable importance. The sharp rise in the incidence of absenteeism throughout the secondary school years suggests that school, and possibly community, influences may become more important as pupils progress through puberty and adolescence. The increase in the incidence of truancy—absence without parents' knowledge or consent—in secondary school pupils is further evidence for this view. Even more cogent is the increasing body of evidence that the school itself exerts an important influence on absence rates.

Another objection is that the categories over-simplify the complexity of their social and psychological correlates to the point of being severely misleading. Taking the same category as an example: "parents unable or unwilling to insist on return" tells us virtually nothing about the parent nor about the child. The child may be quite amenable to the idea of return; continued absence may be attributable simply to a mentally or physically ill parent's inability to get him dressed and ready for school. In contrast the parent may desperately want the child to return, yet lack the physical and emotional strength to insist, against the wishes of a determined youngster. Problems of this sort are, perhaps, inevitable in any system of categorisation. The point at issue is merely that the categories tell us nothing about the social, psychological or educational factors associated with absence.

CHAPTER 4

School and Community Influences

INTRODUCTION

Most of the clinical research on truancy and school refusal described in previous chapters has emphasised the importance of factors in the child and/ or in the family. This emphasis reflects a theoretical model which sees deviant behaviour largely as evidence of an individual's or a family's abnormal psychopathology. Some of the authors reviewed earlier have mentioned sources of stress at school, but have tended either to dismiss them or to rate them as making relatively unimportant contributions to the overall problem.

This attitude was implicitly legitimised both by the Plowden Report in Britain (D.E.S., 1967) and by the Coleman Report in America (Coleman *et al.*, 1966). Both reports considered the importance of a school's influence on children's behaviour and on their educational progress. Both concluded that a school's influence was relatively insignificant compared with that of the home background and the local neighbourhood. The implication was as depressing as it was clear: how quickly and how well a child learnt to read, or whether the child showed signs of "maladjustment" or disruptive behaviour at school, depended partly on the child, partly on the child's family, partly on the home neighbourhood, and hardly at all on which school the child happened to be attending. This essentially nihilistic message was not essentially modified by the Plowden Report's call for positive discrimination in socially disadvantaged areas. The underlying philosophy was not that schools might become more effective by changing existing practices, but that "more of the same" might help to compensate for a disadvantaged background.

The 1960s were a period of optimism in the power of education to create a better, implicitly more equal, society. Schools were seen not as the means for reproducing divisions within society, but as the agents of an increasingly meritocratic society. This optimism faltered in the 1970s and, at least in Britain, is now seen as distinctly unrealistic.

The research of some authors argues that schools do indeed serve to reproduce existing divisions within society. Truancy, they suggest, is a predictable response to this "hidden curriculum". While not altogether sharing this view, Ramsay (1983) points out that throughout the last ten years educational sociologists have been seeking "to develop a sound theoretical basis for the claim that knowledge was being used as a form of social control, and that schools had not advanced much from the days when they began with the chant 'God bless the squire and his relations, and help to keep us in our social stations'".

Another group of researchers, however have argued both that schools and individual teachers vary in their effectiveness. Moreover, they maintain that these variations cannot be dismissed by pointing to differences between the schools' catchment areas. Using measures of pupil performance such as behaviour in school, juvenile delinquency, examination results and attendance they have shown that some schools have much better results than others.

There are, of course, sound practical reasons for considering how the school itself might be able to encourage regular attendance. Hamblin (1977) notes succinctly: "we might well as teachers concentrate on what is modifiable, namely the interaction of teachers and pupils; ... although it would be interesting to trace the origins of the attitudes which seem to be linked with truancy, one can question if this is the most urgent task". A second practical reason for investigating school influences is the predictable inability of child guidance, psychological and child psychiatric services to make any real impact on the problem of poor attendance. We need only note here that although treatment of school refusers, especially of primary age, has a good prognosis, there is scant evidence that the remaining 95 to 98 per cent of persistent absentees have been, or can be, helped by agencies outside the school.

An emphasis on the school's influences over its pupils' attendance should not be taken to imply that individual, family and community factors are unimportant. Indeed a central thesis of this book is that poor attendance can only be understood in terms of an interaction between these factors and the school. An interest in the school's influence does, however, imply an interest in factors within the school which may encourage, or inhibit regular attendances. It also implies interest in pupils' own accounts of their experiences at school and of the reasons for their absences. The remainder of this chapter will discuss research on community and school influences on attendance. It will argue that schools do exert an important influence. In Chapter 8 we shall see how this influence is reflected in aspects of a school's policies, practices and organisation. First, however, we will look at community influences. The reason is that these need to be recognised in order to appreciate fully the importance of the school's contribution—a contribution, incidentally, which can be positive or negative.

COMMUNITY INFLUENCES

Social Class

Several studies have reported an association between attendance and social class. Fogelman and Richardson (1974) used data from the National Child Development Study to show that pupils who were often absent for their first two years at school, but attended regularly thereafter, tended to catch up in their educational attainments unless their parents came from social classes IV or V. The National Child Development Study also showed that only 6 per cent of pupils missing more than 15 per cent of attendances came from social class I, compared with 20 per cent from social class V. With absence rates of less than 5 per cent this tendency was reversed.

In Central Scotland, Mitchell (1972) found that poor attenders tended to come from families where the father was an unskilled or semi-skilled worker. The same tendency was evident in Aberdeen (May, 1975). Here, it was even more marked in the case of absentees regarded by their teachers as truants.

Family Background

Tyerman (1958) demonstrated the multiply disadvantaged backgrounds of his sample of truants. Larger scale studies have confirmed that absentees frequently live in socially disadvantaged families. Tibbenham (1977) showed that over-crowding in all social class groupings was more common in families of absentees. This was consistent with May's (1975) earlier evidence that 38 per cent of truants (defined by teachers) lived in families with five or more children, compared with 26 per cent of non-truant absentees. Mitchell (1972) also found family size to be largest in the case of pupils absent entirely for non-medical reasons. Galloway *et al.* (1981a) noted that children from four samples of persistent absentees came from very large families, the mean number of children per family lying between four and six in each sample.

Financial Hardship

Galloway (1976a,b, 1982a) noted a very strong relationship between the number of persistent absentees from a school and the number of pupils authorised to receive free school meals on account of their parents' low income. This implies simply that knowing the level of poverty in the catchment area, as measured by the number of children authorised to receive free school meals enables one to predict with some confidence roughly how many children will be persistently absent from a school. It does *not*, however, enable us to predict who the absentees will be (Galloway, 1980a). The reason is that free school meal rates are as reliable in predicting the number of absentees who are *not* eligible for free school meals as in predicting the total number of absentees. Rutter *et al.* (1975) obtained a similar result when examining the association between free school meal rates and truancy in their longitudinal study in London.

A separate issue is the validity of free school meals as a measure of disadvantage in a school's catchment area. Tyerman (1958) reported no significant correlation between attendance and free school meal rates in a medium sized Welsh town. Caven and Harbison (1978) found a significant positive correlation in Belfast, but not in the rest of Northern Ireland. Combined with the Sheffield data their results suggest: (i) that free school meal rates are closely associated with absenteeism in large cities; but (ii) that free school meal rates may simply reflect other social problems associated principally with the depressed areas of large cities. Galloway *et al.* (1984) used census data to examine in more detail the association between absenteeism and a wide range of demographic variables. They found that, in Sheffield, free school meals had a much higher correlation with persistent absentee rates than any other demographic variable.

A Cautionary Note

The research consistently shows a relationship between attendance and social class. Just as consistently it identifies a range of factors associated with social and/or financial disadvantages in the families of poor attenders. It is important, however, to note that only a minority of children from disadvantaged backgrounds become persistent absentees. Wedge and Prosser (1973) for example showed that only one child in fifty from socially disadvantaged families missed more than three months' schooling.

Three Theories of Absence

Yet although only a minority of children from disadvantaged backgrounds become persistent absentees, it is clear that overall attendance rates in socially disadvantaged areas are frequently low. The obvious question is: Why?

Three points of view are often put forward. One sees poor attendance as a symptom of stress in the family, or in the child. Advocates of this viewpoint tend to agree that the families require help and support from a variety of educational welfare, educational psychology and social work services. A second point of view sees poor attendance as an indication of child neglect, lack of parental control or general anti-authority attitudes on the part of parents, child or both. Advocates of this viewpoint tend to favour legal proceedings to enforce attendance. A third point of view sees poor attendance as the logical outcome of the school system's inability to cater for working class pupils. Some advocates of this perspective tend to argue that teachers, most of whom are middle class, alienate working class pupils by seeking to impose their own cultural preferences, for example on speech and dress, and by systematically devaluing the culture of the pupils and their families. Other advocates of this point of view place less emphasis on social class and more on relationships within the school.

Teachers are not always enthusiastic about theories of absenteeism which see the causes of poor attendance as lying in the education system in general or in the school in particular. Yet teachers clearly play a central part in any child's experience of school. If teachers do not contribute to poor attendance, either actively or by default, it follows logically that they can do nothing about it. The next section reviews some sociological research relevant to poor attendance.

SOCIOLOGICAL PERSPECTIVES

Case Studies

Willis (1977) carried out a participant observation study of twelve non-academic working class boys from a school in the centre of England which he called Hammertown Boys. Selection was based on the fact that all twelve were friends, and were members of "some kind of oppositional culture" in a working class school. In other words, they saw themselves as belonging to an anti-authority sub-group, and were seen in this light by teachers. "This opposition", Willis vividly demonstrated "is expressed mainly as a style. It is lived out in countless small ways which are special to the school institution, instantly recognised by the teachers, and an almost ritualistic part of the daily fabric of life for the kids."

Truancy was merely one aspect of this opposition. Willis was more interested in truancy *within* the school than in truancy *from* the school. Truancy within the school occurred when "the lads" absented themselves from class after registration. A highly esteemed skill within the group was the ability to get out of any class at will, thus demonstrating control over their own movements. It was a skill which the lads had developed to a fine art. It not only implied control over their own time-table, but also opposition to the school's highly structured and elaborate time-table.

In another participant observation study, Corrigan (1979) argued that truancy should not be seen as a conscious, overt form of opposition to the authority of the school. Fifty-two out of ninety-three boys said they came to school because of some form of compulsion—"it's the law", "I have to", "me Mum would get put in prison".

Corrigan draws an analogy between schools and universities. If an unpopular lecturer made his lectures compulsory because students did not attend, the students would use a variety of tactics to persuade him to change his mind. If argument failed, then petitions, pressure from student unions, interviews with a professor, boycotts, pickets and so on could be tried. These methods are not available to working class pupils, nor, for that matter to any pupils apart from a tiny minority in progressive schools. Fifty-two out of the ninety-three boys claimed to have truanted at least once or twice in the past year. The major restraint on truancy was not liking or respect for school, but fear of sanctions.

Like Willis, Corrigan mentions a high rate of "dolling off" lessons, or absenting themselves from selected lessons after registration. Unlike Willis, he does not see it primarily as an attack on the school's values:

> "It does not seem that truancy is an action which is meant to *attack the school's values* in any way; rather the action seems to have something to do with the boys' protection of themselves from things that they don't like. Thus there are specific actions against specific lessons where the boys absent themselves. None of the boys mention the rights and wrongs of such forms of action, rather they seem to be constantly concerned with the *power* of the school and the law in making them (and attempting to make them) attend school as a whole and certain lessons specifically. This difference between my hypothesis expressed in terms of values and the boys' views expressed in terms of actions led me to change the structure of the research completely."

Education first became free and compulsory, Corrigan argues, because this served the needs of the powerful sectors of society. Through education the working class could be given a "suitable" curriculum which would help to ensure a docile labour force and to prevent social unrest. The system, in short, "had as its hallmark a transference of a system of morality". Corrigan felt that a historical perspective could explain *why* the boys were truanting, even though they could not see *what* they were truanting from.

Both Willis and Corrigan have made an important contribution by directing attention to some of the ways in which "deviant" behaviour at school, including truancy, may be seen as an inevitable result of the way schools are organised. This, in turn, results from what society, or rather the most articulate and powerful sections of society, expects schools to achieve. Three points, though, need to be made about their research. First, most boys in their studies *did* attend school, even though they often skipped lessons; the possibility of family stress as at least a contributing factor in persistent absence remains open. Second, they may underestimate the difference between schools; other research to which we shall turn shortly, suggests that a working class child's experiences may vary substantially from one school to another. Third, their explicit focus on working class culture prevents them exploring some wider issues of teacher–pupil interaction.

Negative Labelling

In recent years educational sociologists have attempted to understand the development of deviant behaviour at school in terms of teacher–pupil relations, with particular emphasis on the positive or negative ways in which teachers label children. The research has not, on the whole, focused specifically on poor attendance. Nevertheless, it seems logical that arguments which explain disruptive behaviour may at least give some pointers in understanding poor attendance.

In a much quoted article, Werthman (1963) suggested that a majority of pupils, and all teachers, accept the teacher's authority by virtue of the teacher's position. In other words, the teacher is both accepted and respected because he is a teacher. Some pupils, however, implicitly demand that respect has to be earned. These pupils will only accept the teacher's authority if the teacher conforms to their own unwritten "rules". Such pupils are likely to be considered deviant.

Once a pupil is regarded as deviant, he can live down to his reputation. Lemert (1967) argued that a society's reactions to an initial act of delinquency could lead an individual to identify himself, and to be identified by others, as deviant. He used the term "secondary deviance" to describe the process of establishing a vicious circle of labelling and deviance. Moreover, this process can start before a teacher has even seen a child. Cicourel and Kitsuse (1968) pointed out how teachers and school counsellors can set a child on course for a school career of delinquency and failure. Well-intentioned labels such as "remedial", "in need of counselling", "disturbed home background" can create a rôle, from which many children can never free themselves. Following in the footsteps of an older brother or sister can have the same effect. (When discussing this point with university students, there is invariably someone in the group who remembers with bitterness how school teachers expected him to live up or down to the reputation of an older sibling.) Most of the literature has focused on the negative effects of labelling. It is important to note, though, that the same process may be used to develop a positive self-image in pupils.

Hargreaves (1967) described an anti-school sub-culture in a secondary modern school in the north of England. He attributed this to the school's streaming system, suggesting that the pupils concerned were reacting predictably to having been rejected as examination candidates. Teachers claimed that streaming was necessary for the benefit of the brighter, more co-operative boys. Against this view, streaming started in the first year and the younger pupils contained no group which was united by opposition to the school's values.

It is not clear, though, how much part streaming plays in facilitating anti-school attitudes. Willis (1977), for example, notes that anti-school groups developed in fourth year pupils after the school had introduced mixed ability teaching in exactly the same way as under the streamed system. It seems likely that the critical factor is not the school's formal organisation, but the extent to which less able or *potentially* disruptive pupils feel that the school values their efforts and achievements.

This implies that schools may indeed vary in their success in winning their pupils' co-operation. The question is not whether attendance rates vary from school to school. They quite definitely do. Rather the question is whether schools *in similar areas* have different attendance rates, and if so how are these differences achieved? A related question is whether schools with high attendance rates tend also to have less disruptive behaviour and better academic results than schools with low attendance rates. If so, this would have important implications both for our understanding of poor attendance, and for the ways that schools and society respond to it.

THE SCHOOL'S INFLUENCE ON ATTENDANCE

In a study of nine secondary modern in South Wales from 1966–1967 to 1972–1973 average annual attendance for all nine schools ranged from 80.7 per cent to 84.1 (Reynolds and Murgatroyd, 1977; Reynolds *et al.*, 1980). The differences between schools were much greater. In one year they ranged between 73 and 90 per cent, and remained fairly consistent from year to year. Initially, analysis of demographic variables in the schools' catchment areas failed to find any satisfactory explanation for the differences, indicating that they were more likely to reflect differences in the effects of the school's organisation than in the pupils they admitted. Subsequently, however, Reynolds *et al.* (1980) noted a tendency for schools with higher attendance rates to admit pupils with higher reading attainments. In addition they found a somewhat less consistent tendency for their pupils to have higher scores on entering secondary school on a maths test and on the extroversion/introversion and neuroticism/stability subscale of the Junior Eysenck Personality Inventory (Eysenck, 1965). To confuse the picture still further, there was evidence that pupils at the schools with high rates obtained lower scores on Raven's (1960) Standard Progressive Matrices—a nonverbal intelligence test.

These results at first sight are conflicting. Schools with higher attendance rates apparently admitted pupils with better educational attainments, who were both more extroverted and more neurotic but less intelligent non-verbally. On the face of it, these results do not suggest that the school differences could be attributed to differences in pupil intake. Nor, however, do they necessarily suggest the reverse. There are three problems in interpreting the results: (i) the intelligence and attainment data were based on small numbers (ranging from seventeen to sixty), and were obtained *after* collection of the attendance data, on a different pupil intake (Reynolds *et al.*, 1980); (ii) given the fairly narrow range of mean Raven's Matrices scores across the eight schools on which information was available, the differences in pupil's educational attainments at age eleven could be attributed to differences between the referring primary schools; (iii) it is possible that demographic variables in the catchment area are more closely related to school attendance than the pupil's attainments at age eleven.

This third point needs developing. Reynolds and Murgatroyd (1977) note that the schools served "a relatively homogenous community with very small differences in the social class composition of the people who live in the catchment areas of the different schools". Yet small social class differences may not reflect other possibly important differences between the catchment areas, such as the nature and adequacy of housing. A predominantly working class community with owner occupied housing may not differ in social class distribution from a council housing estate. Yet there *may* be major differences in school attendance rates. In a study of twenty-two catchment area variables derived from census data, Galloway *et al.* (1984) found virtually all to have a statistically highly significant relationship to school attendance.

These issues do not necessarily invalidate Reynold's results. His work has been of great importance in focusing attention on a grossly neglected area in research on poor attendance. They do, however, illustrate the methodological difficulties in demonstrating that differences between schools are due to factors within the schools and not to factors in their catchment areas. These difficulties are also evident in another highly influential and much quoted study.

Rutter *et al.* (1979) studied twelve schools in the Inner London Education Authority. They found that the average attendance of all fifth year pupils (fifteen- to sixteen-year-olds) ranged from 12.8 to 17.3 out of a maximum twenty attendances over two weeks in September and January. Attendance was related both to parental occupation and to the children's verbal reasoning ability at age ten. The relationship between ability level and attendance was not, however, the same within all the schools. The authors therefore carried out further analyses on results for the middle ability band, since this was the largest single group in each school. In addition they controlled for differences in parental occupation. They found that:

"The adjusted school attendance rates were then found to vary from 11.85 to 16.8 out of 20. ... Thus, when the analysis was restricted to pupils of similar ability, and when the effects of parental occupation had been taken into account, there were still substantial and statistically significant differences between schools."

Differences between schools were most marked in the fifth year, but were also evident to a lesser extent in the younger age groups. The differences were also maintained over a period of three years. This was seen both in the rankings of the nine schools and in the overall attendance rate at each school.

The principal difficulty in interpreting the London study, as in that of Reynolds *et al.* (1980) is the limited data on pupil intake and, more importantly, the school's catchment area. The methodological problems in controlling for catchment area variables are immense. The Radical Statistics Education Group (1982) concluded that the differences between schools found by Rutter *et al.* (1979) would probably remain if the results were submitted to a more rigorous statistical analysis, but would be much smaller.

In view of the problems in comparing schools, it may be more fruitful to look for changes in attendance rates within individual schools. If a school's overall attendance rises or falls, even though the catchment area remains the same, we can legitimately attribute the change to factors within the school. Rutter *et al.* (1979) found very small changes within their twelve schools over a three year period. Other studies, though, have noted substantial changes.

Jones (1980) described how the problem of poor attendance was tackled at Vauxhall Manor School in London (see Chapter 10). Here we need only note that the average September attendance rate rose from 77 per cent in 1974 to 88 per cent in 1977. She noted that attendance declined throughout each term, and throughout the year. This should not, however, obscure the dramatic changes reflected in these figures.

Galloway (1982a) compared persistent absentee rates over three years within each of thirty six mixed comprehensive schools in Sheffield. In the majority of schools the differences between the number of persistent absentees (less than 50 per cent attendance) were not significant. Table 4.1, however shows some interesting variations in seven schools. In five of these schools the number of persistent absentees fell over the three years. In two it rose. Although not shown in the table, changes in the number on roll each year were taken into account in the statistical analyses.

Table 4.1. *Changes over three years in numbers of pupils persistently absent from seven secondary schools*

School	Number of Persistent Absentees			Log Likelihood Ratio (df=2)*
	1974	1975	1976	
03	29	12	15	3.2 (p<.02)
04	35	10	16	20.7 (p<.001)
29	42	26	16	12.6 (p<.01)
22	33	12	16	14.6 (p<.001)
27	75	34	36	17.02 (p<.001)
11	60	96	87	7.5 (p<.05)
23	45	106	86	31.0 (p<.001)

Reproduced from *Educational Research*, Volume 24, p. 194 with the editor's permission.
*This is a statistical test for comparing data from two or more samples. Using conventional criteria, all the results are statistically significant. Taking school 11 as an example, p<.05 means that there is no more than one chance in twenty that the differences could be attributed to chance factors.

As the catchment areas underwent no major changes in these years, there is evidence that the changes reflected developments, or problems, in the schools themselves. The study did not extend to an analysis of the nature of these. In most cases, though, they were fairly obvious, at least superficially. A change of head teacher could have a profoundly disorientating effect, particularly if there was a long inter-regnum. Conversely, a concerted attempt to review the school's curriculum and pastoral care arrangements was reflected in a reduction in the number of persistent absentees from some schools.

Persistent absenteeism has been shown to correlate very highly with overall attendance rates (Galloway, 1980a; Rutter *et al.*, 1979). Monitoring changes in the number of persistent absentees over three years is nevertheless a very crude method of demonstrating a school's influence over its pupils' attendance. Yet if this admittedly crude measure can demonstrate changes, we might expect to find far more substantial changes from more refined measures. There is a notable lack of systematic attempts to monitor the effects of school-based initiatives affecting the curriculum, pastoral care system or general organisation. Nor has much effort been spent in identifying more refined methods for monitoring attendance generally. Using the Sheffield schools in Table 4.1 as an example, it would be interesting to know: (i) whether the numbers of short term absences (e.g. of less than three days) also changed over the three years; (ii) whether the amount of "hidden truancy", when the pupils missed lessons after registering, also changed.

Overall, there is now adequate evidence that schools do have an effect on the pupils' attendance. This conclusion is not invalidated by the methodological problems in comparing schools, nor by the crude measures that have been used to monitor attendance rates within individual schools. On the other hand, there is no doubt that factors in the catchment area also have a very substantial influence on attendance. The critical questions concern the nature both of catchment area and of school variables, and the ways they interact. We return to these questions in later chapters. First we need to consider the relationships between attendance and behaviour, and the evidence for school influences on behaviour.

SCHOOL ATTENDANCE, DELINQUENCY AND DISRUPTIVE BEHAVIOUR

Part of the folk lore of many magistrates and many teachers is that truancy and delinquency are indissolubly linked. Is truancy in fact strongly associated with delinquency and/or with disruptive behaviour at school? If so, this would help to explain why poor attendance is so widely seen as a social problem as well as an educational problem. It would also pose a separate question, concerning the extent of a school's influence over its pupils' behaviour. If some schools seem to protect their pupils from delinquent or disruptive behaviour, while others seem to facilitate these patterns, this could be seen as an additional reason for investigating the nature of pupils' experiences at school. The implication, at least for some children in some schools, might be that regular attendance could "protect" them from delinquency. Conversely, the effect of enrolment at other schools might be to encourage attitudes associated both with truancy and with delinquency.

As early as 1925 Burt was claiming an association between truancy and delinquency. Tennent (1971a) listed twenty studies of juvenile or adult offenders which reported at least 20 per cent of the sample as having a history of truancy. As Carroll (1977b) and Tennent (1971a) rightly point out, though, the fact that many delinquents have a history of truancy does not necessarily imply that a similar proportion of truants will have a history of delinquency.

There is some evidence that truants, as defined by most psychologists and psychiatrists are a high-risk group for delinquency. Tyerman (1958) reported that educational welfare officers had identified 144 pupils appearing in court for non-attendance between 1946–1952 as truants. Of these, 44 per cent had criminal records by the end of 1953. Hersov (1960a) noted that 74 per cent of his truant sample had appeared in court, compared with 2 per cent of the school refusers. May (1975) found that poor attenders regarded by their teachers as truants were more likely to have criminal records than absentees not so defined. Both groups were more likely to have appeared in court than good attenders. Nevertheless, fewer than half of the truants had appeared in court. Similar results were obtained by Ferguson (1952), who concluded that absentees were nearly twice as likely as good attenders to appear in Glasgow Courts. When the absenteeism was due to truancy, nearly 40 per cent of the sample had a criminal record.

In the 1976 study of persistent absenteeism in Sheffield, Galloway (1982a) collected information about all pupils in the survey aged eleven to sixteen known by the police to have been convicted in the juvenile court and/or to have received a formal verbal caution from the police before 1st September 1977. Table 4.2 shows the per cent of all absentees in each age group who were known to the police. Table 4.3 shows the per cent assigned to each category of absence who were known to the police. As expected, both the number and the percentage of offenders increased with age, both for boys and girls. Yet there was no age group in which more than 27 per cent of boys and 15 per cent of girls were known to the police.

The analysis by category shows that boy truants were the most delinquent group. Even so, only 36 per cent were known to have offended. Other noteworthy results from Table 4.3 are that 19 per cent of boys whose absence

Table 4.2. *Persistent absentees aged 11 or over from 1976 survey known to have been convicted in the Juvenile Court and/or to have received a verbal caution from the police*

| | Age Group | | | | | | |
	11	12	13	14	15	16	Total
Number of Boy Offenders	2	1	6	12	21	47	89
As Percentage of Boy Absentees in Age Group	13	6	19	20	25	27	23
Number of Girl Offenders	0	1	1	7	14	34	57
As Percentage of Girl Absentees in Age Group	0	4	2	10	15	15	12
Total	2	2	7	19	35	81	146
Percentage	5	5	9	14	20	20	17

Reproduced from *Educational Research*, Volume 24, p. 194, with the editor's permission.

was attributed mainly to illness were known to have offended. In addition, this was true of 24 per cent in the category of absence with parents' knowledge, consent and approval.

Overall, the evidence suggests that all absentees, including those whose absence is attributed to illness are "at risk" of delinquency. Truants seem considerably more likely than other groups to find themselves in trouble with the law. Thus, the picture which emerges both from clinic studies and from wider ranging surveys is of a consistent association between poor attendance and delinquency. Yet it is perfectly clear that truancy is neither a necessary nor a sufficient cause of delinquency. As both May (1975) and Tennent (1971a) imply, there is a need for studies which show *why* some absentees offend, while others do not.

Since the majority of absentees do not offend, it would obviously be illogical to argue that regular attendance would "protect" them from delinquency. A substantial minority, however, *does* offend. There appears to be no evidence on the likely effect of regular attendance on *these* pupils' delinquent activities. Nevertheless, fairly strong evidence has emerged that schools may indeed play an important part in the development, or prevention of delinquency.

The seminal study in this field was carried out in the London Borough of Tower Hamlets (Power et al., 1967, 1972, Phillipson, 1971). The authors showed that schools varied widely in their delinquency rates, and argued that these differences could not be attributed to differences in pupil intake. Baldwin (1972) criticised Power and his colleagues on methodological grounds. Moreover other studies have claimed that schools with high delinquency rates admit pupils who are already "at risk" by reason of their home neighbourhood (Farrington, 1972; West and Farrington, 1973).

Other longitudinal work, though, found that differences in the prevalence

Table 4.3. *Persistent absentees aged 11 or over in 1976 survey known to have been convicted in the Juvenile Court and/or to have received a verbal caution from the police*

	Boys		Girls		Total	
	Number of Offenders	Percentage of all boy Absentees in Category	Number of Offenders	Percentage of all Girl Absentees in Category	Number of Offenders	Percentage of all Absentees in Category
Absence Mainly Due to Illness	13	19	9	8	22	12
Some Illness, but Other Factors also Present	6	11	6	9	12	9
Absent with Parents' Knowledge, Consent and Approval	16	24	17	17	33	20
Parents Unable or Unwilling to Insist on Action	28	27	12	12	40	19
Truancy: Absence without Parents' Knowledge or Consent	14	36	5	15	19	26
"School Phobia" or Psycho-somatic Illness	4	27	2	7	6	14
Socio-medical Reasons, (e.g. Infestation, Scabies etc.)	3	21	1	6	4	13
Excluded or Suspended from School	2	33	1	100	3	43
Could not be Rated	3	33	4	27	7	29
Totals	89	23	57	12	146	17

Reproduced from *Educational Research*, Volume 24, p. 145, with the editor's permission of psychiatric disorder were attributable to school as well as family conditions (Rutter *et al.*, 1975; Rutter and Quinton, 1977). Both the comparative study of twelve London schools (Rutter *et al.*, 1979) and Reynolds' (1976) study of secondary modern schools in South Wales showed notable differences between schools in delinquency rates. The methodological problems involved in the limited range of intake variables have already been noted. It is interesting, though, that both studies found a consistent relationship between the outcome variables. Thus, schools which had high attendance rates tended also to have low delinquency rates, and, in London, good examination results. Cannon (1970) found some evidence that both the amount and the type of delinquency varied from school to school. This is consistent with the observation that schools' referral to child guidance and juvenile delinquency rates vary independently of the effects of home neighbourhood (Gath *et al.*, 1972, 1977).

Delinquency generally involves offences outside the school. There is evidence that pupils' behaviour while at school varies from school to school, and that these differences are not attributable to catchment area variables. Galloway (1976a) reported that Sheffield comprehensive schools which had incorporated a former grammar school tended to suspend more pupils than former secondary moderns. This suggested that the former grammar schools might be having more difficulty adjusting to the needs of their potentially troublesome pupils.

In a subsequent study carried out over four years we found enormous differences between schools in suspension rates (Galloway, 1980b). These were not associated in any systematic way with any of the twenty-two catchment area variables available for study (Galloway *et al.*, 1984). This, of course, stood in striking contrast to the highly significant relationship between catchment area variables and persistent absenteeism. An intensive study of the schools found evidence that the amount of disruptive behaviour varied dramatically from school to school. Schools with low suspension rates had some exceedingly disruptive pupils, who would certainly have been suspended from other schools. Perhaps because these pupils were in such small numbers at some schools, suspension was seldom considered necessary.

CONCLUSIONS

The research has shown a consistent tendency for absentees to come from disadvantaged backgrounds. The association between absenteeism and delinquency is similarly consistent. Yet the evidence is equally clear: (i) that only a fairly small minority of poor attenders gets into trouble with the police, and (ii) that a much smaller minority of children from socially disadvantaged homes are persistent poor attenders. The evidence that schools themselves exert an important influence over their pupils' attendance, independent of the catchment area, is not particularly extensive but all points in the same direction: it would be as myopic to ignore school influences on attendance as it would be to ignore personal, social and family background influences.

Unfortunately much of the debate has been conducted within narrow theoretical models which sometimes appear almost to be mutually exclusive. Much of the psychological and psychiatric research has tended to underestimate, or even to ignore, the school's contribution. Similarly, much of the sociological literature seems to imply that factors within the individual child or family are similarly unimportant. It would be naive to accept either view as correct. This becomes clear if we consider evidence from the absentees themselves.

It is not in dispute that fifteen- and sixteen-year-olds are more frequently absent than younger age groups. The fact that fifteen- and sixteen-year-olds from socially and economically disadvantaged families are more likely than any other group to be absent does not alter this point. Logically, the increasing absenteeism throughout the secondary school years could be caused by pressures in society and/or their families which affect adolescents more than children. This possibility needs investigating. It is possible, for example, that some adolescents are required to remain at home to look after younger children. Yet it would be absurd and irresponsible not also to investigate the possibility that the climate and curriculum of many secondary schools plays a central part in the sharp increase in absence rates from these schools compared with primary schools.

CHAPTER 5

Persistent Absentees and their Families

QUESTIONS ARISING FROM EARLIER STUDIES

Why the Increase in Secondary Schools?

The sharp increase in absenteeism throughout the secondary school years is well established. Equally uncontroversial is the peak in the final year of compulsory attendance. Theories of absenteeism which see the fault as lying in the family background have a problem explaining these well-documented facts. It is, after all, pretty ridiculous to suggest that adolescents have more disturbed or less privileged family backgrounds than younger children.

Theories which seek causal explanations in the pupils themselves have a similar problem. Before claiming that psychological factors explain the increasing absenteeism throughout the secondary school years, it is necessary: (a) to identify disorders which are particularly common in adolescence, and (b) to demonstrate a relationship between these and poor attendance. Adequate research evidence to support either possibility is conspicuously lacking. Longitudinal studies have shown a slight increase in the prevalence of psychiatric disorder in adolescence (e.g. Rutter *et al.*, 1976) mainly accounted for by an increase in the number of young people with depressed or withdrawn mood. There is no evidence, though, on which to regard these teenagers as poor attenders.

It is legitimate to argue that cognitive and educational factors may become more important as the child grows older. Thus, low intelligence, learning difficulties or reading backwardness may be less of a problem in primary schools than in secondary schools. Yet this merely restates the problem: we still need to know why.

Sociological research such as that of Willis (1977), Corrigan (1979) or Hargreaves (1967) gives a number of pointers but leaves many questions unanswered. The major problem for present purposes, of course, is that most

54

of the boys they studied were not very poor attenders, though they did frequently skip lessons. Moreover, many of their conclusions are at variance with those from clinical research. The "lads" Willis studies, for example, formed a fairly close friendship group. In contrast, most of Tyerman's (1958) truants were lonely, solitary children. Certainly there was no suggestion that they belonged even to a loosely knit anti-authority peer group. Nor was there evidence that the truancy resulted from resentment at the coercion implicit in a compulsory education system.

One way to investigate reasons for the increase in poor attendance at secondary schools is to compare absentees from primary schools with similarly poor attenders at secondary schools in the same areas. It would then be possible: (i) to see whether the two groups differ in any respects in terms of home background, intelligence or educational retardation; (ii) to see whether they differ in the pupils' own attitudes towards school, and experiences of it. Later in the chapter we describe a study which aimed to provide some tentative answers.

The Silent Majority

Psychologists and psychiatrists have spent a lot of time and effort studying school refusers and, to a lesser extent, truants. Yet the Sheffield surveys suggest that truants and school refusers account for a very small proportion of all persistent absentees who lack a legally acceptable reason. It seems quite extraordinary that by far the largest group should have received virtually no attention at all from child psychiatric and educational psychology services. It is almost as if there has been a bland, but unspoken assumption that absentees who are "withheld" by their parents merit neither help nor investigation.

It is surely important, though, to know why so many parents apparently condone, or at least tolerate, their children's absence from school. Parents of poor attenders tend to live in socially and financially disadvantaged circumstances. Yet that statement tells us nothing about their attitude towards education. Nor does it give any indication as to whether these attitudes change following the children's transfer to a secondary school. Equally important, the research has used very crude measures of social and financial disadvantage, for example, eligibility for free school meals. Low income can legitimately be seen as one index of disadvantage. Overcrowding is another. Yet few attempts have been made to investigate the range and nature of stress experienced by families of poor attenders.

Access to Specialist Services

It is clear that the majority of very poor attenders is never referred to psychological or psychiatric services for specialist investigation or help. In theory one reason could be that teachers, family doctors and educational welfare officers are skilled at recognising the school refusers who would benefit from clinical treatment. Again, in theory, it might be the case that children whose parents tolerate or actively condone their absence would not benefit from specialist treatment. There is no evidence either for or against these views.

Nevertheless, there is an obvious possibility that referrals to psychologists and psychiatrists reflect the views of referring agencies, rather than the needs of the children themselves or of their families. Although truants are generally reported to come from social class four and five, many studies have reported a disproportionate number of middle class families in samples of school refusers. This could simply reflect a greater willingness to refer middle class children, perhaps because teachers, doctors and educational welfare officers believe middle class parents are more likely to keep appointments.

No studies appear to have looked specifically at whether poor attenders referred to psychological or psychiatric services do in fact differ in any way from the much larger number who are not referred. The question is of some importance, particularly as evidence in Chapter 6 suggests that *some* children may benefit from specialist attention. In a study of delinquent children, Gath *et al.* (1972) found that children attending a child guidance clinic had similar characteristics to children taken to court. By implication, referral to a child guidance clinic was pretty fortuitous.

A study of children brought before the Leeds juvenile court for poor attendance identified three main groups (Berg *et al.*, 1978). The authors called one "clinical truancy", involving anti-social behaviour and educational problems. The second was labelled "school withdrawal" as it covered adverse social factors and parental complicity. The third was labelled "school refusal", and involved a tendency to social isolation. Most children, however, had features of all three groups, which were all evident to varying degrees. A further point about this study is that it was based on a juvenile court sample, which could therefore be as arbitrarily selected as a sample attending a child guidance or child psychiatric clinic.

Hence, there could be some value in comparing absentees who are referred for specialist help with similarly poor attenders who are not referred. Specifically, we need to know whether referring agencies show a bias towards, or against, particular groups. In addition, we need to know something about the reasons for referral in a depressed urban area. This is because almost all studies of school refusers have been based on predominantly middle class samples.

PLANNING THE STUDY

In planning the study we had to decide whether to interview all absentees in one selected area, or to draw a sample at random from across the whole city. We decided on the former for four principal reasons: (i) the city wide surveys had shown a very strong relationship between persistent absenteeism and financial hardship in the schools' catchment areas; it seemed sensible to concentrate effort on an area where the problem was greatest; (ii) concentrating in one area is the most appropriate way to investigate age differences in the factors associated with absence; selecting one secondary school "pyramid" (i.e. a secondary school and its feeding primary schools) reduces the possibility that differences observed between secondary and primary age groups are caused by neighbourhood differences over which the study has no control; (iii) the influence of school influences could be underestimated by selecting pupils from across the city; extreme dislike of a particular subject, for example, would not come to light unless it happened to be the same subject in all or most schools in the sample; (iv) finally, but by no means least, teachers in the selected area were concerned about pupils' attendance, and willing to co-operate in the project.

The Schools and their Catchment Area

The secondary school had a slightly above average number of pupils of compulsory school age on roll. At the time, the mean for all secondary schools in the city was 1,023. Over 12 per cent of the pupils received free school meals, a very high proportion by comparison with most Sheffield schools. Virtually the whole of the catchment area was characterised by many social problems with few owner occupied houses. It was fairly typical of the decaying districts in many large cities. Prior to the reorganisation of secondary education in Sheffield into a comprehensive system, the school did not have a selective intake. Most children lived within three miles of the school.

The catchment area divided roughly into three sections. Two of these had three primary schools. The third had two. The primary schools ranged in size from nearly 200 to nearly 500 children.

Selection of Children

We identified four samples of children: (i) all persistent absentees aged 12–15 on the roll of the secondary school, excluding children whose absences were attributed mainly to illness by the school's educational welfare officer;

(ii) all persistent absentees from the eight feeding primary schools; (iii) children in one area of the city who had been referred to the local education authority's psychological service on account of poor school attendance; the area of the city included the secondary school pyramid in (i) and (ii), but extended beyond it; (iv) regular attenders from the same class in school as a representative sample of the secondary and primary school absentees.

Each sample contained a roughly equal number of boys and girls. The persistent absentees in the secondary and primary school samples had all missed at least 50 per cent of possible attendances in the Autumn term 1975. None of these children had been referred to the psychological service for poor attendance. The "referred" sample, though, contained several poor attenders from these schools. Regular attenders were defined as pupils who had been present for at least 85 per cent of possible attendances in the term immediately preceding the interview.

Response Rate

We interviewed parents of thirty-nine secondary school absentees, twenty from the primary schools, twenty who had been referred to the psychological service, and twenty-three regular attenders. For the three absentee samples these figures represent more than 90 per cent of the original sample. The acceptance rate from parents of regular attenders was 74 per cent. The lower response rate from regular attenders was possibly because initial contact was by letter from a head teacher. For the absentees, initial contact was a personal request from an education welfare officer or from the psychologist to whom the child had been referred.

The Interviews

At least one parent in each family was interviewed. Most of the children were interviewed subsequently. A few were not available, for reasons such as committal to care or because they were in hospital. The five regular attenders from primary schools were aged less than eight and we did not feel that any conclusions could be drawn from such a small number.

The interviews sought wide ranging information, and are described in full elsewhere (Galloway, 1980a, 1982b). The general approach was "semi-structured". That is to say, the same information was requested from each family, but both the order and the way in which questions were asked depended on the circumstances. In addition, issues which seemed of particular importance to the parent or child were discussed in greater depth. The results are described below. Selected items from the interviews with parents are shown in Table 5.1 and from the interviews with pupils in Table 5.3.

INTERVIEWS WITH PARENTS

Housing, Employment and Family Structure

In all four samples more than 84 per cent of pupils lived in the older forms of council housing, either high-rise flats or estates of semi-detached houses. Most families had been living at their present address for four years or more. At least in this area, there was no suggestion that poor attendance was associated with the disruption of frequent changes of address and school.

In each of the three absentee samples more than two-thirds of the families contained four or more children per family. Only 50 per cent of the regular attenders' families had four or more children. The regular attenders were significantly more likely to be the oldest, youngest or only child in their family than the secondary school absentees. Studies of school refusers have noted that they are frequently the oldest, youngest or only children (e.g. Hersov, 1960a). Moreover, these studies have also noted relatively small family size, at least when compared with that in the Sheffield absentee samples.

Table 5.1. *Selected Items from Interviews with Parents**

	Secondary School Absentees (N = 39)	Primary School Absentees (N = 20)	Absentees Referred to Psychological Service (N = 20)	Regular Attenders (N = 23)*
Neither parent in current employment (%)	53	53	53	9
Parents had received social security in last twelve months* (%)	66	88	63	27
Mothers' mean score on Health Questionnaire*	6.8	8.8	6.3	4.2
Fear of particular teacher (%)	67	10	45	22
Dislike of particular subject (%)	46	5	35	39
Mean number of measures of disadvantage or potential stress	7.7	7.9	8.4	4.9
Mean number of behaviour problems reported**	6.8	6.1	10.2	4.9

*The sample sizes refer to the total numbers interviewed. Complete information was not obtained in all cases, but each result given here is based on at least N = 36 (secondary absentees), N = 16 (primary absentees), N = 18 (absentees referred to the psychological service) and N = 19 (regular attenders)
** The difference between the four groups is statistically significant for each item. For full details see Galloway (1982b)

There was no statistically significant difference between the four samples on overcrowding, defined as three or more people per bedroom, apart from the parents. Nor were any significant differences found in family structure, though fewer of the regular attenders were not living with both parents, than of the absentees. Separation or divorce and/or the death of at least one parent was reported of 27 per cent of the regular attenders' families, and 53 per cent of the primary school absentees'. The secondary and the referred absentees were between these two points.

The regular attenders were less likely to live in families with neither parent working than children in any of the absentee sample. Similarly: (i) their parents were significantly less likely to have received social security at some stage in the previous twelve months than those of both secondary and primary school absentees; (ii) their father or stepfathers were more likely to be supporting the family financially. The general picture to emerge was clearly that persistent poor attendance was associated with financial problems to a degree not found with families of regular attenders. Yet here, too, the obvious question is: why?

Health and Early History

There was a tendency for the referred absentees to have had more separations from both parents than children in the other absentee samples or the regular attenders. At least 30 per cent of children in each sample, including the regular attenders, suffered from some chronic illness requiring regular or frequent medication, such as asthma, bronchitis or migraine, and/ or had in the past suffered a serious illness or accident requiring in-patient treatment. "Socio medical" problems such as infestation or scabies had affected 70 per cent of the primary school absentees, a much higher proportion than in any other sample.

Parents' Health

We wondered whether parents of poor attenders might more often be in poor health than parents of regular attenders. If so this could have obvious relevance to the children's school attendance. We therefore asked parents about their own health. The results indicated that regular attenders were less likely than the referred absentees to have both parents suffering from chronic illness. There were no significant differences between the three absentee samples in the incidence of chronic illness in either parent, nor in the incidence of severe illnesses or accidents in either parent.

At the end of the interview we asked parents to complete a twenty-three item Health Questionnaire (Rutter *et al.*, 1970) on their own health. This questionnaire was originally designed as a screening instrument to identify people likely to be diagnosed in a psychiatric interview as suffering from some clinically significant form of psychiatric disorder. The questionnaire items focus on possible symptoms of minor psychiatric disorder, such as: "Do you feel tired most of the time?" "Do you often have bad headaches?" "Are you easily upset or irritated?" Answers to each question were simply "yes" or "no". Scores of seven and over indicate an increasing possibility that a person will be experiencing significant psychiatric problems. Analysis of the results was confined to the mothers' responses, as fathers were not sufficiently often present at the interviews to justify comparisons.

We calculated the mean scores of mothers in each of the three samples. The results showed mothers of the regular attenders to have significantly lower mean scores, indicating better mental health, than mothers in any of the three absentee samples. We were also able to compare the scores obtained by our four samples with those obtained by two samples of women on the Isle of Wight where the questionnaire was developed (Chadwick, 1976). The two Isle of Wight samples were a control group of mothers who were all known *not* to be suffering from any form of psychiatric disorder, and a "psychiatric" sample who had been diagnosed at interview as suffering from some form of psychiatric disorder (Chadwick, 1976). The results showed that mothers in all the Sheffield absentee samples were significantly more likely to have scores of seven or higher than mothers of the Isle of Wight control sample. More interesting, though, was that roughly the same proportion of mothers in the three absentee groups obtained these high scores as of mothers of the Isle of Wight psychiatric sample.

The majority of parents with high scores in the Health Questionnaires reported symptoms associated with depression. At one level this is not altogether surprising. Epidemiological research on the health of mothers of young children in inner city areas has consistently found a high rate of such symptoms (e.g. Rutter *et al.*, 1975). The results do, nevertheless, suggest two possible links with poor school attendance: (i) parents who are themselves feeling ill or depressed are likely to have little energy for ensuring their children's regular attendance; it may be much easier simply to let the child stay at home; (ii) the possible effects of a parent's poor health, particularly poor psychiatric health, on children's adjustment are well known (e.g. Rutter, 1966); well justified anxiety about a parent's health may be a powerful inducement to remain at home.

Contributing Factors at School

We asked parents about eight problems at school which might have contributed to their children's poor attendance. The eight problems were: bullying; fear of a teacher; extreme dislike of any particular subject; boredom; a sense of academic failure; difficulty with social relationships with other pupils; influence of peers; anxiety or self-consciousness related to sexual development or relationships.

Parents of secondary absentees reported fear of a particular teacher and extreme dislike of a particular subject in the curriculum significantly more frequently than parents of the primary pupils. Fear of a teacher also distinguished the secondary school absentees from the regular attenders, though this was not true of dislike of a particular subject. Indeed parents of regular attenders, a majority of whom attended the secondary school, regarded dislike of a particular subject as a substantial source of stress for their children more frequently than parents of the primary school absentees.

Thus, information from parents confirmed the prediction from the city-wide surveys. Parents of primary school absentees seldom considered that problems at school had contributed to their children's poor attendance. Parents of secondary school absentees noted this much more frequently. A further point is that the referred group was characterised by a much greater frequency of difficulty in social relationships with other pupils. The picture was more often of a socially isolated child who felt lost in a large secondary school.

Parents' Observations on their Children's Behaviour

We asked parents about ten possible indications of "disturbed" or difficult behaviour out of school. They were: child shows anxiety about harm befalling parent/about parents' health; history of anxiety about leaving home; psycho-somatic symptoms associated with school attendance; abdominal pains; eating difficulties, sleep disturbance; history of enuresis; history of stealing; history of lying; history of wandering (e.g. staying out late, or not coming home).

There was a general tendency for parents of regular attenders to report problems less frequently than parents of the absentees. This was particularly true of a history of stealing. Perhaps the most notable result, though, was that 36 per cent of the secondary absentees and 45 per cent of the primary and referred absentees were said to have shown anxiety about their parents' health. Similarly, a slightly higher proportion was said to have had a history of anxiety about leaving home. This is, of course, consistent with a recurring theme in the clinical research on school refusal. The research on school refusal, however, sees separation anxiety as an essentially "neurotic" problem. Many of the children in our study had good reason to be concerned about their parents' health. We return to this point later.

Multiple Stress

In addition to knowing about individual indices of stress, it is important to have a broader picture. This is because of evidence that the effect of stress is cumulative (e.g. Rutter, 1978, 1981). A family may, for example, be able to cope with poor housing, *or* bereavement, or financial problems, *or* one member's illness. If all these are combined at the same time the effect may be much more severe, both for the family as a whole and for individual members.

Following the interviews with parents we listed the items which indicated social disadvantage and/or potential stress in the family. They are listed in Table 5.2. Certain items were omitted to avoid possible overlap. For example, "father unemployed, or alive but not supporting family" would have over-lapped with "parents receive social security, or have done so within the last twelve months. Conversely, "not living with both parents" and "child has been/is in care" were both included, since it was felt that being in care constituted an additional risk factor over and above the fact of not living with both parents. We ascribed a value of 0 or 1 to each item, depending on whether a parent reported it. This enabled us to calculate a total for each child, and hence a mean for each sample.

The results were unequivocal. The range was from a mean of 4.9 items for the regular attenders to 8.4 for the referred absentees. On average, children in

Table 5.2. *Measures of Disadvantage and/or Potential Stress from Social Histories*

1. Live in high-rise or tenement flat, or older-type estate of semi-detached council houses.
2. More than 3 children per bedroom.
3. More than 4 children in family.
4. Not living with both parents.
5. Child has history of chronic illness.
6. Child has history of severe illness or accident.
7. 1 or more sibling has history of chronic illness.
8. 1 or more sibling has history of severe illness or accident.
9. Mother has history of chronic illness.
10. Mother has history of severe illness or accident.
11. Father has history of chronic illness.
12. Father has history of severe illness or accident.
13. Bereavement of close relative.
14. Child has been/is in care.
15. 1 or more sibling has been/is in care.
16. Parents are on Social Security/have been within last 12 months.
17. More than 2 weeks' separation from mother.
18. More than 2 weeks' separation from father.
19. History of "socio-medical" problems.

each of the three absentee samples were living with significantly more measures of disadvantage and/or potential stress than the regular attenders. We found no significant differences between the three absentee samples.

Multiple Behaviour Disturbance

We also thought it important to note the number of indications of behavioural disturbance that parents reported for each child. Just as the effect of social disadvantage may be cumulative, so may the effect of a child's behaviour. At a common sense level, parents or teachers who can cope with *one* form of difficult behaviour may have great difficulty when they find *several* aspects of the child's behaviour difficult.

Behaviour items were drawn from three sources: (i) items reported as "definitely" applying on the "Behaviour Statement" part of Rutter's (A2) scale (1970). This is a questionnaire for parents, designed to identify children showing "clinically significant" symptoms of psychiatric disorder; (ii) items from the contributing factors at school, noted above, and items from the parents' observations of their child's behaviour, noted above. We felt some doubt as to whether the school items should be included. The decision to do so was based on the view that, implicitly or explicitly, they described disturbing aspects of the child's behaviour at school, and in the case of the absentee pupils were frequently cited as contributing reasons for absence. The same principles were used in analysing the data as for analysing the evidence on multiple stress.

The results differed from those for multiple stress. The range was from a mean of 4.9 items for the regular attenders, to 10.2 for the referred absentees. The referred sample differed significantly from the other two absentee samples and from the regular attenders in the high number of problems reported by parents. The secondary school absentees also were reported as presenting more behavioural problems than the regular attenders.

We would stress, though, that not all the items included in this analysis would necessarily have been considered a problem by parents. Thus, a child's anxiety about a parent's health could be seen as evidence of sympathy. This becomes more likely if it leads an older child to remain at home in order to help the parent. It does not, however, invalidate the overall impression both from the statistical analysis and from the interviews that parents of children in the referred sample tended to report a high number of problems from their children.

INTERVIEWS WITH CHILDREN

The interviews with the children covered some of the same ground as the interviews with parents. This was partly because we wished to discuss their attendance with them as well as with their parents, and partly as an informal check on the validity of information provided in the interviews. A high level of agreement between the information provided by children, for example, on possible pressures at school, and the information from parents would indicate that these were problems of some duration, and not simply the result of a recent, perhaps isolated incident. In fact the agreement between children and their parents was generally high.

Table 5.3. *Selected Items from Interviews with Pupils**

	Secondary School Absentees (N = 34)	Primary School Absentees (N = 18)	Absentees Referred to Psychological Service (N = 19)	Regular Attenders (N = 17)
Fear of harm befalling parent/ anxiety about parents' health (%)	74	56	47	24
Sense of academic failure (%)	44	44	79	24
Reading age at least two years below chronological age* (%)	77	50	83	94
Mean verbal scale I.Q.**	89	86	86	86

*N = 31, 18, 19, 16
**N = 34, 18, 19, 16
For full details of statistical analyses see Galloway (1982b)

More children in each of the three absentee samples expressed concern about their parents' health and safety than the regular attenders. A similar tendency was evident in the absentee pupils' statements about staying at home to help their parents or to look after young siblings. Compared with the regular attenders, significantly more of the referred group expressed anxiety about academic failure as a contributing reason for their poor attendance. Another source of anxiety expressed by these children was their difficulty in social relationships with other children. More than half of both the secondary and the referred absentees expressed extreme dislike of a particular subject. Nearly two-thirds of the secondary absentees claimed to stay away from school on account of fear of a particular teacher. The regular attenders stood out sharply from the primary and the referred groups, and to a lesser extent from the secondary sample in being more likely to have interests outside the home.

Fifty per cent of children in the primary sample were at least two years backward in reading. This applied to 77 per cent of the secondary absentees, 83 per cent of the referred group, and an astonishing 94 per cent of the regular attenders. The mean verbal scale on a short form of Wechsler's (1974) Intelligence Scale for Children was between 86 and 89 in all four samples.

The results on reading backwardness were, to put it mildly, a bit disconcerting. One possible explanation comes from the way the sample was selected. Many of the secondary absentees were in a "remedial" class. Hence, many of the regular attenders were also drawn from remedial classes. It is at least possible that some poor attenders were placed in these classes partly because of their absence, while the regular attenders were placed in them because of their lack of ability.

Whether or not this was the case, the prevalence of reading backwardness raises some interesting questions about the nature of the pupils' experiences at school. The regular attenders *did* attend, although most of them were seriously backward in reading. Yet this does not make it any less probable that the absentees would have experienced a good deal of frustration at school had they started to attend regularly.

Certainly, the majority could never realistically have hoped for useful passes in the Certificate of Secondary Education (i.e. passes which would have improved their career prospects). This is not to say that C.S.E. would have been an unrealistic goal in different circumstances. Our point is simply that regular attendance at *this* stage in their school life would have done little or nothing to improve either examination or career prospects for most of the secondary age pupils.

We asked the secondary school absentees and the pupils of secondary age in the referred and regular attender samples to fill in the Health Questionnaire that their parents had completed. With adolescents, a score of six has been found the most reliable cut off point when using the questionnaire as a screening instrument to identify "clinically significant" psychiatric disorder (Chadwick, 1976). Fifty-three per cent of the secondary sample obtained scores at or above this criterion, compared with 31 per cent of the secondary age children in the referred group, and 18 per cent of the regular attenders.

The results imply that many persistent absentees of secondary age experience a range of health problems. These may be seen as symptoms of stress, and could be regarded as evidence of minor, non-psychotic psychiatric disorder in a medical interview. It does not follow from the way Rutter and Graham (1968) define psychiatric disorder that referral to a psychiatrist would be either beneficial or even necessary. Nevertheless, it is clear that the evidence does not support a Tom Sawyer theory which regards poor attenders as happy, well-adjusted young rebels escaping from the tyranny of school.

SUBSEQUENT ATTENDANCE

We obtained details from school records about the attendance of all children whose parents agreed to take part in the project. We covered a six term period, from the Autumn term 1975, up to and including the Summer term 1977. A small number was lost to the survey, either through committal to care, or (in the Summer term 1977) through having left school the previous Easter.

Table 5.4 shows the mean attendance of pupils in each sample over the six terms. Apart from a small improvement in 1976, the secondary school absentees continued to attend school infrequently over the two year period. In contrast, the primary sample improved slowly but consistently. By the Summer term of 1977 their average attendance was nearly 60 per cent, or more than 20 per cent higher than two years previously.

In the course of the two years 1975–1977, nine pupils in the referred sample were transferred to special schools. Two went to schools designated for the maladjusted, two to schools for maladjusted children who also had "moderate" learning difficulties, i.e. the ESN(M), and five to schools for delicate children. Before transfer they averaged 34 per cent attendance. Subsequently they averaged 69 per cent. This compares with an overall average of 42 per cent for the eleven pupils in the referred sample who were not transferred to a special school. Attendance of four children in the special school groups may have been improved by provision of a taxi for transport to and from school. For two other children, transfer to the special school coincided with removal from grossly disturbing and unsatisfactory home backgrounds by reception into care.

Table 5.4. *Mean Per Cent Attendance of Pupils in Each Sample, 1975–1977*

	Autumn 1975	Spring 1976	Summer 1976	Autumn 1976	Spring 1977	Summer 1977
Secondary school absentees	31	41	40	43	32	31
Primary school absentees	38	49	51	54	56	59
Referred absentees	47	46	35	45	55*	55*
Regular attenders	91	92	92	94	93	91

*These figures reflect improvement in some pupils' attendance following transfer to a special school (see text).

THE MEANING OF POOR ATTENDANCE FOR THE PUPILS AND THEIR FAMILIES

There is no shortage of ideas on the reasons for poor school attendance. Teachers, magistrates, psychologists, sociologists and psychiatrists have all had plenty to say. Yet the explanations frequently seem to reflect the discipline and/or the bias of the writer as much as the experience of the children or their families. Superficially this is inevitable. The information a researcher or a clinician obtains depends, at least to some extent, on what he looks for; the answers he gets depend on the questions he asks. Someone whose professional background and training leads him to regard school experiences as lying at the root of poor attendance will seek quite different information to that sought by a psychoanalytically-orientated therapist.

This problem is compounded by the widespread observation that asking absentees *why* they have missed school is seldom a fruitful exercise. More often than not, the question simply does not seem to relate to their personal experience. The question implies the possibility of a conscious, rational decision. Further, it implies that the pupil is aware of different factors influencing her attendance, can weigh them all up and decide which is of most importance. A glazed incomprehension is a frequent response to the question: "Why don't you go to school?" Some children, of course, can articulate their reasons. For the majority, if the reply extends beyond "don't know" it is influenced by what they think the adult authority figure will consider acceptable.

Yet we found in our research in Sheffield that these same pupils would talk freely about their activities at school and at home. They participated freely in interviews with their parents, and later agreed willingly to talk about their lives in and out of school. Most were willing, and many eager, to talk about circumstances they found difficult or unpleasant either at home or at school. As they talked it became clear why the question: Why don't you go to school? was so inappropriate. For a family on social security a skiing holiday in Switzerland would not be a realistic option. Nor, for many of the children we interviewed, would regular school attendance. Faced with the reality of their day to day experience, it became futile to expect reasons for poor attendance. Rather, poor attendance was part of the process by which they adapted to their current situation.

At first sight this argument seems to deny the school's influence on attendance. We argue that this is not the case. In many middle class families regular school attendance is the accepted norm. Yet unsatisfactory experiences at school can encourage, or at least facilitate, absence. For many families in our study erratic attendance was the norm. Yet as we saw in Chapter 4, some schools seem to encourage better attendance than others, irrespective of their catchment areas.

Truancy and Condoned Absence

When talking about their absence from school several pupils spontaneously distinguished between absence with their parents' knowledge and truancy. Asked about his day-time activities when not at school, a boy in the secondary sample used the local term for truancy in his reply:

Stay in house, or go out with me mates if they're not at school. More often I stay in house. (But) I often wag it, either on my own or with me mates.

A girl in the secondary sample explained why she stayed at home with her parents, especially when her mother was ill, but insisted:

I've never wagged it.

Another girl in the secondary sample, when asked if her friends ever encouraged her to stay off school replied firmly:

No, I've never played truant.

This girl, too, stayed at home to help her mother. Doing so was not only the logical, but also the rational, proper thing to do. Truancy, or "wagging it" was recognised as being against the law. That, however, implied absence without parents' consent. Staying at home to help, or simply to be with parents was seen in an entirely different light. Certainly, the local education authority could, and sometimes did take legal action to enforce attendance. Yet that did not mean they had done anything wrong. It was merely another of life's unpredictable hazards.

The fact that the pupils themselves distinguished between truancy and being at home in school hours with their parents' knowledge suggests that truants might differ from other absentees. This would, of course, be predicted from the clinical research on truancy and school refusal. In the next chapter we describe a comparison between truants and other absentees.

Parent–Child Dependency

Psychiatric studies of school refusers have frequently noted mutually dependent relationships between parents and children. The mother of a primary school boy in the sample referred to the psychological service said:

I made him dependent on me. . . . I do it (dressing him) because it's easier.

The social worker of an extremely withdrawn twelve-year-old boy in the referred sample described a home visit in which she found the boy sitting on his mother's knee having his hair and back stroked. This boy was subsequently committed to care and stayed in a children's home for five months. During this period he missed no school, although the attendance of some other children in the home was highly erratic. His attendance declined immediately on return home, presumably because his mother's behaviour towards him remained unchanged.

The relationships were seldom as complex as in these two examples, though. More characteristic was the secondary school boy whose father said:

He doesn't like his mother going out—always wants to know when she's coming in. (He's) a bit protective towards her.

The mother of a sixteen-year-old girl said:

The children think they owe me something, with their dad leaving.

The girl herself agreed that she stayed at home with her mother. She also made clear that there were things she disliked at school. She particularly disliked one teacher, and in the past had stayed at home to avoid P.E. She was embarrassed both at having no kit and by having to take a shower afterwards. Concern about her mother, who was overweight and had chronic chest troubles was also relevant. Mother and daughter apparently had a close relationship, enjoying each other's company during the day.

Parental Health

A parent's poor health is inevitably a source of anxiety to any child. The anxiety implies neither that the child is over-dependent on the parent nor vice versa. It can, however, be compounded by conflicting messages from a parent. Thus, the solo father of a fifteen-year-old girl in the secondary absentees sample said he could not understand why his daughter did not like going to school. Yet he spoke at length of his own health problems, and admitted that in the past he had kept her away from school because of them. This girl's mother had died seven years earlier and the previous year her grandfather, to whom she had been close, had also died. In the circumstances this girl would have had to be highly insensitive to take at face value her father's stated concern that she attend school.

Even when no conflicting messages were evident, it was frequently not necessary to look very far for a motive in remaining at home. The father of a secondary school girl in the referred sample had died suddenly five years earlier. At the time everyone thought she had "got over it marvellously" because she had neither cried nor stayed away from school, even though she had had a close relationship with her father. The mother had become depressed after her husband's death. In addition she suffered from chronic bronchitis which had several times necessitated in-patient treatment. This girl's fear that her remaining parent might also die was not unrealistic.

Several of the children were acutely aware of, and worried by, their parents' mental and/or physical health. A fourteen-year-old boy in the secondary absentees' sample said:

Before my dad went (i.e. died) I stopped in with my Mum; she got nervous and that; she's still suffering with her nerves.

This boy, too, had few friends at school. In addition he was virtually a non-reader. For him, "stopping in with my Mum" was not so much part of a conscious decision to avoid school as the most obvious course of action available. Given his circumstances at home and at school, he might indeed have felt some difficulty in explaining a decision to attend.

Not all the children whose parents were ill showed obvious signs of anxiety. Some seemed to accept the situation in a matter of fact way. A twelve-year-old girl in the group of primary school absentees denied that she was influenced by other children, explaining:

> I only stay off when my Mum knows. She's poorly, you see.

Her mother was indeed "poorly", appearing extremely depressed, and suffering from agoraphobia and chronic backache for which she refused to see a doctor because of her fear of hospitals.

Occasionally a particularly strong-minded child would take responsibility for other children. A nine-year-old girl in the primary sample was the second child in a family of eight. Her mother described her as the dominant child who always did what she wanted to, but spent a lot of time helping look after her younger brothers and sisters. The mother was awaiting an operation. The girl regarded fear of something happening to her mother as the main reason for her absences from school, explaining:

> Me Mother's got something in her stomach that's got to be taken out.

She made clear, however, that she had never discussed this with her mother.

Other Family Stress

As noted earlier in the chapter, many families were living in multiply disadvantaged circumstances. That, however, is a statement about their circumstances relative to other groups in society. It says nothing about how they themselves regarded their situation. During the interviews it frequently became extremely clear that both parents and children were experiencing a great deal of stress. One mother described how her daughter's poor attendance had started two years earlier, following her father going to live with another woman. Since then the mother had felt depressed, sometimes spending the whole day sitting in a chair weeping. She had been "summoned" to appear before the l.e.a.'s school attendance sub-committee to explain her daughter's absence (see Chapter 7) and became very agitated when describing what she saw as the intimidating, threatening manner of councillors and teacher union representatives. Perhaps as a result of the generally depressed mood she had got into financial difficulties, and was heavily in arrears with her rent, with the council threatening eviction from her flat. This woman described her own school attendance as good:

> I had to go.

Yet there was a real sense in which her daughter "had" to stay at home, not because her mother explicitly required her to do so, but because getting up and going to school required a conscious, deliberate decision, and she lacked any incentive to make such a decision.

Occasionally the family problems seemed to have overwhelmed the child to the extent that school simply became an irrelevance. An eight-year-old boy in the sample of primary school absentees had spent a lot of time wandering by a canal and vandalising cars. His mother had received in-patient treatment for depression. She described a series of harrowing experiences in the first four years of his life, which culminated in her "kidnapping" him from an elderly relative. She was in arrears with rent and items bought on hire purchase, and had recently taken an overdose. Her common law husband himself suffered from a serious chronic illness, but was having an affair with another woman. Both for the mother and for the child, school attendance was a very long way down their list of priorities.

Some children became involved in parental friction which was not of their own making. The mother of a boy in the secondary sample described her husband's violence and drinking habits. The only child for whom he showed any liking was apparently his youngest daughter. Because of this, the mother explained that she had been indulgent to the boy over his absences from school, concealing them from her husband.

School

The stress experienced at home by many of the absentees in our samples was both chronic and severe. This does not, however, mean that schools had no influence on their attendance. Three possibilities are worth considering: (i) that experiences at school may, for some pupils, to some extent compensate for the stress they experience at home, or at least, enable them to cope with it; (ii) that experiences at school provide an additional source of stress, thus compounding the stress some pupils feel under at home; (iii) that experiences at school are simply irrelevant to anything that happens at home.

For teachers the first possibility is perhaps the most important. It is also the most difficult to investigate. The evidence we reviewed earlier suggests that schools do affect their pupils' attendance. Whether the most successful schools do in fact help their pupils cope with stressful family life remains very much an open question.

In the Sheffield studies we found little evidence that experiences at school were seen as helpful, either by the absentees or by the regular attenders. In retrospect, a limitation of the interviews was that they focused on sources of potential stress at school, and made little explicit attempt to assess positive experiences. There was, however, plenty of evidence that some pupils and some parents regarded school simply as an irrelevance, while others regarded it with active hostility.

Most frequently, persistent absence could be seen as the product of experiences both at school and at home. A boy in the secondary school sample explained:

> I don't go if I'm late because I get done by Mr. Y. (a senior teacher) ... If you're late more than three times in a week he canes you.

Boys at the school *had* been caned in the past for persistent lateness, though this punishment was certainly not used routinely. The boy himself was a nervous child who would easily have been intimidated by an angry teacher. His mother seemed far too tired and depressed to help him and his younger brothers and sisters get up in time for school. In addition, as both the boy himself and his mother explained in interview, the mother often kept him at home to help her in the house. The senior teacher's wrath at lateness was, at the same time, a genuine source of anxiety and a convenient reason for staying away.

Some parents made clear that they regarded education, at best, with considerable scepticism. The mother of a primary school boy noted dryly, talking about the infant school he had attended:

> They didn't learn him anything at that school.

The boy's reading age, incidentally, was above his chronological age. The parent of a sixteen-year-old girl was in no doubt about what could be done to improve school attendance:

> Let 'em leave at fifteen!

These parents did not regard absence from school as any sort of problem. With some justification, they considered their daughter an adult, and thought she should be allowed to leave. The parents of a sixteen-year-old boy expressed a similar point of view. School attendance was only a problem to the extent that the authorities made a fuss about it. As the mother exclaimed while completing the Rutter (A2) scale:

> All this trouble just because he doesn't go to school!

A minority of pupils, though, expressed intense resentment towards their school. A girl in the secondary sample explained that she sometimes stayed at home when absent from school. More often she "wagged it" with her brother or with other girls. She was determined to get away from school:

> The lads used to call me names ... other kids always making me go red ... I used to have fights with the lads; they used to call me slag ... didn't hardly know the teachers. The form teacher used to say: "Put the flags out—Smith's come to school today!" Other kids used to laugh, so I went mad and walked out.

School was not the only source of stress for this girl. She and the other children in her family had all spent a period in the care of the local authority, but were now living at home again.

A boy in the secondary sample was eloquent about two particular teachers:

> She goes on and on about Jesus and things. I don't like it, it gets me mad . . . (another) teacher . . . I can't stand him—he says he will try and get my lessons changed but he hasn't . . . he doesn't reason with you; I can't really tell him: "I don't come to school because I hate you"! He thinks he's an ex copper. He goes: "oh, I've put some kids in Shirecliffe (A local social services home for boys on remand) today", and things like that.

Some of the regular attenders, too, had complaints about school. One secondary school girl expressed considerable doubts and fear of a teacher, but insisted that her mother made her go. Another insisted that he would not come to school if his mother was ill or had an accident; he would have to stay at home to look after her.

COMMENT

When we did our research unemployment was a relatively minor problem in Sheffield. Most school leavers could find jobs. Since then the position has changed dramatically. For the overwhelming majority of pupils who do not progress to further or higher education the only realistic prospect is unemployment. The old adage, beloved of teachers even before education became free and compulsory, that a good school report and a scatter of examination passes were the prospects to a good job is now manifestly untrue.

This might seem to legitimise the views of those parents who regarded pressure from the local education authority as the only problem arising from their children's poor attendance. If school is quite obviously not a preparation for work—since there is little or no work available—why bother to attend school? From a teacher's point of view the answer, of course, could be that the threat of unemployment makes school attendance doubly important. Teachers could argue that they have an essential role in preparing pupils for the pressures they will face on the dole. Or, more plausibly, they might argue that positive experiences at school can have a beneficial effect on a pupil's self-esteem, and that this is intrinsically desirable, irrespective of what the future holds.

The trouble with these arguments is not that they are necessarily false. Teachers in some schools *may* be able to help pupils prepare for the pressures they will face on leaving. They certainly *can* offer experiences which are intrinsically desirable. The trouble with the arguments is rather that few, if any, of the absentees in our study saw them in this light. Nor did their parents.

Only a few pupils expressed a strong sense of alienation from school. The majority expressed dislike of *some* aspects of school. The overwhelming impression, though, was not that they were consciously rejecting the school and its values. Rather, the school and its values seemed peripheral to their lives. School for these families was not a place for learning, discovery or personal growth. It was a place children were supposed to attend during the day because "they" said so. Some teachers were disliked but not the majority. Indeed many children made clear that they liked individual teachers, as well as some subjects. Yet attendance was seldom seen in terms of co-operation between parents and teachers. For these families the impersonal "they" who made school attendance compulsory were as faceless, nameless, as the councillors who set the rents to their houses or flats, or the officials who sent out the electricity bills.

As a result, the problem of school attendance was often treated in the same way as a demand for payment of an electricity bill or a hire purchase demand—something to be deferred for as long as possible. For a majority of families, living in multiply disadvantaged, acutely stressful circumstances, school attendance was low on the list of priorities. For parents the higher priorities were more basic: housing, heating, food, their own health and the health of their children. Many parents simply lacked the energy to pack a reluctant child off to school. The children, too, regarded school attendance as a low priority when faced with the more immediate problem of a chronically depressed parent, younger brothers and sisters who needed looking after, food that needed to be bought.

School was seldom seen as an active source of advice, help and support. Instead, school attendance was normally seen as just one more burden to be born. In the last three chapters of the book we argue that this is neither necessary nor inevitable. First though, we must consider the possibilities and the limitations in some of the well tried, if conventional approaches to absence from school.

CHAPTER 6

Partial Solutions? I. Clinical Treatments

INTRODUCTION

The distinction which psychiatrists make between school refusers, truants and pupils withheld by their parents has already been noted (Hersov, 1977). In practice, the great majority of poor attenders referred to child psychiatrists are "diagnosed" either as truants or school refusers. There is not the slightest doubt, however, that children who are referred constitute a very small proportion indeed of all unauthorised absentees. In Sheffield, for example, the number of pupils thought to have missed over half their schooling, illegally, in the autumn term was roughly the same as the *total* number of children seen by all the l.e.a.'s psychologists in the whole year. Hence, most persistent absentees were never referred to educational psychologists.

The proportion of poor attenders referred to specialist agencies is almost certainly highest in socially privileged middle class districts. In such areas overall attendance rates are high. A poor attender stands out, and both teachers and family doctors may be tempted to seek a medical, or psychiatric, explanation. Just as certainly, the proportion of poor attenders referred for specialist treatment is probably lowest in socially under-privileged inner-city areas. In these areas overall absence rates are high, leading teachers and general practitioners to regard the problem as a social one. This view may be reinforced when clinic or hospital appointments are not kept.

The very small proportion of children referred for investigation and treatment should not, however, lead us to overlook the *possible* usefulness of such treatment for some children. Appropriate questions are: Which children apparently do not benefit? Is there evidence that many of the "silent majority" of absentees who are never referred might in fact be helped by treatment from psychologists and psychiatrists or under their supervision? If not, why not?

Definition of Clinical Treatment

In this chapter the term "clinical treatment" does not necessarily imply that treatment was carried out in a child guidance clinic or hospital, nor that the treatment was carried out by a psychologist or psychiatrist. The term is used in a broader sense to include approaches in which the basic treatment method has its origin in the theory and practice of psychiatry or applied psychology. Hence, case-work carried out at a child's home by a social worker would be included, since it has its origins in psychotherapeutic theory, even though social work is a discipline in its own right. Similarly, a behaviour therapy programme carried out by a teacher would be included. In this chapter we first discuss clinic and hospital based approaches, and then consider wider applications in schools and in the community.

Availability

All local educational authorities employ educational psychologists. The number of psychologists in any l.e.a. depends not only on its size but also on the generosity and/or priorities of the Education Committee. In Sheffield there has since 1974 been a ratio of one educational psychologist to every 8,000 children of school age. A few l.e.a.s are more generously staffed. Several still expect their psychologists to provide a useful service with a ratio of one to 12,000.

Educational psychologists are trained and experienced teachers who have taken an Honours degree in psychology and a higher degree or a diploma in the applications of psychology in school and other professional work with children. Until recently educational psychologists had no statutory responsibilities. In practice, the Department of Education and Science (1975) made clear that they should advise the chief education officer whenever special education is being considered. Moreover, the 1981 Education Act placed a duty on l.e.a.s to identify and assess children with special educational needs. They cannot perform this duty without the services of educational psychologists.

Educational psychologists vary very widely both in the amount and in the nature of the clinical work they carry out. In the last few years many members of the profession have become dissatisfied with a clinic-based approach, and have been exploring alternative ways of working. Some have argued that their first priority should lie in working with teachers to identify problems in school organisation or teaching method (e.g. Gillham, 1981). Others have concentrated on in-service education for teachers (e.g. Cox and Lavelle, 1982), while others have developed observation scales to help teachers identify children with special needs and develop effective programmes for them (e.g. Lindsay, 1981).

In many, but by no means all, authorities, educational psychologists divide their time between the l.e.a.'s school-orientated psychological service and a child guidance clinic. The clinic team consists of a social worker, usually seconded from the local social services department, a child psychiatrist employed by the area health authority and an educational psychologist. Child guidance clinics accept referrals from teachers, parents and doctors. The same, incidentally, applies to l.e.a. psychological services which have no involvement in clinics. In practice, though, child guidance clinics tend to receive a higher proportion of referrals from doctors than "independent" educational psychologists.

Educational psychologists' joint involvement with a child guidance clinic and the l.e.a.'s psychological service still receives a good deal of support (Cline, 1980). In some areas, though, child guidance clinics have been phased out in favour of hospital based out-patient departments of child psychiatry. When this happens educational psychologists spend their whole time working for the l.e.a., but some continue to offer individual clinical treatment when appropriate. The out-patient departments are staffed by a child psychiatrist, social worker and clinical psychologist. Clinical psychologists differ from educational psychologists in not having teaching experience, and having less extensive training in work with children. On the other hand they are more familiar with medical settings, generally have longer postgraduate training which often includes more training and experience than educational psychologists in therapy with individual children and with families.

Poor school attenders form a fairly small minority of children referred to child guidance clinics, varying from one per cent (Chazan, 1962) to eight per cent (Kahn and Nursten, 1962). There is no reason for thinking that this picture would be different either in out-patient psychiatric departments or in children referred to l.e.a. psychological services.

Services which are more readily accessible to teachers than child guidance clinics or hospital departments are the area health authority's school health service and the l.e.a.'s education welfare service. All schools are visited regularly by a doctor from the school health service, though secondary schools receive more visits than primaries. The doctors do some routine screening for visual and hearing defects, but increasingly see their principal function as an advisory one. Thus teachers should be able to seek advice about the medical implications of a child's condition for his management in the classroom. In addition some doctors spend much of their time counselling parents or children.

The l.e.a.'s educational welfare service is concerned principally with school attendance, and is always involved in any decision to take legal action. Later in the chapter we discuss some developments in the work of educational welfare officers. Here we need only note: (i) that teachers should be able to consult their school's e.w.o. about any child *before* the problem becomes severe (though in practice some head-teachers make informal liaison between e.w.o.s and class teachers extremely difficult), and (ii) that their increasing professionalism enables some e.w.o.s to offer their clients social case-work and counselling skills which differ substantially from their traditional "truant catcher" image.

It will be clear from this overview of existing services that they vary from area to area, and within a service from individual to individual. There is remarkably little consensus either on priorities or on methods. Some clinics have a strong psychodynamic orientation, emphasising the importance of therapy in uncovering unconscious motivation. Some l.e.a. psychological services have a strong behavioural orientation, aiming to help clients, whether children, parents or teachers, tackle their immediate problems. Most larger l.e.a.s and the larger hospital out-patient departments contain individuals with a range of theoretical orientations. Occasionally one person specialises in work with a particular group of clients. In addition some people establish a reputation for work with a particular group, even though they do not deliberately specialise.

The way some agencies differ in their priorities is best illustrated by the distinction between treatment and support services. Psychologists who wish to offer a treatment service will encourage teachers to refer the children who are most likely to benefit from the treatments they can offer. These children may not, and indeed are unlikely to, be children that the teachers themselves find most disturbing. In contrast, psychologists who aim to offer a support service will encourage teachers to refer the children they find most difficult. Their aim is to work with teachers in investigating the children's needs, and in exploring approaches that may help the teachers in their future work with them.

TREATMENT OF SCHOOL REFUSAL

Aims and Methods

Many different approaches have been described, but until the development of behaviour therapy their conceptual underpinning generally came from psychotherapeutic practice (Hersov, 1977). This was consistent with theories of development which emphasised abnormal psychopathology in the family, or less frequently, the child.

Initially, the principal aim of treatment was improvement in the relationship between mother and child (Johnson *et al.*, 1941; Kahn and Nursten, 1962), but other work has placed a higher priority on the family relationships in general, rather than the mother–child relationship in particular (Hersov, 1960b; Eisenberg, 1958; Bowlby, 1973). These studies also recognised the possible influence of the father's attitudes or personality. This was reviewed by Skynner (1974) who argued in favour of conjoint family therapy in which the therapy sessions aim to loosen the over-close tie between mother and child by involving the rest of the family.

Although the majority of studies advocate out-patient treatment, hospital admission is a recognised possibility. Of Hersov's (1960b) 50 cases, 22 were admitted as in-patients. Treatment was more intensive than with the out-patients. It consisted of three psychotherapy sessions per week, dealing with anxieties about family and school. Play therapy was used with younger children, and interpretative face-to-face discussion with older children and adolescents. Berg *et al.* (1970) stressed the importance of a therapeutic community with a generous staff–patient ratio in an adolescent in-patient unit. They also noted that although 50 per cent of patients showed obvious difficulties in accepting a temporary stay at the unit, these cleared up in all cases.

The timing of return to school has been the subject of controversy. Davidson (1960) argued that premature pressure would result in panic or even attempted suicide, though firmness was appropriate at the right moment. A similar view was taken by Greenbaum (1964) in criticising advocates of early return (Klein, 1945; Rodriguez *et al.*, 1959). In general, the argument against early return is that it reduces the chances of resolving the hypothesised underlying conflicts which lie at the root of the problem. The arguments in favour of early return are that prolonged absence results in educational retardation, loss of friendship (though most studies have reported school refusers as socially isolated anyway), and the emotional gains from being at home.

There is associated controversy about the relevance of school factors. Several studies have mentioned the possibility of pressures at school precipitating school refusal (Hersov, 1960b; Chazan, 1962; Klein, 1945), though greater emphasis is generally laid on family relationships. Bowlby (1973) regarded complaints about school as a mere rationalisation, but was criticised by Hersov (1977) who maintained that:

> Complaints by children and parents about any aspect of the school situation should be taken seriously and investigated as carefully as possible before discarding them as important factors in aetiology and treatment. ... It seems reasonable to explore in depth the child's own perception of the school situation if one is to fully understand the reasons for non-attendance.

If overt pressure for return to school is exerted in the course of psychotherapeutic treatment, it is reasonable to ask whether success, as judged by subsequent attendance results from this pressure or from the psychotherapy. Eysenck and Rachman (1965) pointed out that methods of gradual return have much in common with behaviour therapy treatment, even if the aim is to bring into the open anxieties or conflicts that can later be resolved in clinical interviews (Talbot, 1957). Chazan (1962) noted the possible usefulness of change of school, in combination with other forms of treatment such as psychotherapy, play therapy or remedial teaching.

Behavioural Treatments

Treatments derived from social learning theory and to a lesser extent from applied behavioural analysis have increased in popularity in the last fifteen years. Typically, treatment is based on a thorough analysis of the presenting problem with a general agreement on return to school at the earliest opportunity. There has been considerable disagreement amongst behaviour therapists, though, on the ways to achieve this goal. Scherman and Grover (1962) insisted on a gradual approach, combined with training in relationship techniques. Weinberger *et al.* (1973) saw school refusal essentially as a power struggle between child and parents. Treatment consisted of helping the parents to reassert their authority by winning a confrontation over school attendance.

The trouble with this sort of approach is the naive way it conceptualises school refusal. While appropriate for some school refusers, treatment plans often need to take greater account both of stress at school and of tensions in family relationships. Blagg (1977) insisted on the initial interview taking place at school. This enabled the child to remain at school once a treatment plan had been worked out. This approach is interesting partly because return to school was abrupt and partly because it constituted only one part of the treatment plan. Although early, if not immediate return to school was considered essential, the overall treatment plan took account of information from the school, the parents and the child. The approach is also interesting on account of the successful return to school in the majority of cases (Blagg and Yule, 1984).

In his article, Blagg described how Robert, aged fourteen, was initially to be excused games, having expressed concern about changing. In addition, he would be collected from home by a teacher in the morning. Having agreed to return on these terms Robert was less than delighted when his parents were asked to leave. Although he had to be restrained physically, he calmed down quickly after they had left and maintained regular attendance subsequently.

Dealing with anxiety associated with school attendance can be effective, even when no direct attempt is made to improve attendance as such. Galloway and Miller (1978) described eleven-year-old Harry who had regularly missed school on days when he might have to undress for games or swimming and to take a shower afterwards. It was thought that his mother was not firm enough to insist on his attendance. In four sessions of forty minutes he was asked to relax while imagining increasingly stressful situations, ranging from "standing in changing room on own" to "have shower with other children". After imagining each situation he was required to practice it. After three more shorter sessions he was able to participate in games and take a shower with the other boys subsequently. For the next five weeks there were no further problems with school attendance.

Some behaviour therapists have distinguished between different groups of school refusers. Kennedy (1965), for example, accepted the views of Coolidge *et al.* (1957) who regarded "Type I" school phobia as a neurotic crisis, seen as a response to the separation involved in school attendance. "Type II" in contrast was seen as a chronic "way of life" phobia, in which the school phobia was merely one of several maladaptive patterns of behaviour which had developed over time, associated with serious emotional problems in at least one parent. In treating Type I cases, Kennedy insisted on immediate return to school, followed by an interview with parents and support from clinic staff. Parents were told to be firm, not to discuss school attendance with the child, and to compliment him when he stayed in school. He considered this rapid treatment procedure less effective with Type II cases, but did not make clear how often he did in fact use it with them. Rines (1973) described a twelve-year-old girl with many Type II characteristics who responded to the rapid treatment procedure, attending regularly and making good academic progress even though the family pathology remained unaltered.

In an important and thorough review of behavioural treatments of school refusal Yule *et al.* (1977) identified five groups: (i) children whose school refusal starts on entry to school, and usually indicates separation anxiety; with these children a gradual return to school aims to reduce (or "desensitise") the fear; (ii) children whose refusal occurs shortly after a major change of schooling; this is most frequent following transfer to secondary school; treatment requires a graded re-entry to school, with particular attention to aspects of school which the child finds stressful; (iii) school refusal in adolescents after nine or ten years of good attendance; this may be associated with the onset of a depressive or schizophrenic illness; treatment requires more individual work with the patient than is often necessary with younger children, and may involve acceptance of the young person's reasons for non-attendance, though alternative coping strategies should be explained; (iv) children of any age who have been at school for only a short time; these children generally respond to a variety of simple, straight forward techniques (e.g. Kennedy, 1965); (iv) children whose refusal is associated with a combination of stresses; thus, a bullying incident may be shrugged off by many children, but can precipitate school refusal in a child who is already anxious about separation from home; this underlines the need for a detailed inquiry into the child's experiences of separation from either parent, as well as of death, either of family members or friends.

It will be clear that behavioural treatment requires a thorough understanding of each child's circumstances, as well as familiarity with the range of treatment techniques available. Yule *et al.* (1980) conclude their review:

> New facts emerge during treatment, and in particular we clarify any situations which produce the fear reaction in the child. Once they are more clearly delineated, then we can help the child confront them more openly. Our approach is predominantly behavioural yet with close attention to other personal and family factors. In a similar way to Miller, Barrett and Hampe (1974) we agree that there are four stages in an overall treatment approach: (i) establishing a good, trusting relationship with the child and his family; (ii) clarifying the stimulus situations which give rise to anxiety; (iii) desensitising the child to the feared situation by using imagination, relaxation or merely talking, whichever is appropriate; and (iv) confronting the feared situations. We prefer, when we have a choice, to adopt a gradual rather than a sudden approach to the latter. Nevertheless we try to remain firm and we have learned that in most cases the fears and tantrums which destroy the resolve of many parents soon subside when the child makes progress. The art is to know what is progress in the eyes of the child.

Outcomes

Superficially the research suggests that the outcome for school refusal is good, whatever treatment is used. Most studies have reported success rates well over two thirds (e.g. Davidson, 1960; Hersov, 1960b; Coolidge *et al.*, 1964; Clyne, 1966), though Kennedy's (1965) 100 per cent success rates with Type I school phobics is exceptional. A closer look, however, is not quite so reassuring. Kennedy made clear that he considered the prognosis for Type II school phobics much less satisfactory. Yule *et al.* (1980) concluded that treatment was easier when the problem was reported at an early stage. While their advice that schools be encouraged to recognise school refusal at an early stage is undoubtedly appropriate, teachers could be forgiven for feeling cynical and discouraged at the lengthy waiting lists in many clinics. Further, the outlook for treatment is better with younger children. Berg's (1970) follow-up of adolescents who had left an in-patient unit reported 51 per cent "undoubted failures" and Rodriguez *et al.* (1959) found the prognosis for pupils aged more than eleven was much less favourable than for younger children.

A recent detailed study of sixty six school refusers has reported widely disparate results, depending on the type of treatment (Blagg and Yule, 1984). Thirty pupils received Blagg's (1977) behavioural treatment approach, described above. Sixteen received in-patient hospital treatment, and twenty home tuition with psychotherapy. Using fairly stringent criteria, 93 per cent of the behaviour therapy group were judged successes at follow-up over one year after the end of treatment, compared with 37.5 per cent of the hospital group and 10 per cent of the pupils receiving home tuition with psychotherapy. These results are particularly interesting as the mean age of the behaviour therapy pupils at the start of treatment was just under thirteen, and 43 per cent were classified as Kennedy's Type II school refusers. The results following home tuition with psychotherapy were worse than those reported in any other published study, leading the authors to question "whether home tuition with psychotherapy actually inhibited spontaneous remission".

To conclude, treatment for school refusal has an excellent outlook provided: (a) the child is pre-adolescent; (b) the child is referred very soon after the problem has started; (c) there are no long-term social problems or particularly complex relationship problems in the family. There does not appear to have been any investigation into how many of these children would have improved without treatment, though Kennedy (1971) accepted that his 100 per cent success rate with Type I school phobics was helped by good family backgrounds which made the chances of successful return to school high irrespective of treatment. Research on the "spontaneous improvement" of behaviour problems without treatment suggests that a high proportion do in fact clear up (e.g. Levitt, 1957). This is particularly true of children with "neurotic" and emotional problems (Levitt, 1963). A separate point is that the children with a good prognosis, meeting the three criteria listed above, certainly account for less than 5 per cent of all unauthorised absentees, and probably for less than 1 per cent. This does not mean that none of the others will benefit. It does mean: (i) that treatment is likely to take longer; (ii) that a more comprehensive approach will be needed, perhaps tackling several aspects of the problem consecutively or simultaneously; (iii) that the outlook is much less certain.

Two retrospective studies have investigated the prevalence of school refusal in adult psychiatric patients. Berg *et al.* (1974) asked agoraphobic women about their school attendance and found a history of school phobia was associated with early onset of agoraphobia, though only in a small proportion of cases. Similarly Tyrer and Tyrer (1974) found a history of school refusal in more adult psychiatric patients than controls, but concluded that most school refusers will become normal adults.

TRUANCY AND OTHER REASONS FOR ABSENCE

Compared with the extensive literature on the treatment of school refusal, there is a remarkable absence of published work on the treatment of other forms of absence. It may be that child psychologists and psychiatrists have assumed that pupils withheld by their parents do not require specialist help, though as we saw in Chapter 5 it is clear that many of these come from highly stressful backgrounds. Yet this does not explain the apparent lack of interest in the treatment or management of truancy.

Brooks (1974) described the use of contingency contracts with truants. The school counsellor drew up a written contract between pupil, parent and school in which attendance was reinforced by previously agreed rewards. Brooks reported improvement but his cases seem to have been fairly straightforward as it was not thought necessary for the contract to require active intervention from the school, for example helping the child overcome his sense of educational failure by teaching him to read.

Only two studies have been traced which focused on poor attenders without distinguishing them from truants. Morgan (1975) compared three behaviour modification procedures with elementary (primary) school children. He found a combination of material rewards and social reinforcement from peers the most effective procedures, but his follow-up period was unfortunately very short. Hoback (1976) placed more responsibility on the school, emphasising the need to create an environment and curriculum which pupils and parents see as relevant to their needs.

Counselling procedures have been used both by teachers and outside personnel. A number of small-scale studies with truants have reported encouraging results, though again the follow-up periods were short (Law, 1973; Sassi, 1973; Cain, 1974; Beaumont, 1976; Tumelty, 1976). In a much more extensive programme of action research, Rose and Marshall (1974) reported improvement in attendance and reduction in delinquency when counsellors or social workers were introduced into schools.

An important American study has suggested that poor attendance from school is often followed by a wide range of anti-social behaviour in adult life (Robins and Ratcliffe, 1980). The authors followed up a sample of black school boys until they were in their thirties. The results indicated an association between poor attendance and subsequent problems such as unemployment and low status employment, alcohol abuse, criminality, and fathering an illegitimate child or failing to support a legitimate one. Violence was more frequently reported in men with a history of absence from high school than from elementary school, but scarcely ever reported of men with *no* history of truancy.

The relevance for this study for poor attenders in Britain is open to question. Gray *et al.* (1980) found a strong relationship between poor attendance and educational level in their study of London pupils. This was not due to the poor attenders having lower general intelligence. On the other hand, they also found "no associations between fifth year absenteeism and job skill level, job satisfaction, number of jobs, dismissal from jobs, or further training, once examination achievements had been taken into account". In other words, absenteeism in the final year of compulsory schooling was *not* associated with subsequent failure in the first year of work. It remains an open question whether poor attendance in younger age groups is associated with later employment problems, and whether the fifth year absentees have any longer term adjustment problems.

These studies were based on samples of poor attenders, with no attempt to distinguish between specific groups. Poor prognosis may be one of the main reasons for the relative lack of treatment research on truancy as defined in the clinical studies. While school refusal is generally seen by psychiatrists as the main expression of a neurotic disorder, truancy tends to be regarded as just one aspect of a more wide ranging pattern of anti-social behaviour. So-called conduct disorders have a worse prognosis than neurotic disorders, both for treatment and for spontaneous remission (Levitt, 1963; Robins, 1966, 1972; Mitchell and Rosa, 1981). Moreover, truants and their families have a much higher incidence of social problems than those school refusers who are referred for treatment. These may make them less able or less willing to co-operate with clinical services.

There is a detailed theoretical literature on school refusal, but this is not so true of truancy, and still less of the much larger number whose absence is condoned or tolerated by their parents. Clinicians are in general agreement about the neurotic nature of school refusal, though they have differed on points of detail, for example the relative significance of depression, separation anxiety and avoidance conditioning (Davidson, 1960; Chazan, 1962; Ross, 1972). The point is that the literature offers a number of conceptual frameworks within which to plan treatment programmes for school refusers, but not to the same extent for truants or other absentees.

There is another way of looking at this. Most school refusers described in the treatment literature have been well able to cope with their school work. In returning children to school a treatment agency is tackling the principal behavioural problem. This not only "teaches" the child that he can cope with school, which he had previously found impossible, but may also establish the clinician's credibility in tackling any relationship or management problems within the family. Truants, though, seldom regard return to school with the same anxiety as school refusers. The "lesson" they learn from enforced return may simply be that they are continuing to feel bored, to get into trouble, and to fail educationally. Moreover, if truancy is only one aspect of a more wide ranging pattern of anti-social behaviour, successful return may require an equally wide-ranging treatment programme, tackling the problems at home, in the child and in the community which maintain the overall pattern.

Yule (1977) reviewed studies which suggest that behavioural methods have been successful with a variety of behaviour problems both in the school and in the home. As with behavioural treatments of school refusal, the common conceptual underpinning of these studies is an analysis of ways in which the child and other people, adults or children, interact with each other in creating or maintaining the presenting problem. This approach is suitable for the study and treatment of a problem in which the evidence suggests a highly complex interaction between precipitating factors in the family, the neighbourhood, the child himself and the school.

Seen in this way, clinic treatments may have an important role in the treatment of some truants, but are unlikely to be effective unless combined with other approaches which tackle the problem in its social context. In view of the complexity of reasons for truancy and "condoned" absence, it is highly doubtful whether any *single* method, such as individual psychotherapy or a behaviour therapy technique, is often likely to be helpful. Clinical treatments, whether carried out by an untrained teacher, a counsellor, a psychotherapist or a behaviour therapist, may nevertheless form part of an overall programme based on a thorough initial assessment.

The difficulty here lies in the necessarily close liaison between teachers and members of the child guidance clinic team. Schools vary in their willingness to co-operate with specialist agencies. The problem is not fully overcome by an educational psychologist having responsibilities both in schools and in a clinic, though hospital psychiatric out-patients departments often have even greater difficulty in this respect. A more basic point is that the centralised child guidance clinic team of psychologist, psychiatrist and social worker has come under attack on the grounds that it is expensive, ineffective and too remote from school (Tizard, 1973; Loxley, 1974). Consequently, it is being replaced in some areas by a more loosely knit network of services as proposed by the Court Committee on Child Health Services (D.H.S.S., 1976).

COMMUNITY BASED APPROACHES TO MANAGEMENT

There is little question that the child guidance clinic team is as effective as a hospital child psychiatry out-patient department in treating the minority of school refusers who have a good prognosis. The problem, as indicated above, is that these children constitute a tiny minority of all poor attenders. The desire to provide a service more responsive to the needs of schools and of their local community led some clinic teams to co-operate in school-based projects to help teachers work more effectively with difficult children (Labon, 1973; N. Jones, 1973, 1974), disadvantaged children (Boxall, 1973) and their parents (Gorrell-Barnes, 1973). These early projects did not aim specifically at poor attenders. They did, however, aim to enable social workers and psychologists to extend their professional skills to a wider group than could be reached within the confines of the child guidance system. The need for services to become more readily available where the need was greatest was evident both in the Seebohm Report (D.H.S.S., 1968), which led to the 1969 Children's and Young Person's Act, and in the Court Report (D.H.S.S., 1976).

There is little doubt that more social workers and more psychologists are working in inner-city and other socially disadvantaged areas than was the case fifteen, or even ten years ago. Unfortunately, systematic descriptions of their work with poor attenders are hard to find. Nor is it clear how much influence they have had either on policy and practice within schools, or on the attendance of the pupils.

Social Work and Educational Welfare Teams

The generally favourable results of an action-research project which introduced counsellors and social workers into school have already been mentioned. Jones (1980) too, favoured the appointment of a social worker to a secondary school, though only as part of a comprehensive programme of change (see Chapter 8). Social work in school nevertheless remains a controversial topic, with a multitude of opportunities for accidental or intentional misunderstanding on both sides (Saltmarsh, 1973; Fitzherbert, 1977a).

In principle, the educational welfare service is well placed to provide an advisory service to schools as well as a social work service to absentees and their families. The educational welfare service is the branch of the l.e.a. responsible for investigating cases of poor attendance, and applying the formal sanctions described in Chapter 7. In practice, the service is still the Cinderella of the social services (Fitzherbert, 1977a,b) in spite of the recommendation of the D.E.S. sponsored Ralphs Report (Local Government Training Board, 1972) which concluded that its members should have social work training. Although some l.e.a.s, have made notable attempts to recruit trained staff and to extend the role of the service, in many areas its members are still seen as "school policemen", with responsibilities limited to school attendance in its narrowest sense. This makes it difficult for e.w.o.s in these areas to work as equals with teachers in drawing up programmes for absentees' return to school, since such programmes must tackle the complex interaction between educational, social and emotional factors that is so often seen.

A model which is gaining favour in a number of l.e.a.s is for the support services of school health, educational psychology and e.w.o.s to base themselves on secondary school catchment areas. As the service responsible for cases of poor attendance, e.w.o.s co-operate with teachers in preliminary investigations. Ideally, these include a home visit, generally from the e.w.o., and an interview with the child about possible difficulties at school. Sometimes study of the attendance register shows a consistent pattern of absences, for example from certain subjects, or at the start of the week. When a pupil has frequent absences due to minor illnesses, advice is sought from the school's visiting doctor, who may involve the educational psychologist or child psychiatrist if he thinks the illnesses may be symptomatic of other problems. Other children may be referred directly to the visiting psychologist, or discussed informally with him at a weekly staff meeting on pupils' welfare.

Liverpool l.e.a. extended this approach. Each area had a social education team headed by an "education guidance officer" whose job was to co-ordinate the efforts of all the available educational, social work and medical agencies to help both child and school (Brandon, 1974). Although the teams were based in the education department, it was hoped that they would be able to draw on the skills of other personnel, and thus prevent overlap in service provision. It is not clear how far this was in fact possible, and Brandon's account placed the emphasis squarely on the child's and family's problems rather than on contributory factors in school. Nevertheless, the social education team constituted an interesting attempt to extend and co-ordinate the available resources for dealing with truancy and related problems.

TREATMENT NEEDS: TRUANTS AND OTHER ABSENTEES

An inter-linked network of support services, both within the l.e.a. and outside it, should, in theory, make available to all families who might benefit the skills which formerly were available only to the minority that was referred to the clinic-based services and willing or able to co-operate with them. Further, the quality of support available to schools should enable teachers to identify at an early stage children who might benefit from support or treatment. In practice, things have not always worked out quite like this. Before considering the reasons, though, it is worth taking another look at the sort of problems facing teachers and members of the support services in areas where absenteeism is highest.

In the last chapter we described a study of persistent absentees from an inner-city part of Sheffield. We showed that the pupils tended to come from such multiply disadvantaged families that school attendance was relegated to a fairly low position on their unspoken list of priorities. In addition we showed that many pupils had special educational needs which would require intensive and skilled teaching, at least in reading. We made no attempt in describing these families to distinguish between the diagnostic categories described in this chapter and Chapter 3. The reason, of course, was that we were concerned to see: (i) how the secondary absentees differed from the primary group; (ii) how both differed from the children referred to the psychological service because of their poor attendance; and (iii) how all three groups differed from the regular attenders.

There is, however, another way of looking at the information obtained from the absentees and from their families (Galloway, 1983a). In 80 per cent of cases children and their parents independently gave similar replies when we asked about the child's activities when absent from school. From the replies we were able to distinguish between truants and other absentees. Truants were children whose parents "seldom" or only "occasionally" knew their whereabouts when absent from school. Parents of the other absentees "generally" knew their children's whereabouts. By comparing the two groups, we hoped: (i) to see whether the truants would differ from the other absentees (even

though both groups came from the same disadvantaged, high-absentee area),
as would be suggested by the clinical literature on truancy and school refusal;
(ii) to establish how far the other absentees showed the characteristics of
school refusers described in clinical studies. We hoped that the results would
shed further light on the relevance of research carried out with children
referred to clinics, for people working with poor attenders in socially
disadvantaged areas with high absentee rates and, perhaps, less tradition of
co-operation with specialist agencies. The results are described below, and
summarised in Table 6.1.

Table 6.1. *Truants and Other Absentees: Summary of Results*

	Truants (N = 31) per cent	Other Absentees (N = 48) per cent
One or both parents dead	3	18
Parents had received social security within previous twelve months	57	80
Mother or stepmother in paid employment	47	29
Mother had history of chronic illness	33	64
Mother* had Health Questionnaire score of at least 7	50	57**
Child had shown anxiety about parents' health	13	58
Child had shown anxiety about leaving home	29	65
Child at least two years backward in reading	89	58
Parents regarded a sense of educational failure as contributing to absence	7	23
Mother considered over protective	39	72
Child considered over dependent	32	60
Warm, mutually satisfactory mother–child relationship	48	75

* or father in 3 cases where he was the sole informant
** this is the only set of results which was *not* statistically significant: full details are given elsewhere (Galloway, 1983a)

Social Background, Early History and Health

Truants and other absentees did not differ in the type of housing their
families occupied, nor in the period they had lived there. The truants were
more likely to have lost a parent through death. On the other hand, their
parents were less likely to have received social security, or similar payment
within the last twelve months, and their mother or step-mothers were more
likely to be in gainful employment.

There were no differences in the children's health, nor in their history of separation from parents or bereavements. Social work agencies were involved equally with both groups. More of the other absentees' mothers had a history of chronic illness than of the truants'. Mothers of 57 per cent of the other absentees and of 50 per cent of the truants obtained scores of at least seven on the Health Questionnaire, indicating a high probability of clinically significant psychiatric disorder.

Behaviour at Home

As would perhaps be expected, the truants were significantly less likely to stay at home in the evenings and weekends. Parents of the other absentees more often reported a history of anxiety about leaving home and anxiety about their parents' health, even though, as noted above, there appeared to be no important differences between the two groups in terms of parental health. The truants' parents more frequently reported a history of lying, stealing from within or outside the home and wandering from home.

Behaviour and Progress at School

There were no significant differences in the accounts each group gave of contributory factors at school. Nor was there any noteworthy difference in the mean verbal scale IQ of the two groups. More of the truants, though, were at least two years backward in reading ability. This was particularly interesting as significantly fewer of the truants' parents than of the other absentees' regarded a sense of educational failure as a contributing factor in their children's absence.

Family Attitudes and Relationships

After each interview, parents' attitudes and relationships were coded on a form designed for the study (Galloway, 1980). In practice, we coded the child's relationship with her or his mother, except in three cases when the father was the sole informant. An observer was present at thirty interviews and coded the form independently. This enabled us to demonstrate a high level of reliability between the observer's and the interviewer's ratings.

There were no important differences in family attitudes and relationships when comparing the original four groups of secondary absentees, primary school absentees, absentees referred to the psychological service and regular attenders. However, a different pattern emerged when comparing truants with other absentees. The mothers of absentees were more frequently con-

sidered over-protective towards their child. Conversely, the children themselves were more frequently considered over-dependent on their parents.
More of the other absentees were thought to have a warm, mutually
satisfactory relationship with their mother (75 per cent, compared with 48 per
cent). There was a tendency for truants to be rated more frequently as having
a tense, mutually unsatisfactory relationship with their mother, but the
numbers in both groups were small (19 per cent and 6 per cent). The two
groups tended to regard school with equal hostility.

Delinquency and Subsequent Attendance

There was a tendency for more truants to have committed offences known
to the police than other absentees and for truants who offended to offend more
frequently than other absentees who did so. In the Autumn term 1975 both
groups averaged 37 per cent attendance. By the Summer term 1975 (five terms
later) the other absentees averaged 49 per cent and the truants 44 per cent. At
one stage in the two year period the truants' average attendance rose to 50 per
cent, but that was due entirely to three total non-attenders being lost to the
sample when they were committed to the local authority's care by the juvenile
court.

COMMENT

Clinical studies have described a wide range of treatments for school
refusal, but have largely ignored truancy. Treatment of school refusal is often
successful, but children with the most favourable prognosis (pre-adolescent,
referred very soon after the problem starts, and from families without major
social problems) constitute a very small minority indeed of all unauthorised
absentees. On theoretical grounds we would predict less satisfactory results
from clinical work with truants. The reason is that truancy, as part of a more
wide-ranging pattern of anti-social behaviour, more obviously results from
the interaction between the pupil and the people in his environment. As a
result, it is the *interaction*, often involving teachers and peers which needs to be
"treated", rather than the child. School refusal is often seen as a symptom of
disturbed family relationships. It is easier for treatment services to tackle the
child's anxiety, or the family's problems than the wider social and educational
problems associated with truancy.

There is a notable lack of accounts on how community based social work
and medical services work with poor school attenders. The Sheffield study
suggests that truants in a socially disadvantaged area differed from other
absentees in their responses to stress at home or at school. The results did not

show many differences between the families. Thus, Health Questionnaire scores suggested that pupils in both groups might have felt anxiety about their mothers' health. In fact, the other absentees expressed greater anxiety. The truants tended to show less anxiety about their educational attainments, although they were more frequently backward in reading than the other absentees. There was a fairly consistent tendency for parents of other absentees to report anxiety related problems, and for parents of truants to report problems involving anti-social behaviour.

In these respects the other absentees resembled the school refusers described in numerous psychiatric studies. On the other hand the general lack of tension between the other absentees and their parents is quite out of keeping with the consistent picture of disturbed family relationships in clinical studies. Nor does it make any sense to label as a "neurotic" symptom the anxiety which so many of these children expressed about their parents' health. The evidence suggests overwhelmingly that the anxiety was both predictable and rational. In many cases the multiple sources of stress experienced by these families had had the effect of uniting families, making members more dependent on each other rather than less. As they grew older, secondary pupils found the apparent irrelevance of the school system to their immediate concerns more irksome than when they were younger. The older pupils had many more complaints about school than the younger children. In the last analysis, though, the incentive to *stay at home*, because of factors within the home, was as strong as to opt out of school because of stress at school. Given their current family situation school attendance was just one more problem to worry about. The problem for the pupils and their families was not school attendance as such, since regular attendance held no prospect of relieving their immediate worries, but rather the fuss the authorities made about it.

Viewed in this way it becomes easier to understand why treatment and support services had little to offer the families we interviewed in Sheffield. These families exist in the depressed areas of all large cities. There is no reason to doubt that the picture would be substantially different in other areas with very high rates of persistent absence from school. At the simplest possible level, it makes no sense to offer a family treatment for a child's poor attendance if neither child nor parents see poor attendance as a problem.

There are three possible ways out of this impasse.

(1) Social workers and psychologists may devote their energy to helping families either to accept or to change the social conditions which made the children's poor attendance highly probable in the first place. Two objections are immediately apparent. First, these conditions should be seen as a problem *of* society, and not simply as a problem for it. Most professional people would consider it grossly unethical to use their skills to "help" their clients accept social injustice. Second, the economic structure

of society, reflected, for example, in the level of unemployment and social security benefits, presents enormous practical difficulties to professionals who aim to help their clients change their own social conditions. We are not denying that change is possible, nor, emphatically that it is desirable. The point is that professionals can work intensively only with a small number of families at a time. Moreover, their efforts may do little to change attitudes in schools and nothing to change the structure of society.

(2) The authorities may try to persuade poor attenders and their families to place a higher priority on school attendance by threatening legal action. In the next chapter we list practical and ethical arguments against this.

(3) Teachers may acknowledge school attendance as *their* responsibility. The approaches described in this chapter see poor attendance essentially as the child's or the parent's problem. In the short term teachers may feel relieved at an opportunity to "pass the buck" to other professionals who are paid to investigate, and just occasionally to sort out, the problems facing children and their families. In the long run they feel frustration, and ultimately disillusionment. Other professionals manifestly lack a solution to the problem of poor attendance. Moreover, having once passed responsibility on to the "experts" teachers have to some extent lost control, or at least sight, of solutions which are closer to hand. It need not happen like this. In Chapters 8–10 we consider in more detail what teachers themselves can do, and are doing, to "sell" education to families who might otherwise treat it with the same low priority as many families in our Sheffield study.

CHAPTER 7

Partial Solutions? II. Administrative and Legal Sanctions

INTRODUCTION

We can't teach them anything if they don't come. If they start attending we'll see what we can do. Meanwhile we're just going to concentrate on the ones who do turn up.

These quotes from senior pastoral care staff in a secondary school reflect a not uncommon attitude towards attendance, namely that the responsibility is someone else's. They also implicitly reject an interactive model of learning. It is as though pupils are seen, as Dickens' Thomas Gradgrind saw them in the novel *Hard Times*, as little pitchers to be filled with knowledge. The teachers' role is to wait, with the jug of knowledge ready, for the little pitchers to turn up.

Criticism, though, is modified by recognition of the impossible position in which the present system has placed teachers. The empty rows in many classes of fourteen- to sixteen-year-olds in socially disadvantaged areas are inevitably demoralising, even when the teacher recognises that full attendance would bring several of the potentially most disruptive elements back into the class. Frustration is increased by feeling, incorrectly as we argue in the remaining chapters, that teachers themselves can do little to solve the problem. Attendance, after all, is seen as the responsibility of the educational welfare service. E.w.o.s frequently resent teachers making home visits. Moreover, many teachers feel that they have neither the time nor the training for investigating and acting on cases of persistent poor attendance. Many e.w.o.s, incidentally, might say the same of themselves.

A further point is that legally responsibility for attendance rests squarely with parents. In law it is not the school's job to create a climate which ensures full attendance. Indeed, the school's ability to provide its pupils with education appropriate to their age, ability and aptitude, is taken for granted in the 1944 Education Act. Neither pupils nor teachers may always share the Act's endearing, but probably necessary confidence in the ability of all schools to fulfill this responsibility. Nevertheless, the law is clear.

As long as education remains free and compulsory the question of legal sanctions against defaulters will continue to arise. Section 40 of the 1944 Education Act empowers l.e.a.s to prosecute parents for failure to ensure their child's regular attendance. Section 1(2)(e) of the 1969 Children's and Young Person's Act enables children to be brought before the juvenile court, where poor school attendance may be used as evidence in "care proceedings". The intention here is generally to have the child removed from the home. This is achieved if the magistrates make a care order. In practice, in most parts of the country they are at least as likely to make a supervision order, under which the child will be supervised by a local authority social worker or, less frequently, by a probation officer.

Although clear in theory, there are many areas of confusion in practice. Moreover there is evidence of increasing attempts to control poor attendance both from the fringe of the legal system and from outside it. These attempts involve the police, teachers, members of support and treatment services and elected local councillors.

This chapter describes the bureaucratic and legal sanctions in use against poor attenders and their families. We analyse anomalies in their use, and in the way pupils and parents are selected for action. We report the generally dismal failure of all these sanctions to exert any beneficial effect on subsequent attendance, but identify two apparent exceptions to this general picture. The first, which has received a great deal of publicity involves a special procedure in the juvenile court. We argue that major legal objections must be raised against this procedure, and that in any case the claims made on its behalf have been overstated. The second involves no legal procedures, yet achieves similar results to those obtained from the special procedure in the juvenile court. We conclude that the evidence suggests, very tentatively, a more constructive approach for teachers and society to adopt towards poor attenders.

PRELIMINARY, OSTENSIBLY PREVENTIVE ACTION: A GROWTH AREA

Overview

Pratt (1984) points out that hearings against parents in the magistrates' courts have declined slightly in recent years, while juvenile court hearings have remained virtually static. In contrast:

there has been a widespread and rapid growth of an administrative network of interventions
... i.e. the administrative sector may increasingly be acting as an alternative to the legal.

Figures on this growth, however, are notoriously difficult to collect. Neither schools nor l.e.a.s like to publicise that they have a truancy problem. Moreover, the individuals involved invariably have many other responsibilities and lack both the time and the inclination to keep detailed records or to publicise what they are doing.

Police Involvement

Children who are absent from school are not, technically, breaking the law. If anyone is breaking a law it is their parents. Absentees are without doubt a high risk group for delinquency, but the evidence reported in Chapter 4 showed clearly that a majority is *not* known to have committed any offence. Hence, the question of police involvement in school attendance is contentious. However, inter-agency co-operation is a largely unchallenged goal amongst members of the helping and teaching professions, and in most parts of the country police officers involved with juveniles have been eager to co-operate with their colleagues in these professions. Superficially, the nature of the juvenile justice system makes such co-operation both inevitable and desirable. The police have no power, for example, to prosecute children under ten. Moreover, they know that juvenile court magistrates are required to act in what they consider the child's best interests.

Hence, it was probably inevitable that the police should sooner or later become involved in school attendance. It was equally inevitable that their involvement would be controversial. Pratt (1984) quotes a Home Office (1980) circular which describes one initiative:

> in Cheshire, with the agreement of the various services concerned, the police Juvenile Department have sought the help of heads of certain schools in identifying first to third year truants. Those identified are visited at home by police officers, and the importance of regular school attendance is discussed with them and with their parents. Places where truants congregate are visited by the police, sometimes in company with an education welfare officer, and in certain instances children thought to be truanting are taken home or back to school.

The practices described here raise a number of interesting questions. First, parents might legitimately object to schools giving their children's names to the police when the children have committed no offence. With some justification they might fear that giving their child a police record, albeit an informal one, will make him a prime target for suspicion in the future. As a way of establishing a co-operative trusting relationship between parents and teachers the Cheshire practice leaves something to be desired.

The second point concerns the extent of police knowledge about school attendance. The assumption behind the scheme would appear to be that the problem of non-attendance is due principally to truancy—i.e. to absence without parents' knowledge or consent. This is a false premise. The majority of absentees are at home with their parents' knowledge, and in many cases with their consent. At the very least there would seem to be considerable scope for police and parents to talk at cross purposes. Moreover, it is hard to see how a visit from the police is conducive to unravelling the complex personal, family and educational issues involved in many cases of persistent poor attendance.

The Home Office is not altogether insensitive to these points. The same circular (Home Office, 1980) acknowledges both that the effectiveness of the schemes have been questioned, and that they might be operating with inadequate legal powers. The circular noted that the Home Office and the other departments involved were currently giving the matter their "consideration".

Units and Special Centres

We describe the curriculum and organisation of school-based centres catering for poor attenders in the next chapter. Here the aim is to discuss their role on the fringe of the legal system. Two principal groups merit attention.

Social Services Departments are empowered to provide "intermediate treatment" facilities for children and adolescents. These aim to offer "treatment" either on a day or a residential basis, thus preventing the need for formal and perhaps long-term reception into care or committal to care. One form of intermediate treatment is provision of alternative schooling, either on a full-time or a part-time basis. In theory poor attenders come voluntarily, though attendance can be linked to a supervision order made by the juvenile court. Kenny (1981) noted that seventeen of thirty-one London boroughs had established such schemes, and that others were discussing the possibility of starting them.

L.e.a.s and individual schools are also active in this field. Recognising the rapid and undocumented growth of units for "problem" children, H.M.I. (1978) carried out their own investigation. They reported that seventy-two out of ninety-six l.e.a.s surveyed had established some form of unit. Their inquiry almost certainly underestimated the number of school-based units set up without special assistance from the l.e.a.

Units vary widely in their aims, curriculum and methods. At this stage we need note only four recurring themes: (i) admission procedures are frequently more simple than discharge; many units start with good intentions of returning pupils to the mainstream, but subsequently develop, or regress, into a long-term alternative to the mainstream; (ii) parents are not always consulted about their child's admission, and seldom if ever have a right of veto, (iii) to the extent that units are seen ostensibly as a "last chance" before committal to care, or a "half way house" back to the mainstream, pupils are under some pressure to attend; (iv) the curriculum is frequently orientated towards "non academic" topics, with few pupils taking public examinations; hence, attendance is unlikely to enhance greatly a pupil's chances in the job market on reaching school leaving age, though teachers in many units make energetic efforts to arrange employment; a related point is perhaps that few pupils admitted to units would have been examination candidates had they remained in the mainstream.

Separate provision in the form of units may therefore be seen as an alternative to legal action. Yet it may also be seen as a form of control, seeking to contain truants, who might otherwise be involved in anti-social activities, or at least wasting the time of professionals assigned to investigate the reasons for their absence! In this sense they may be seen as a "liberal" alternative to legal action.

Investigation by Committee: Teachers and Social Workers

We noted in the last chapter members of the support services were basing themselves in many places on secondary school catchment areas. Brandon's (1974) description of the Liverpool education guidance officer as coordinator of medical, educational and social work services is consistent with this. Systematic accounts of what is popularly known as "inter-agency coope-ration" are rather infrequent. Acceptable evidence on their effectiveness in improving attendance is almost non-existent.

The rationale behind formation of these committees is less straightforward than appears at first sight. Superficially they may be seen as commendable efforts to avoid duplication of effort by different agencies and to ensure that help is given where it is needed. They may also be seen as a laudable attempt at preventive social work, aiming to identify problems before they become firmly established.

As always, other points of view are also possible. At least five arguments can be put forward as a critical commentary on inter-agency co-operation in the field of school attendance.

(1) Although intended to identify "cases" at an early stage, the committees are in fact only concerned with crises or with the most prolonged and intransigent problems. It is not hard to see why. In some classes in inner city schools at least a third of all final year pupils miss more than half their possible attendances without any legally acceptable reason. Doubling the number of professionals in the school attendance industry would still not enable them to give more than cursory attention to the most severe cases.

(2) Uniformly, the committees appear to be child and family orientated. The emphasis is on the child's and the family's problems, which are seen as the reason for the absence from school. Even when the school's possible contribution is recognised by some members of the team, for example social workers or educational psychologists, it is not always recognised by the teachers on the committee. Hence, the committee's efforts are spent in persuading children to return to an unchanged situation at school. Neither children nor parents are always clear why they should view the prospect with enthusiasm.

(3) Even more speculatively, and cynically, committees may be seen as a way of sharing responsibility for failure. As the evidence reviewed in Chapter 6 showed, psychological treatment is likely to solve attendance problems in no more than a tiny proportion of all cases. Teachers and e.w.o.s feel under attack on the subject of absence rates. Social workers are generally acutely aware of the difficulties inherent in persuading a reluctant child to return, even when the juvenile court has made a supervision order for this specific purpose. A problem shared may not be a problem solved. Yet sharing the problem does have two functions: (a) responsibility for failure, and less often for success, is more widely spread; (b) failure to accept the "help" which has been offered places responsibility for the attendance problem unequivocally on the family:

> they *still* won't get their kids to school, even after all we've done to help them!

(4) Related to the last point, the committees may also act as an unofficial screening system for identifying parents or children against whom the l.e.a. should take legal action. Thus, if clients "fail to respond" to offers of help, then the more openly coercive arm of the law should be invoked. Moreover, a "successful" prosecution may be more likely if the l.e.a. can demonstrate that everything possible has already been tried.

(5) The final argument is that truancy committees may sometimes be seen not as a prelude to legal action, but as an alternative. Opposition may take two forms: (a) some professionals object on ideological grounds to invoking legal sanctions against families whose problems they see as the product of an unjust or unsatisfactory system; (b) others regard legal sanctions as necessary and desirable in theory, but inadequate in practice. Objections focus on the delay in bringing parents or children to court, on the procedures adopted in court which are seen as favouring the defendants, and on the action available to the courts.

We return to these points later. Here, we need only note that the most apparently caring and liberal initiatives may be seen from different perspectives. The aim is not to argue that committees of professionals concerned about school attendance constitute a sinister, devious attempt to discredit the very people they are purportedly trying to help. Rather we are arguing that care committees cannot be seen in isolation from the legal system, irrespective of their members' wishes. The point is not simply that many members of these inter-professional networks have the responsibility either for initiating legal action or for submitting evidence in court. The more complex point is that their existence may often serve to disguise the tensions within schools which facilitate poor attendance even if they do not actually cause it.

The Home Office (1980) notes that some secondary schools have set up their own committees, consisting of head teacher, pastoral care staff and governors to investigate cases of poor attendance. These could be seen either as an alternative to the inter-disciplinary committees discussed above, or as complimentary to them. The involvement of head teachers and of school governors, however, suggests a rather high level of formality in the proceedings. The primary aim, it might be expected, would be return to school, rather than "treatment" or resolution of family or educational problems. It is difficult to imagine how this sort of committee could fail to act as a screening device to identify clients for more intensive, or coercive forms of action. The involvement of school governors raises many of the same issues as are raised by that of Education Committee councillors in this field.

INVESTIGATION BY COMMITTEE: LOCAL COUNCILLORS

Organisation and Administrative Framework

The legal justification for the Education Committee's school attendance section in Sheffield and for similar committees elsewhere lies in Section 40 of the 1944 Education Act. This requires l.e.a.s to initiate legal proceedings whenever "in their opinion, the institution of such proceedings is necessary". Officers of the l.e.a are answerable to the education committee, which appoints the school attendance section to oversee the activities of the educational welfare service. Galloway *et al.* (1981a) describe the system operating in Sheffield:

> Parents, and sometimes older children, may be invited to attend a meeting of the Education Committee's school attendance section. This body ... consists of elected councillors and coopted representatives of the teachers' associations. It is serviced by senior members of the educational welfare service. The proceedings are formal. The educational welfare officer states his views about the reasons for the child's absence from school. Members of the school attendance section then interview the parents and the child. Subsequently parents and child are asked to withdraw while members deliberate on their recommendation. Finally, parents and child return and are informed of the recommendation. Surprisingly, though, recommendations from the school attendance section have no binding force on the educational welfare service. The chief educational welfare officer is free to accept or reject advice from the school attendance section, and is under no obligation to consult it at any stage.

That, at least, was the theory. In practice councillors required the educational welfare service to produce sufficient clients for interview or discussion at their regular meetings. Councillors would undoubtedly have considered the chief educational welfare officer answerable, through the chief education officer, to the Education Committee's school attendance section. Hence, the section acted as a stringent form of control over the educational welfare service. Probably no other branch of the l.e.a., and certainly no school, is subjected to so close an oversight by elected councillors as this service. It was extremely rare for officers not to follow the advice they received from their political masters. On the only occasion which came to our notice, a senior member of the welfare service had discretely followed his own judgement, without drawing the matter to the committee's attention. Some education welfare officers pointed out that their agreement with the committee's decision was because *they* had advised the committee! In this case, though, it is hard to see why the case was referred to the committee in the first place.

Aims

The aims of the school attendance section have been described in four ways (Galloway *et al.*, 1981a):

(i) a final attempt by the l.e.a. to prevent the necessity for legal action in connection with poor school attendance by bringing home to parents the seriousness of the position;
(ii) an advisory committee for the educational welfare service;
(iii) an opportunity for members of the Education Committee to assist, monitor and influence the work of one of its support services;
(iv) an opportunity for senior members of the education welfare service to maintain contact with and advise elected representatives, and representatives of the teachers' associations.

These aims contain some curious inconsistencies. Although in theory educational welfare officers were not required to seek approval before taking legal action, there was evidence from interviews that they sometimes invited parents to attend for just this purpose. It was not clear who was supposed to be advising whom. Councillors and teacher union representatives clearly thought that they were taking the decisions, which would subsequently be followed. Members of the educational welfare service, however, frequently asserted in an interview that *they* were the only people professionally competent to take the necessary decisions. Taking legal action was, they argued, a matter of professional judgement. Several members of the service had received specific training in this sort of decision-making skill through successful completion of the Certificate of Qualification in Social Work, as recommended by the Local Government Training Board (1972).

This is not the place for discussion of the sociology of professions, except to note that exclusivity is an invariable stage in any profession's development, carried to its highest, or lowest form in the medical and legal professions. The "closed shop" is not, in its literal sense confined to working class trades. The confusion which e.w.o.s felt about the aims of the school attendance section was caused by two conflicting attitudes. On the one hand they felt that the section's existence gave them status within the l.e.a., and an opportunity to express their views to people in high places. On the other hand they recognised that receiving professional advice from a "lay" committee could only underline their lack of status.

Frequency of Use

In 1976–1977 the parents of 227 pupils were invited to a meeting of the school attendance section. The following year the parents of 245 were invited. Fig. 7.1 shows: (i) that the school attendance section was used more frequently than either the juvenile or the magistrates' court; (ii) that numbers involved showed little variation throughout the primary school years, but rose sharply thereafter with a peak in the penultimate year of compulsory schooling. Absence from school is highest in the final year of compulsory education (see

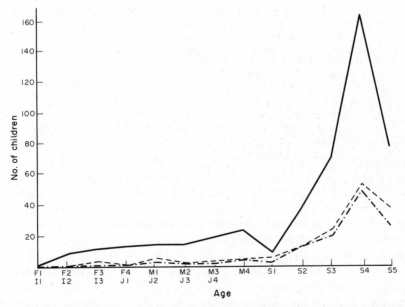

Fig. 7.1.   Age of children involved in legal or administrative action for poor school attendance over two years, 1976–1978.— School Attendance Section; --- Magistrates' Court; ----- Juvenile Court. Reproduced from the *Durham and Newcastle Research Review*, Vol. IX, No. 46 with the editor's permission.

Chapter 2). Formal procedures are used less frequently then because it is felt too late to apply them.

Committee Recommendations

The committee's decisions are shown in Table 7.1. By far the most common was to warn the parents, and to tell them that their child's case would be kept under review. In view of the stated aim to prevent the need for legal action, it is perhaps surprising that the committee recommended educational welfare officers to prosecute 14 per cent of parents following their first appearance. There are two possible explanations: (i) some welfare officers used the committee to seek approval for legal action, even though this was not theoretically necessary; (ii) members of the committee sometimes felt so incensed by the attitude or behaviour of parents appearing before them that they decided on prosecution without further delay.

Compared with the number of recommendations to prosecute parents, recommendations for juvenile court proceedings were infrequent. This pattern was not altered by taking into account the committee's eventual recommendation when a case had been kept under review, following the first appearance. Of the reviewed cases, only 2 per cent were directed to the juvenile court, compared with 12.5 per cent to the magistrates' court.

The evidence suggests that the school attendance section saw its function

Table 7.1. *Recommendations made following Parents' First Appearance Before the School Attendance Section over Two Years 1976–1978*

Recommendation	(No. of children = 472)* Per cent
(1) Warning given/case to be kept under review:	64.6
(2) Parents should be prosecuted in magistrates court:	14.0
(3) Child should be taken before juvenile court:	1.3
(4) Case referred to chief e.w.o. and to go directly to court without review if no improvement:	3.2
(5) Parents re-invited to next S.A.S. meeting:	5.3
(6) Case referred to Probation Service or social services department:	3.8
(7) Child referred for medical reports/ill:	1.5
(8) Child referred to psychologist/psychiatrist:	2.8
(9) E.w.o. to undertake further casework:	2.5
(10) Other:	1.5

*Total of recommendations exceeds 100 per cent because of 4 dual recommendations.
Reproduced from the *Durham and Newcastle Research Review*, Vol. IX, No. 46, with the editor's permission.

primarily in terms of sanctions against parents, seldom opting for care proceedings which aimed to remove the child from home.

A notable absence from the recommendations in Table 7.1. is discussion with teachers on ways to encourage better attendance. Referral to specialist social work, medical or psychological agencies was seen as appropriate, with the implicit assumption that these services might be able to help the family with its presumed problems. Nowhere is there any suggestion that the problem might lie in the school. Nor is there any suggestion that their previous experiences at school may have provided some adolescents with little incentive, or even an active disincentive, to regular attendance.

We are not suggesting that the committee should have focused its attention wholly on schools. Any coherent explanation of poor school attendance needs to consider the relevance of factors within the child, the family, the local community *and* the school. Yet the committee's apparent failure to consider the school's contribution demands explanation.

It would be unjust to attribute this solely to the presence of teacher union representatives who might be expected to resist any implicit criticism of teachers. Nor should it be attributed solely to the fact that councillors have a degree of accountability for the l.e.a.'s school system, and thus have an interest in defending it against criticism. An equally plausible explanation is that members of the school attendance section regarded school attendance as "normal", quite apart from any legal requirement. By definition, therefore, poor attenders must be in some way abnormal. Those who did not require help from specialist agencies would presumably be encouraged by prosecution or the threat of prosecution.

This reasoning undoubtedly contains more than one *non sequitur*. Yet it is hard to spot a consistent philosophy in the establishment of bodies such as Sheffield Education Committee's school attendance section. If some of their decisions seem to be one-sided, and others to contain contradictions, this is only to be expected from a committee with such conflicting aims. Members of the committee and the e.w.o.s who served it believed sincerely that they were acting in the best interests of the child. Because they had no agreed idea as to how these should be defined, let alone met, the committee's approach was frequently idiosyncratic, with proceedings dominated by one or two particularly vocal individuals.

Several of the parents who were interviewed in the study described in Chapter 5 had appeared before the school attendance section. There was no doubt that some of these parents had found their appearance traumatic. One depressed mother burst into tears when recalling her appearance before the committee eighteen months previously. The education welfare officer admitted later that this woman had indeed been "bashed by ROTA" (the local name for the school attendance section). The interviewing psychologist believed that another such incident might precipitate a suicide attempt.

Another parent said she would rather face the magistrates' court again than another appearance before the school attendance section.

It is clear that the constraints imposed by the legal system upon magistrates and prosecution counsel did not operate in the proceedings of the school attendance section. The greater flexibility and informality appeared to be seen by members of the school attendance section as an advantage. Unfortunately members were untrained in interviewing people who might have major personal and medical problems. As a result the proceedings sometimes intimidated parents, without helping them to effect any change.

PROSECUTION IN THE MAGISTRATES' COURT

Rationale

L.e.a.s are empowered to prosecute parents under Section 40 of the 1944 Education Act for failure to ensure their child's regular attendance. They are also empowered to take care proceedings in the juvenile court. In practice they seldom, if ever, follow both courses of action simultaneously. The reason is probably that it could appear vindictive to prosecute parents over school attendance *and* to press for their child's removal from home.

It is doubtful whether criteria for prosecution of parents are always clearly recognised. Logically, however, prosecution would seem to have little point unless three conditions are met:

(i)   the parent is thought to be guilty of an offence, *and*
(ii)   the offence is caused by the parents' wilful decision or by apathy, *and*
(iii) it is thought that the parent is capable of exerting proper care and control *and* that a court conviction and consequent penalty will encourage him to do so more effectively. If conditions (ii) and (iii) are not met, the prosecution could not be expected to result in any improvement in school attendance, and the l.e.a. would pursue the matter in the juvenile court. The theory is not, however, always translated into practice.

Frequency of Use and Outcome

Figure 7.1 shows the number and age of children whose parents were prosecuted by Sheffield l.e.a. in 1976–1978. At the time the school population was just over 100,000. We do not know how representative these figures are of the country as a whole. Tyerman (1968) reported 5,544 prosecutions nationally in 1963–1964 for truancy or for withholding a child from school, representing .07 per cent of the total on roll, or roughly the same proportion as in Sheffield in 1976–78.

Table 7.2 shows what happened to the parents prosecuted by Sheffield l.e.a. in 1976–1978. A fine was by far the most frequent outcome, either with or without a direction that the child should be brought before the juvenile court. This was followed by conditional discharge, again with or without a direction that the child be referred to the juvenile court.

Table 7.2. *Final Outcomes of Parents' Appearances in Magistrates' Court over Two Years, 1976–1978* *†

Outcome	(No. of children = 157)	Per cent
Fine only:		41.4
Fine and direction that child should be referred to juvenile court:		36.9
Conditional discharge only:		7.6
Conditional discharge and direction that child be referred to juvenile court:		6.4
Absolute discharge only:		0.6
Absolute discharge and direction that child be referred to juvenile court:		1.3
Other, e.g. case adjourned *sine die*, withdrawn, dismissed, etc.:		5.7

* 18 cases were brought back for a second hearing before a final decision was reached.

† 2 cases were brought back for a third hearing before a final decision was reached.

Reproduced from the *Durham and Newcastle Research Review*, Vol. IX, No. 46, with the editor's permission.

In law there is no question about the magistrates' right to direct the l.e.a. to bring the child before the juvenile court. The extensive use of this sanction does, however, raise some interesting questions. The l.e.a. makes a conscious decision to prosecute parents, rather than take the child directly to the juvenile court. In theory at least, the l.e.a.'s decision is taken after making detailed inquiries into the circumstances of each case. Generally acting on less information than is available to the l.e.a., the magistrates then decide to order that care proceedings be initiated in the juvenile court.

Bewilderingly, when we questioned educational welfare officers, they seemed to see nothing odd about this. Some officers felt that their cases would be strengthened in the juvenile court if the parents had already been convicted in the magistrates' court. Others pointed out that reporting restrictions are invariably imposed in juvenile court hearings. Conviction in the magistrates' court was thus the only way to secure publicity in the local press, which might act as a deterrent to other parents.

The double punishment implicit in fining the parents and directing their child to juvenile court was also seen as uncontroversial. In theory juvenile court action is intended purely to promote the child's interests. Hence, it was quite logical, some educational welfare officers pointed out, to fine parents for their activities, while also making an order which might benefit the child. From a parent's perspective the position must have been different. The magistrates were in effect saying: "Not only are we going to fine you, but we are also going to make an order which may result in the juvenile court taking your child away from you".

In law, magistrates are able to discharge parents without a conviction if they feel that the parents have done everything in their power to secure their child's attendance. In such cases the magistrates would direct that the child be brought before the juvenile court. However, this option is only open to parents who plead not guilty: you cannot be discharged after pleading guilty. In practice scarcely any parents plead not guilty.

In view of the evidence in Chapters 3 and 5, a plea of not guilty might well succeed in a substantial proportion of cases, i.e. those children who remained at home because their parents were unable to insist on return. There are probably two reasons why guilt is so seldom denied. First, a plea of not guilty on the grounds that the *child* refused to attend school would certainly result in an order that he be taken before the juvenile court. Second, very few parents have the benefit of legal advice, and therefore have no knowledge of the options open to them.

Until September 1977 the maximum fine in school attendance cases was £10 per child for a first offence, £20 for a second offence, and £20 and/or one month's imprisonment for a third or subsequent offence. The 1977 Criminal Law Act raised the penalties to £200 for the first two offences and £200 and/or one month's imprisonment for subsequent offences. Thus, if a parent was charged with the absence from school of five children the maximum fine would be £1,000.

In 1978 Sheffield magistrates did in fact fine a parent £200. We were carrying out field work in schools at the time, and found that the news spread throughout the city's schools in a matter of days. At last, teachers told us, the magistrates were getting tough. Now, perhaps, parents would realise that they couldn't get away with not sending their children to school.

The reality was sadder and more predictable. The father was already in debt. He had been unemployed for years due to chronic depression. The family was typical of the multiply disadvantaged families described in Chapter 5. The fine did nothing to improve the children's attendance, since it merely added to the family's already overwhelming burdens without doing anything to help the parents to cope with them.

CARE PROCEEDINGS IN THE JUVENILE COURT

Rationale

As with a decision to prosecute parents, the logic behind a decision to bring a child before the juvenile court on the grounds of poor attendance is fairly clear. The underlying theory is the same, whether the l.e.a. brings the case on its own initiative or at the order of the magistrates' court. Three conditions apply (Galloway *et al.*, 1981a):

(i) the parent is thought to be guilty of failing to secure the child's attendance at school, and hence could be prosecuted under Section 40 of the 1944 Education Act; *and*
(ii) the child is thought to be beyond the parents' care and control; *and*
(iii) *either* it is not thought that punishing the parents will enable them to regain sufficient care and control to ensure their child's resumed attendance; *or* it is not thought that punishment by the court will provide sufficient incentive to compel the parents to exercise the care and control of which they are nevertheless capable.

It is important to note that in bringing a child before the court for non-attendance at school, the l.e.a. is often seeking a care order. This has the effect of transferring parental responsibilities to the local social services department until the child is eighteen. The department *may* then decide not to move the child from his parents. In practice, though, they are likely to take him into care, for an initial period of assessment. This is generally followed by transfer to a children's home. Eventually, the child is likely to return home.

The court can also make a "supervision order" for a specified period, usually one or two years. This confers responsibility on a local authority social worker to supervise the child, with an implicit requirement to ensure that regular school attendance is resumed. The child will generally remain at home, but the supervising social worker can bring him back to the court if progress is unsatisfactory and seek a care order as an extension to the supervision order.

Extent of Use

Returning again to Fig. 7.1, the general picture in Sheffield is similar to that of parents prosecuted in the magistrates' court: the number of children concerned increases in the secondary school years, with a sharp peak in the penultimate year of compulsory education. Combining juvenile court cases with children whose parents are prosecuted accounted for roughly .15 per cent of all pupils on role in 1976–1977.

Evidence from elsewhere is sparse. Tyerman (1958) noted that in one medium sized Welsh town 405 children from 321 families were taken to court over a six-year period, representing 1.4 per cent of the total on role. In the whole of the United Kingdom 750 children were brought to court in 1954 (Anon., 1955). Tennent (1970) found that .2 per cent of pupils from ordinary schools in London were brought before the courts for school attendance reasons, the highest incidence being .7 per cent amongst fourteen-year-olds.

There is evidence that juvenile court action is taken more frequently in Leeds than in other parts of the country (Pratt, 1983). We discuss this evidence later in relation to the decisions reached by the juvenile court, and the special circumstances operating in Leeds. No other important regional variations are known.

Juvenile Court Decisions

If the magistrates find the child to be in need of care, protection or control they are likely to make either a care order or a supervision order. They are also able to make an interim care order before reaching a final decision. This has the effect of remanding the child to the custody of the social services departments. The intention of the Act is to enable the magistrates to obtain specialist advice and reports in the child's needs. Such advice may be needed as magistrates are required to act in what they consider the child's best interests. In practice interim care orders appear sometimes to have been used to "encourage" more regular attendance in the future (Berg *et al.*, 1977). It is clear, though, that this consciously punitive use of interim care orders was neither intended nor anticipated by the authors of the 1969 Children's and Young Persons' Act.

Table 7.3 shows the decisions reached by Sheffield juvenile court over a two-year period. The table shows that the court placed a supervision order on more than half the poor attenders brought before it by the l.e.a. and a care order on fewer than a quarter. The remaining cases were either adjourned *sine die* or

Table 7.3. *Final Outcomes of Children's Appearances Before Juvenile Court Over Two Years 1976–1978**

Outcome	(No. of children = 126)	Per cent
Supervision order		45.7
Supervision order following interim Care order		3.1
Supervision order with intermediate treatment		2.4
Care order		20.5
Care order following interim Care order		3.1
Case adjourned *sine die*		14.2
Case withdrawn or dismissed		11.0

*Before a final decision was reached, 33 children were brought back to court once, 6 children were brought back twice, and 2 children were brought back 3 times.

Reproduced from the *Durham and Newcastle Research Review*, Vol. IX, No. 46, with the editor's permission.

dismissed. Adjournment *sine die* is considered appropriate when the child's attendance has improved, but the magistrates do not wish the case to be withdrawn or dismissed altogether. The possibility of the l.e.a. bringing the child back to court on the original grounds is thus left open. In contrast, if the case is withdrawn or dismissed the l.e.a. would need to obtain fresh evidence before bringing the child back to court.

HOW DOES THE L.E.A. DECIDE WHO TO PROSECUTE?

In the Autumn term 1976 all Sheffield schools reported 737 pupils missing at least 50 per cent of possible attendance without a legally adequate explanation. In the same term about 800 primary children missed at least 25 per cent of attendance without an adequate reason. Other unpublished work in Sheffield suggests it is safe to assume at least a proportionate increase in the number of secondary school pupils missing 25 per cent of attendances. This would result in 4000–5000 children missing at least 25 per cent of their schooling throughout the city. These figures, moreover are based on the beginning of the school year, when attendance is highest. Yet in the two years 1976–1977 and 1977–1978 the parents of only 157 children were prosecuted by Sheffield, and 126 children were brought before the juvenile court (Tables 7.2 and 7.3), with considerable overlap between the two groups.

Clearly, therefore, some form of selection procedure was operating. One obvious possibility was that educational welfare officers simply selected the worst cases. Some, indeed, claimed that this was the case. A careful analysis of children's attendance records, however, showed that it was not. For every child over whom formal action was taken, there were several other similarly poor attenders against whom the l.e.a. had taken no formal action. To find out more about how the decisions were made we identified four groups of children. Parents of the first group had been invited to attend a meeting of the Education Committee's school attendance section. Parents of the second had been prosecuted in the magistrates' court. The third had been brought before the juvenile court, and the fourth had not been involved in any formal action even though their attendance compared with that of children in the other groups. We then interviewed each child's e.w.o. to find out why the action had been taken, or why no action had been taken (Galloway *et al.*, 1981c).

We first asked about school and family factors which the officers thought might have contributed to poor attendance. Family problems were more frequently reported than problems at school. It became clear, however, that most e.w.o.s had not investigated possible sources of stress within the school as carefully as they had investigated sources of stress with the families. In this connection it was noteworthy that the majority thought they had a good relationship with their clients' parents. They showed greater variation in.their relationships with the children themselves.

The only striking variation between the four samples was that the juvenile court group were more frequently considered out of their parents' control than children in the other three groups. Conversely, parents in these three groups were more often said to be able to control their children, even though they did not insist on attendance.

E.w.o.s differed in their reasons for inviting parents to meetings of the School Attendance Section. Some saw this as a way of avoiding legal action, others as a way of securing approval for legal action. Three-quarters of the magistrates' court group had first been involved with the school attendance section. Seven of the twenty parents were prosecuted following a recommendation made at the request of the e.w.o. Seven were prosecuted, though, following a recommendation which was *not* made at the e.w.o.'s request. This alone indicates that e.w.o.s have by no means as much freedom to make their own decisions in practice as they do in theory. However, they are themselves under pressure. Thirty per cent of e.w.o.s admitted that pressure from the school was a significant factor in their decision to prosecute. Juvenile court action resulted, in a majority of cases, from an instruction from the magistrates' court following conviction of the parents, or from advice from the school attendance section.

There was a fairly strong tendency for e.w.o.s to report truancy in fewer of the children over whom they took no formal action. Other research has shown that these children are less likely to have a record of delinquency than children in the other groups (Galloway *et al.*, 1981c). In addition e.w.o.s tended to consider unnecessarily prolonged illness a cause of these children's absences more frequently than in the other groups. Nevertheless these tendencies were by no means universal. The conclusions (Galloway *et al.*, 1981b) were that:

> There appear to be no clear and consistent principles governing the selection of cases for formal action. The individual judgement of e.w.o.s, their own attitudes towards legal and administrative sanctions, the nature of the schools and catchment areas they serve and pressures from within the educational welfare service itself are more accurate explanations of action than are a set of principles.

SUBSEQUENT ATTENDANCE

Unless attendance improves subsequently, it is hard to see any justification for the elaborate and expensive procedures described in this chapter. In view of the time and money spent on these procedures the shortage of information on the progress of the children concerned is surprising. To shed some light on this question we investigated all children over whom Sheffield l.e.a. took any form of legal action in the school year 1976–1977. We collected details about four groups of children aged less than fifteen at the start of the year:

(i)   ninety children whose parents were invited to a meeting of the school attendance section in 1976–1977;

(ii)   thirty-one children whose parents were prosecuted for the first time in 1976–1977;

(iii) thirty-three children whom the l.e.a. brought before the juvenile court for the first time in the same year;

(iv)   107 children against whom the l.e.a. had taken no formal intervention.

These children were selected from the city-wide persistent absentee survey (see Chapter 2), omitting those who had been involved in administrative or legal proceedings in the previous twelve months; thus they had all illegally missed at least 50 per cent of possible attendances in the Autumn term 1976.

The sex and age distribution was similar in all four groups. There was, however, some overlap between the groups. This was caused by the tendency which we have already noted for the school attendance section to recommend prosecution of parents or care proceedings in connection with the child. Similarly the l.e.a. took action against 24 per cent of pupils in the "no formal action" group in the follow-up period because of their continued poor attendance. The overlap between groups makes statistical comparison between them impractical. Hence, the results must be studied in their own right and not for the purposes of comparison with the others.

We followed up all the children's attendance until the Autumn term 1978. Table 7.4 shows the average school attendance for each group before and after formal action was taken. We have not included in these results periods spent in custodial care. This could result from a care order or an interim care order; the children concerned would attend classes in a social services department institution. On the other hand, we have included children who were placed in non-custodial care. This too could result from a care order or an interim care order, but the children were placed in an "open" setting, such as a children's home from which they would be expected to attend one of the l.e.a.'s day schools.

The table lends no support to the view that formal action encourages parents to ensure that their children attend more regularly in future. On the contrary, attendance a year later was virtually unchanged in the two court samples, and only marginally improved in the school attendance section group. In contrast, the "no formal action" group improved their average attendance from 34 per cent in the Autumn term 1976 to 60 per cent in the Autumn term 1978. It is, of course, possible that the mean attendance figures given in the table conceal important differences within each group. Some children, for example, might have improved dramatically after court action, while others dropped to zero attendance. There was, in fact, a slight drop following intervention in the proportion of pupils attending less than 50 per cent of the time in all samples except that of children before the juvenile court

Table 7.4. *Average School Attendance Before and After Formal Intervention**

School attendance	School attendance section per cent	Magistrates' court per cent	Juvenile court per cent	No formal intervention per cent
Attendance one complete term before intervention (where available) and leading up to intervention in the term it took place (attendance in Autumn term 1976 for N.F.I. sample)	46	34	37	34
Attendance for remainder of term following intervention	58	44	40	N/A
Complete term immediately following formal intervention (Spring term 1977 for N.F.I. sample)	56	50	34	40
Summer term 1978	58	41	37	55
Autumn term 1978	54	38	35	60

*There is some fluctuation in the number of children for whom information was available from term to term. This is because school registers were not available, or were incomplete, or the child had been temporarily placed in custodial care. However, there was no period in which results were calculated on the attendance of less than: (1) 86 children out of the 90 in the S.A.S. sample; (2) 30 out of 31 in the magistrates court sample; (3) 28 out of 30 in the juvenile court sample; (4) 101 out of 107 in the no formal intervention sample.

Reproduced from *Educational Review*, **33** (1), with the editor's permission.

(Galloway *et al.*, 1981c). The reduction was greatest, paradoxically, in the no formal intervention sample.

During the follow-up period 105 children changed schools. These children's attendance is shown in Table 7.5. Normal age-related transfer seemed to have no effect on attendance. In contrast, transfer to a special school, and to a lesser degree transfer to another school for some special reason was associated with a very considerable improvement. We had no detailed information on why these children transferred, nor by whom the transfer was arranged. The results do, however, suggest that an arranged transfer, based on recognition of the child's educational needs, may be considerably more effective than any form of legal action.

THE LEEDS JUVENILE COURT PROCEDURES

The Procedure

A much publicised experiment in Leeds has used the procedure of repeated

Table 7.5. *School Attendance of Pupils who Changed Schools*

Period of attendance	Normal transfer, e.g. primary to secondary N = 45 per cent	Transfer to special school N = 18 per cent	Transfer to another school for some special reason N = 42 per cent
Final complete term at old school, plus any fraction of term before transfer	60.9	15.3	37.1
First complete term at new school, plus any fraction of term after transfer	59.3	70.4	63.5
Second term at new school	50.5	68.3	62.2

*Several of these children made their transfer towards the end of the follow-up period. As a result information on attendance in the second term at the new school was available on only 20 of the children who made ordinary transfers, 12 of the children who transferred to special schools and 31 of the children who had specially arranged transfer.

Reproduced from *Educational Review*, **33** (1), 106, with the editor's permission.

adjournment to encourage attendance (Berg *et al.*, 1977, 1978; Berg, 1980). Under this procedure the court repeatedly adjourns the case, reviewing attendance each time the child re-appears. The adjournment period may be a week, a fortnight or several weeks, depending on progress. If attendance does not improve, an interim care order is made as an "encouragement" (Berg *et al.*, 1977). If this does not work a full care order is made. According to Cross (1983) children are left in no doubt about the requirements and the likely sanctions. The chairman tells them:

> Now go away and come back here in a week's time. If you've missed any more school without a very good reason you can bring a bag with your night things—you'll be going away for a bit.

Results

Two studies have been reported. The first was retrospective, and compared children on whom the adjournment procedure had been used, with children placed on a supervision order (Berg *et al.*, 1977). The results clearly favoured the adjourned group. As the study was retrospective, though, it was possible that the two groups might have differed before the children came to court. The Leeds researchers, therefore, carried out a controlled trial in which cases were allocated at random to supervision or to the repeated adjournment procedure (Berg *et al.*, 1978).

The results were slightly less impressive than in the retrospective investigation, but still favoured the adjournment group. Before their first appearance, both groups had averaged 25 per cent attendance. In the first six months after their first appearance the adjourned group averaged 65 per cent attendance, compared with 50 per cent for the supervision group. In the second six-month period the adjourned group averaged 75 per cent attendance, compared with 50 per cent in the supervision group. The results were not affected by age or sex in any consistent way, though older pupils in both groups tended to miss more school than younger pupils.

In addition court convictions for delinquent activities were examined as a further possible measure of progress. Before the l.e.a. first brought them to court, children in the adjourned group had averaged 1–2 appearances, and in the supervision group 1–3. In the six months after their first appearance the average conviction rate was 0.2 and 0.9 respectively. As with the attendance figures, the differences were statistically significant.

The Leeds research has attracted wide-spread attention. It has been criticised by social workers (e.g. Reynolds, 1976), but applauded by critics who challenge social work services because of their supposed political leanings, expense and ineffectiveness. Brewer *et al.* (1981), for example, are enthusiastic about the implied possibilities for behaviour change in the Leeds experiment. Yet before extending the procedure to other areas, it is worth taking a more critical look at what the Leeds court has been doing.

Validity of the Results

Berg *et al.* (1978b) claim:

> Subsequent school attendance would be most satisfactory if the adjournment procedure was used on all truants coming to court.

The evidence they present does not, however, justify this claim. There are two problems. First, the two samples were not representative of all children brought before the Leeds court for poor attendance in the period under study. Nearly 42 per cent were excluded because they had less than six months left at school or for special circumstances, "such as social factors of overriding importance, the existence of offences which needed to be taken into consideration or the child's adamant refusal even to consider returning to school" (Berg, 1980). Hence, it would appear that the most difficult cases were simply excluded from the experiment. Moreover, Berg *et al.* (1978b) make clear that the adjournment procedure has more effect with children under the age of thirteen and a half. Its effectiveness with older pupils was considerably less.

A second problem is that Leeds social services had been under pressure before the experiment began to bring youngsters placed on supervision back to court if their attendance did not improve. As a result, two interim care orders and five full care orders were made on this group. Berg *et al.* regarded any period in care as 100 per cent absence. Without the court's pressure, these children would have remained in the community, attending school for at least some of the time (on the author's own figures perhaps for an average between 25 and 50 per cent). This would substantially have reduced the gap between the adjournment and the supervision groups, though the effect of the adjourned children committed to care would also have to be taken into account.

Legal Questions

Two legal objections have been raised against the Leeds procedures (Pratt, 1983). The first concerns the legality of the random-allocation to adjournment or supervision. Section 44 of the 1933 Children and Young Persons Act requires the courts to "have regard to the welfare of the child or young person". The Leeds court was selective in who they included in the experiment. Even so, it is questionable whether random allocation is consistent with due regard for the child's welfare.

The second objection concerns the legality of repeated adjournment. Pratt (1983) argues that this has no basis in law. The reason is that the courts are only empowered to adjourn cases in order to make further inquiries into the child's background, or to enable parents to produce further evidence in the light of a report which has already been submitted. Pratt comments:

> We found no power to adjourn the case in the hope that a particular sequence of events will or will not take place, backed up by threat of custody (i.e. interim or full care order) if the wishes of the magistrates are not complied with by the defendant.

Why, then, has the Leeds procedure not been challenged in court? The random allocation experiment could not be challenged because it was kept secret both from defendants and from the professional personnel involved until the experiment was over. Challenge to the adjournment procedure is most unlikely. All the evidence suggests that the families of persistent absentees in urban areas live in socially and financially disadvantaged conditions (see Chapter 5). The overwhelming majority of children brought to court by the l.e.a. come from families where the parents have neither the personal nor the financial resources to mount a sustained challenge to the legality of the procedures.

Changes in juvenile court procedures from May 1984 may possibly change the situation. Due to possible conflict between the child's interests and the interests of the parents, the court is now empowered to order separate legal representation for each party (Lockley, 1984). The child in such cases is eligible for legal aid. It remains to be seen whether these new arrangements will facilitate a sustained challenge to the Leeds procedure. As legal aid has to be granted by the court, this may not be a foregone conclusion.

Practical and Financial Questions

In the random allocation experiment, attendance of the adjourned group was somewhat less satisfactory than in the earlier retrospective study. Berg *et al.* (1978b) attributed this to greater difficulty in obtaining places in assessment centres, with a consequent reduction in the number of interim care orders. If the procedure depends on punitive use of interim care orders, and if these are only available for a limited number of children, the procedure clearly has a very restricted application.

This has not, however, stopped the Leeds court from placing much larger numbers of children in care for poor school attendance than courts in other areas. Table 7.6 shows the number of care orders made on school attendance grounds in five towns. The actual numbers are provided by Pratt (1983) and the estimated numbers from the Personal Social Services Statistics (1981) which he quotes. It is clear that the use of care orders in Leeds is heavy compared with other areas. In the same paper Pratt shows that care orders on school attendance grounds represent a higher proportion of all care orders in Leeds than in other areas.

Table 7.6. *Care Order Under Section 1(2) (e), 1969 Children's and Young Person's Act*

Juvenile Court	1977		1978		1979	
	Actual number	Estimated number based on Leeds population aged 5–17	Actual number	Estimated number based on Leeds population aged 5–17	Actual number	Estimated number based on Leeds population aged 5–17
Leeds	59	59	57	57	62	62
Sheffield	17	20	7	8	6	7
Doncaster	9	26	10	29	3	9
Calderdale	5	20	6	23	13	51

Adapted from Pratt, J. (1983). Folklore and Fact in Truancy Research: Some Critical Comments on Recent Developments. *British Journal of Criminology*, **23**, 336–353.

Residential places cost £89.31 per child per week (Personal Social Services Statistics, 1981). We have no evidence on how long poor attenders committed to care by the Leeds court actually spend in care. The period is unlikely to be less than three months, and may often be a great deal longer. If and when the child returns home on trial, a social worker will be required to maintain contact with him. The supposed, but questionable, efficacy of the Leeds procedure should be considered in the light of its undoubted expense to the tax payer and its possible side-effects on the children concerned, and hence, indirectly on society.

Possible Side-effects: Educational and Social Questions

The Leeds court does not appear to have given much publicity to the possibility that its highly publicised adjournment procedure may have unwelcome side-effects. In medicine any procedure which harms patients more than it benefits them would be considered unethical. In juvenile law such a procedure might be illegal as well as unethical, in view of the court's requirements to act in the child's best interests. In adopting a new and controversial procedure, the magistrates have a moral, if not legal, obligation to explore unwelcome side-effects. As yet there is little evidence that the Leeds court has accepted this obligation. There are, in fact, three areas of potential concern. The first deals with the child's welfare in the family, the second with his welfare at school, and the third with the children who are committed to care.

Parents are required to attend juvenile court hearings. On average adjourned cases are brought back to court seven times before a decision is finally reached. Leeds is a high unemployment area. One wonders how many parents have established an unenviable reputation for absenteeism, or even been sacked, as a result of the procedure. Leeds has similar social problems to Sheffield. Hence, many parents of poor attenders will be living both in chronically and in acutely stressful circumstances. The adjournment procedure must add to this stress. One wonders how often this extra stress has precipitated a crisis, such as marital breakdown or violence towards a child in the family. The Leeds court cannot claim to be made aware of such dangers by skilled and sympathetic e.w.o.s. Berg (1980) has summarised quite clearly the limitations of the service they can offer.

There is more than adequate evidence, reviewed in earlier chapters, that poor attenders tend to be educationally backward, and frequently of below average intellectual ability. Their educational needs are rarely straightforward, and require detailed planning. The only aim for the Leeds court appears to be return to school. Again, the Leeds magistrates cannot rely on e.w.o.s. Berg has recognised their limitations. Moreover, in Sheffield, Galloway *et al.* (1981b) have noted the infrequency with which schools are actively involved with e.w.o.s in planning poor attenders' return to school. There is no doubt that for some pupils, especially in the older age groups, return to school involves a daily diet of frustration and failure. One can respect the determination of the Leeds court to uphold the law. Nevertheless their obligation is to act in the child's interests. It is not clear what specialist advice the Leeds court routinely obtains to ensure that the school both recognises and is able to meet the child's educational needs. The court may sometimes be adding to his problems rather than reducing them.

The final area of concern is the most serious, and has the most supporting evidence. Committal to care is highly disruptive of family life. It is also highly disruptive educationally. Typically, the child will spend three weeks in an assessment centre, from which he will attend the local school. He will then transfer to a long-stay or medium stay children's home, with another change of school. On return home, generally from three months to two years later, he is likely to return to his original school. It is hard to see how any child can make any progress given such an unsettled regime. If the Social Services Department places the child in a residential school, known in the jargon as community home with education on the premises, he is also likely to receive a highly inadequate education. A report by H.M.I. (1980) has drawn attention to major deficiencies in the curriculum provided in many such schools, and to their failure to cater adequately for the pupil's special educational needs.

A further and even more serious problem is that a high proportion of children in residential care have a history of delinquency, even in medium-term non-custodial children's homes. At best, residential care is notoriously ineffective in changing delinquent attitudes and behaviour, and at worst may provide pupils, who had not previously been involved in delinquent behaviour, with unrivalled opportunities for acquiring delinquent attitudes and behaviour patterns (Tutt, 1974, 1981; Cornish and Clarke, 1975). We found the school attendance of many pupils in children's homes in Sheffield to be highly erratic. Committing poor attenders to care may, in effect, give them a very thorough, very expensive, apprenticeship in criminal behaviour.

Overview

We do not dispute that the Leeds procedure appears *prima facie* to be successful with *some* poor attenders. The published evidence does not, however, justify a conclusion that it would be effective with all, or even with a majority. The procedure raises serious questions concerning its legality, practicality and morality. Its morality will remain in doubt until the magistrates are able to demonstrate that it gives rise to none of the side-effects suggested above. A cursory reading of the literature on absence from school and on the progress of children in care suggests that they may not easily be able to do this.

CONCLUSIONS

What place, then, do legal sanctions have in the management of poor school attendance? We do not dispute that education is, and should remain, compulsory. Consequently we do not dispute the existence of legal sanctions, either as an expression of disapproval of parental attitudes or as a way of protecting the child's interests. In Chapter 10 we suggest the very limited circumstances in which they may be appropriate, when discussing cooperation between teachers and other professionals. Our aim here is to draw conclusions on the extent and usefulness of legal sanctions in dealing with the numerically large problem of poor attendance.

They are, quite simply, at best peripheral. We have noted evidence that in Sheffield alone, 4000–5000 pupils illegally miss at least 25 per cent of possible attendances. Even when considering pupils with less than 50 per cent attendance, legal action is only taken against a small proportion. Parents and children are selected in an arbitrary, unsystematic way. Further, legal action is ineffective in improving attendance. Too many question marks hang over the Leeds juvenile court's reported adjournment procedure to advocate its continued use.

Teachers and magistrates who see legal sanctions as the solution to the problem of poor attendance might be more happily occupied in search of the Holy Grail. The failure of these sanctions to secure much improvement is predictable, since they are seldom based on a clear understanding of the complexities of poor attendance. Teachers cannot absolve themselves from responsibility for the massive increase in absenteeism in the secondary school years. Forcing unwilling pupils back into an unchanged system is a recipe for frustration and resentment, both for pupils and for their teachers. Legal procedures, like clinic-based treatment, may be appropriate for a very small proportion of all poor attenders. Any hope for a solution, or even partial solution to the attendance problem, however, lies in the school.

CHAPTER 8

Using Resources: Analysing and Planning

OVERVIEW

This chapter and the next suggest that we already have an abundance of information about poor attenders, their families and even their schools. The problem is not lack of information but the interpretation and use of what is already known. Poor attendance, we argue, is primarily a problem for schools. The educational, social work and medical support or treatment services may contribute towards solving this problem in cooperation with teachers. They cannot, however, solve the problem for teachers. Yet a cooperative partnership between teachers and other professionals will, in itself, do little to improve overall attendance unless accompanied by a rigorous analysis of what the school is trying to achieve, not just for its less willing customers, but for all its pupils.

TOWARDS A CRITIQUE OF EXISTING SERVICES

It is worth asking whether l.e.a. and social work support services can, or are expected to, have any substantial impact on the problem of absence from school. The educational welfare service, after all, is predicated largely on the existence of attendance problems. E.w.o.s could reasonably claim that a reduction in absenteeism would free them for more valuable forms of welfare and social work, as advocated by Fitzherbert (1977a,b). Whether a cost-conscious education committee would see it in the same light is another matter. Clearly, support services are required to respond to problems identified by the school. Just as clearly, this implies the continued existence of problems to be identified. However successful the support services might be in "treating" absentees, a continuing supply of cases for treatment would prove that the problem still existed.

This point is perhaps better illustrated with reference to disruptive behaviour. Many schools have set up special groups to cater for disruptive pupils. In point of fact, the groups appear not to have been particularly successful; at least in Sheffield, Galloway *et al.* (1982) noted that they had had no impact on suspension rates in the schools concerned. Yet however successful they might be, a continuing supply of pupils for admission would prove that the problem remained.

In practice, if not in logic, the only successful "treatment" of disruptive behaviour, or absenteeism, is prevention. Schools have been described both in Britain (Galloway *et al.*, 1982) and in New Zealand (Galloway and Barrett, 1983) which experience few problems from disruptive behaviour. The notion of treatment, therefore, becomes largely redundant.

Whose Problem?

The idea that teachers are paid to meet pupil's educational needs, while social workers or e.w.o.s are paid to investigate and meet their families' social needs has a certain naive attraction. In practice teachers cannot teach effectively without an understanding of the child's cultural, including social, background. Nor can e.w.o.'s work effectively without: (i) a clear idea of potential sources of stress which the child may experience at school, and (ii) agreement on some plan for meeting them. Almost everyone agrees on the necessity for inter-professional cooperation; especially when other people are the subject of exhortation. In practice professionals do not find it easy to cooperate with each other, and teachers perhaps find it more difficult than most. The reasons lie in the nature of teaching, which is too often a lonely activity, with little support from colleagues.

In their study of twelve London schools, Rutter *et al.* (1979) found that cooperation between members of a subject department in curriculum planning was associated with favourable outcomes. Conversely, the less effective schools were characterised by lower levels of cooperation both between teachers and between teachers and pupils. When teachers do not adequately cooperate with each other, they can hardly cooperate with external agencies.

Cooperation implies willingness to consider the other person's point of view, and if necessary to change one's own practices. In other words, it implies joint planning. The nature of interaction between tachers and e.w.o.s and between teachers and social workers makes joint planning virtually impossible. We consider each case in turn.

Galloway *et al.* (1981b) noted that many parents of poor attenders had never visited their child's school, and that even more frequently the e.w.o. knew of no home visits from teachers or contact between the family and specialist l.e.a. support services. In addition the e.w.o.s themselves seemed to see their role primarily in working with the family:

> On this evidence it seems as though many e.w.o.s may see themselves as case workers operating in parallel with the school rather than as catalysts in establishing closer, more constructive relationships between parents, children and teachers.

Case conferences are intended to formulate a coherent plan in meeting the client's needs. Their usefulness is unfortunately often limited by three scenarios which will be familiar to most senior teachers and members of support and treatment services. In the first scenario the case conference is used simply in order to exchange information. At worst such meetings act as an opportunity to exchange gossip. Pratt (1984) describes a discussion in the Education Committee's school attendance section in Sheffield before members interviewed a parent:

> One educational welfare officer introduced her case by stating that: "I won't mention this when the parents are in here, but the other boys (in this family) have a bad history. I don't want the father to think that this child is being judged by their standards."

To which one might ask: really ...? Yet even when discussion rises above this level, the purpose of exchanging information is not always clear. Unless information has implications for future planning it should be considered redundant.

In the second scenario the case conference deteriorates into a hand-wringing session in which everyone commiserates on the insolubility of the problem. This frequently follows an unproductive exchange of information. It engenders a comforting, if illogical, feeling that since everyone agrees, the problem really must be insoluble, and therefore no-one's personal responsibility.

The third scenario is quite different, but no less destructive, being character-ised by professionals "talking past each other" (a term for which I am indebted to Metge and Kinloch's (1978) study of communication barriers between Maoris, other Polynesians and white New Zealanders). This happens when participants in a case conference adopt incompatible positions, seeing each other in a stereotyped manner. Thus, social workers may see teachers as insensitive and authoritarian, concerned only that the pupil cogs should slot neatly into the well-oiled machine of the school. For their part teachers may see social workers as sentimental and impractical, lacking any understanding or concern for the child's educational needs or for those of the wider school community.

Deliberately, these three scenarios are themselves stereotypes. They will nevertheless be recognised by anyone with much professional experience in school attendance. The first occurs most frequently when teachers and e.w.o.s meet. The second occurs most frequently in meetings between teachers and social workers. These examples are not, of course, an argument against inter-professional cooperation. Case conferences are a necessary aspect of this. Effective planning often requires more information than is available to any one individual. It also requires an equal partnership between professionals and between professionals and their clients. In order to see why so many case conferences are unproductive we need to look more carefully at the nature of relationships involved.

The educational welfare service is the Cinderella of the social services. Although members in some services now have a professional social work qualification, this has not substantially changed their status or their image as "school cops". Their activities are subjected to closer "political" scrutiny by elected councillors than those of any other branch of the l.e.a. Very few e.w.o.s have had teaching experience, and they are emphatically not considered competent to offer educational advice. Historically, they have mainly been expected to investigate and deal with cases of poor attendance. A recent survey by H.M.I. has described divergent views about their role and about the training they should receive (D.E.S., 1984).

An e.w.o.'s arguments that schools should accept responsibility for the sharp deterioration in attendance in the final two years of compulsory education are unlikely to be well received. Teachers guard their autonomy jealously, claiming the knowledge and professional judgement to cater appropriately for poor attenders if only they would turn up. While they will listen sympathetically to explanations of mitigating circumstances, they are often, perhaps understandably, less receptive to implicit criticism of their own organisation and performance especially when coming from a member of a group considered to have low status, such as e.w.o.s.

In theory, e.w.o.s have a good deal of autonomy. In practice, criticisms from head teachers will make their life extremely difficult. Moreover, they know that their chances of gaining cooperation from teachers in arranging a child's return to school is entirely dependent on their acceptance as members of an extended staff team. Hence, any actions or suggestions which might threaten acceptance have to be regarded with great caution. Accepting the school's perception of poor attendance—for example that it is illegal, and/or that it results from individual or family deviance or psychopathology—thus becomes a necessity, at least initially. The reasons are twofold: (i) acceptance depends on "not rocking the boat" too much; (ii) without acceptance they are in no position to negotiate changes in the school to facilitate a child's return. The contradiction in the argument is that the procedures adopted to gain acceptance largely negate the e.w.o.'s role as change agent or child advocate within the school.

A similar socialising process applies to educational psychologists on their regular visits to schools. They, however, have two potential advantages. First, almost all educational psychologists were qualified graduate teachers before taking a higher degree or diploma in the applications of psychology in education. Consequently, their status in schools and within the l.e.a. administration is higher. Second, they are required by the 1981 Education Act to advise the l.e.a. on the requirements of children with special educational needs.

The 1981 Act is by no means an unmixed blessing either for teachers, educational psychologists or pupils (Newell, 1983). Nevertheless, it does require l.e.a.s to identify and cater for children with special educational needs, and these needs are defined, at least in part by educational psychologists. Moreover, they are generally the professionals to whom the l.e.a. turns for monitoring the progress of children with special educational needs. That, however, is simply another way of saying that they have some responsibility for monitoring the school's success in meeting the special educational needs which they have previously helped to define.

In practice the psychologists' task is less straight forward. They are under similar pressures to e.w.o.s, and know that their recommendations will not be endorsed by unwilling teachers. They, too, are often under pressure to individualise school attendance problems, by seeing them as evidence of personal or family instability. Nevertheless their teaching background and professional status may give them greater scope for gaining cooperation from teachers as equal partners in identifying and analysing ways in which the school may itself start to reduce its attendance problems.

If educational psychologists and e.w.o.s think they have an uphill task, this applies with much greater force to social workers with responsibility for supervision orders imposed by the juvenile court following legal action by the l.e.a. Galloway *et al.* (1981d) point out that poor attenders are seldom easy or rewarding children to teach. They frequently need intensive and skilled remedial teaching. Although teachers may need guidance in this, they may also feel reluctant to allocate scarce resources to children who have not cooperated in the past. The school may have no special education facilities for older pupils. Although it may seem logical to concentrate resources on the younger age groups, this will increase the sense of frustration and failure facing a fifteen- or sixteen-year-old with limited reading ability. For such a pupil return to school will be a depressing experience. The authors summarise the social worker's plight:

> A persistent absentee's return to school is not a smooth or easy path. It can raise important questions about both the adequacy and the allocation of the school's resources. At the best of times these are exceedingly sensitive areas. At times when teachers face increasing demands with decreasing resources, they become even more sensitive. It therefore seems unfortunate that the social worker with the thankless task of negotiating this minefield with the school's head or senior teachers does not work in the education department, and is generally on the first rung of his professional ladder.

Thus, the 1969 Children's and Young Person's Act enables the juvenile court to require social workers with neither training nor experience in education to negotiate a child's return to school and subsequent regular attendance. The requirement is utterly unrealistic, and has done a disservice both to social workers and, indirectly, to their clients. One can only assume that the Act is based on a naive understanding of school attendance problems, assuming that they can be solved by social work skills. Before accepting this we would have to ask why social work skills are needed so much more frequently by fourteen- to sixteen-year-olds than by other age groups. The answer that these older pupils are most frequently absent does nothing to explain *why* they might need social work help, nor does it explain *what sort* of help they might need.

Case-work Procedures

Social workers and qualified e.w.o.s are trained in various forms of individual and family case work. Some social workers, but few e.w.o.s undertake work with groups of parents or children. Although behavioural approaches are slowly becoming more widely accepted it is probably true that a majority of social workers still adopt a fairly non-directive approach to counselling and case work. They offer practical assistance, for example over welfare benefits or housing, and aim to establish a trusting relationship within which their clients will acquire sufficient insight and confidence to tackle their problems. In addition they generally make clear to clients the likely consequences of their actions, for example if they are charged with offences in the juvenile court.

This, however, places them in a difficult position with respect to supervision orders for non-attendance. It is not the police, the l.e.a. or society which can take the child back to court if attendance does not improve. The decision rests squarely with the social worker. Magistrates and teachers may both expect that the child should be returned to court so that the magistrates may replace the supervision order with a care order. The social worker, though, may have at least four reasons for considering further action inappropriate. He may feel (i) that it might interrupt therapeutic work with the family; (ii) that teachers are making no effort to cater satisfactorily for the pupil, and that he should not enforce return to a school which only offers his client further experience of boredom and failure; (iii) that other children have more urgent need of the limited number of residential places available; (iv) that committing the child to care is likely to make his behaviour worse rather than better by disrupting family life which may already be fragile, and by providing close association with other, more delinquent, young people.

Social workers' training seldom equips them to carry out therapeutic work with children, adolescents and adults. They may be supervising absentees aged from five to sixteen. Their quite understandable sense of frustration arises as much from the limitations to what they can offer their child clients as from resentment at what they see as the intransigent behaviour of teachers in some schools.

THE LEVEL OF ANALYSIS

One-Sidedness

An implication of the discussion so far is that the professionals most frequently involved in school attendance lack the training to carry out a comprehensive analysis of the problem. Thus, neither e.w.o.s nor social workers have teaching experience. Similarly, teachers lack training in the social work skills necessary to understand the complex family relationships which exist in a minority of cases.

We have argued, though, that the problem does not stop there. If it did, cooperation between other professionals and teachers would ensure a comprehensive programme to cater for each pupil's needs. The ethos of each professional group makes active cooperation very difficult indeed. Teachers are sensitive to implicit criticism from outsiders. For their part the outsiders feel vulnerable when visiting schools. They cope with this feeling of vulnerability either by accepting the staff room ethos, becoming kind of adopted honorary members, or by withdrawing into a quite separate professional group, for example of social worker colleagues, in which teachers are the "out group".

The level of this problem can be understood by considering some questions which anyone investigating a case of poor attendance needs to ask. As an example we consider a fifteen-year-old girl, Elaine, whose occasional absences increased in frequency at the start of her final two years of compulsory schooling. She is in a class from which no more than 20 per cent of pupils collect more than two fairly lowly passes in the Certificate of Secondary Education. Even with full attendance, she herself is not likely to rise to this level. She has a boy friend who is also frequently absent from school. She is the oldest child remaining at home, and has four younger brothers and sisters. Her father's whereabouts are unknown and her mother is said to be suffering from depression and to be in poor physical health. She is thus fairly typical of many absentees in inner city areas with low school attendance rates.

A legitimate question to ask first is whether the domestic situation has recently become more stressful. This, however, is not the case. Her mother has been in poor health for a long time and has not deteriorated recently. Hence, Elaine's absenteeism cannot sensibly be attributed simply to home circumstances.

Yet in an interview Elaine expresses anxiety about her mother's health, pointing out that she gets exhausted by the noise of the younger children. Her anxiety appears genuine; moreover, it is perfectly legitimate, since her mother *is* depressed and in poor health. Elaine agrees that her mother has not got any worse recently, but points out, quite reasonably, that that doesn't make her happy and healthy. Just as reasonably she points out that she can help her mother during the day by staying at home. She does not see herself as a domestic drudge. She and her mother enjoy each other's company, and Elaine's presence has undoubtedly resulted in a tidier house, and in the whole family being better cared for and fed. In other words, by staying away from school, Elaine is doing something to relieve the stress which *all* members of the family are feeling at home.

So far, though, we only have half the picture. Elaine denies that she has any major problems at school. She dislikes one or two teachers, "but not enough to make me stop off if I wanted to go". She does not actively dislike any subject in the curriculum, but considers them all boring. Her attitude is not one of intense resentment, but rather of apathy: it's boring, what's the point? She makes two further points. One is that going to school "won't do me any good". The second is that her boy friend in the year above her has been treated badly at school. The teachers know she is his girl friend, and if she returns to school she thinks she might receive similar treatment. These two points are worth considering separately.

Elaine says school won't do her any good. At two levels she is probably right. Even with full attendance, her teachers agree that she is unlikely to pass even one or two subjects in the Certificate of Secondary Education. Even if she astonished everyone by passing three or four subjects, this would do nothing to improve her chances of a job after leaving school. Nor can her teachers claim with honesty that a good reference from the school will help her in the job market. The sort of unskilled job to which Elaine aspires is won by a friend or relation putting in a word for you. She and her family have neither hope nor expectation that the school can help her find a job. "Sometimes they help the bright kids, but not ones like us". Her assessment is realistic.

Teachers might indignantly deny the premise on which Elaine's argument is based; passing public examinations is not the only, or even the primary, aim of education. Some teachers might add that preparation for work is incidental to the school's aims, which they describe in terms of personal and social development. Such aims are not only legitimate, but necessary. The problem for Elaine, or her teachers, is that they are not reflected in her experiences at school. She receives suggestions that school attendance might have other benefits than preparation for employment with a mixture of amusement and incomprehension: "you mean we should be learning to be more like the teachers?" As far as Elaine is concerned, she can read and write well enough for her immediate needs. She has already gone through nine years of schooling, and cannot see two more making that much difference. From her point of view, she is acting reasonably.

Her boy friend's treatment at school raises even more difficult questions. Teachers and e.w.o.s would say, that this has nothing to do with her attendance. It is a rationalisation for her own poor attendance, and a thoroughly weak one at that. It undoubtedly *is* a rationalisation, since Elaine herself has never complained of the sort of gross unfairness which, she claims, her boy friend suffered. Elaine, though, might be excused for seeing the matter from a different point of view. Loyalty to friends and colleagues is a quality which the school, in theory, aims to promote. Elaine points out the following facts: (i) in spite of nine years of regular attendance her boy friend's schools have failed to teach him to read; he is obviously not stupid, though, because he is good at maths and tackles any handyman jobs around the home; (ii) the year tutor "has it in for him"; when he last returned to school the year tutor made a sarcastic remark in assembly about people who were trying to give us all a bit of a shock by turning up for a change; the same year tutor had caned him the previous year for missing afternoon school to attend a football match in another city; when he claimed to have had permission from the head, the year tutor replied that he would get an extra stroke for lying; it was not a lie, but he never received an apology from the year tutor.

All these "facts" were correct. Although the head had taken the matter up with the year tutor, at the request of a psychologist to whom the boy had complained, no apology had been forthcoming. Further, the year tutor was quite explicit in regarding the boy as a "bad 'un", and made no secret of the fact, either to the boy, other pupils, his colleagues or the psychologist. Elaine admitted readily that this year tutor had always been quite fair towards her. Yet she did resent his well-intended advice to stop seeing her boy friend and find someone better. She also suspected, probably rightly, that this teacher attributed her own absences to her boy friend's influence. In the circumstances she was not behaving unreasonably, *from her point of view*, in anticipating a degree of unpleasantness if and when she returned to school.

A legitimate reply from the teacher's point of view might be: "well what does she expect, a red carpet, with a welcome from the school orchestra?" Both Elaine and her teachers have a perfectly valid point of view from their own perspectives. For her teachers, school attendance is compulsory and must be enforced. For Elaine school attendance is at best of peripheral importance in her life. Her time is more pleasantly and profitably spent at home or with her boy friend. Full-time schooling has nothing more to offer her, particularly as she now thinks herself likely to attract the same hostility as her boy friend.

The problem is that Elaine and her teachers are on different wave-lengths. Each sees a different reality, and is either unable to see or unable to comprehend that of the others. The school, it is true, can resort to legal action to enforce its version of the facts. If Elaine, or more probably her friendship with her boy friend, arouses sufficiently strong feelings in teachers they may press the e.w.o. to do just that. Yet care proceedings in the juvenile court are statistically unlikely to be followed by improved attendance. Even if legal pressure does result in return to school, it will do nothing on its own to reduce the validity of Elaine's assessment of the situation from her point of view.

Perhaps more important, Elaine is only one of several poor attenders at her school. The l.e.a. cannot take legal action against all poor attenders without swamping the courts. If the decision to prosecute is perceived as arbitrary, the moral authority both of the school and of the court is weakened. Far from encouraging the others (as Voltaire cynically observed in a different context, more drastic measures have been used in the past *"pour encourager les autres"*) legal action may foster a climate of mistrust and resentment amongst pupils which may promote poor attendance. Elaine's story illustrates the ease with which teachers and children can "talk past each other", adopting mutually incompatible criteria to justify both their attitudes and their behaviour. Assessments based on one set of criteria are inevitably one-sided. Elaine's teachers probably attribute her absence to her own attitudes, her boy friend's influence and, to a lesser extent, her disadvantaged home circumstances. After all, her mother willingly condones her absences. Elaine places her absence in a different light. She identifies areas of concern at school and argues that her time is better spent at home. Although she would be bemused by the term, she is in effect denying the school's moral authority to enforce attendance.

Naïve Levels of Analysis

An obvious objection at this stage is that teachers and educational psychologists do in fact make strenuous efforts to identify sources of stress at school. They are not oblivious to the pupil's perspective. Indeed, a major function for pastoral care staff is investigating problems which pupils are experiencing at school. Most educational psychologists could also deny that their aim is to identify "causes" of poor attendance which lie in the child or the family. Indeed they could point out that they aim to suggest ways in which the school may cater for the child more effectively.

It would be both unfair and incorrect to reply: "Methinks thou dost protest too much". Teachers undoubtedly make conscientious efforts to identify problems their pupils are experiencing at school. Nor would it be fair to say that these efforts focus mainly on finding ways to "help" the *child* adjust to the *school's* needs, though this is undoubtedly an aim of most of what poses for counselling in schools. Most schools go further than this, stretching a complex time-table to the limit to find ways of catering for pupils with special needs. The real problem lies not in the existence of such efforts, but in the fact that they are at best palliative. At worst they obscure the more fundamental areas of tension that have created the climate in which, from the pupil's point of view, absence becomes a legitimate alternative.

Elaine's boy friend, Peter, illustrates the different levels at which analysis of the reasons for poor attendance can take place. Although he is a year older, Peter's attendance, like Elaine's, deteriorated at the start of his last two years of compulsory schooling. At the age of fourteen, after nine years fairly regular attendance, he read as well as the average seven-year-old. He can handle money reliably, though, and has a Saturday job serving on a stall in the local market. He is well-liked by many teachers at the school, but has clashed, as we have noted already, with his year tutor. His father left school at the age of fourteen with no qualifications and no regrets. He thinks the law stupid in not allowing Peter to do likewise. Provided Peter attends regularly enough to avoid the l.e.a. taking legal action, his parents see no need to worry about his absences.

Asked about his poor attendance, Peter complains bitterly about his year tutor, and points out that he is unlikely to make much progress in reading now. Most of his time in class is spent copying what the teacher and other children have written. It holds neither interest nor meaning. He feels he has been labelled an educational failure and a social misfit. He is not alone here. Other pupils in his age group are regarded just as negatively by some of the school's senior staff. They no longer believe that their own efforts will bring them success on the terms set by their teachers. Moreover, they do not believe that their teachers' goals, focusing principally on public examination passes, have any relevance to their present or future life.

Criticism and punishment from teachers have given these pupils a corporate sense of identity. Membership of their particular group is maintained by being seen to challenge authority. It so happens that Peter is genuinely fond of Elaine. Being criticised by his year tutor for leading a younger, formerly well-behaved girl astray raises his status in his peers' eyes. From Peter's perspective, the year tutor's antagonism to his friendship with Elaine is an important bonus.

Looking more closely at Peter's backwardness in reading, some interesting points emerge. First, his reading age has not changed since transfer to his secondary school. In other words, three years fairly regular attendance appears to have resulted in no progress. This cannot entirely be dismissed as due to lack of cooperation. We need to know why Peter often did not cooperate, or rather why his teachers were unable to enlist his cooperation.

On leaving his primary school Peter was recognised as an extremely backward reader. His class had had between two and five changes of teacher in each of his last three primary school years. The last of Peter's long list of primary teachers noted that he seemed easily embarrassed by his lack of reading ability, and tended to conceal his embarrassment behind a display of indifference.

The secondary school placed Peter in one of two full-time "remedial" classes. The experienced and perceptive head of department recognised, from her very limited contact with Peter, the validity of what her primary school colleague had written. Unfortunately Peter was taught mainly by the remedial department's other two teachers, who were less experienced and less perceptive than their senior colleague. Peter gradually acquired a reputation, first for indifference and later for trouble-making.

As the remedial department contained a high proportion of the school's most troublesome pupils, Peter was not particularly exceptional. However, he quickly recognised that the "remedial" classes contained pupils who were widely regarded throughout the school, both by teachers and by pupils, as dull or troublesome. He neither disliked the remedial teachers nor blamed them for his lack of progress which in an ill-defined way he considered his own responsibility. Of his own status, though, he was in no doubt.

The remedial department catered only for the first three secondary school years. By the fourth year, it was argued, pupils should be able to fit into an ordinary lower ability class pursuing a two-year course of work leading to the Certificate of Secondary Education. There were two snags. First, some of the pupils, including Peter simply did not fit neatly into one of these classes. Second, although they catered for lower ability pupils, these classes still contained children with widely varying interests and aptitudes. Many subject teachers considered themselves untrained to teach the least able pupils. There was a dearth of resources suitable for these pupils, and few teachers had the knowledge or the time to develop suitable programmes themselves.

Seeing assessment in this light teachers could be forgiven for saying: "Well, where are we supposed to start?" The most obvious and the easiest starting point is with a thorough diagnostic assessment of Peter's reading skills. Admittedly, the school has no formal provision for meeting special educational needs in his age group, but with goodwill and ingenuity something may perhaps be arranged. A second step may perhaps be tactfully to by-pass the year tutor. This would require considerable diplomacy on the part of the head, but is not impossible. The assistant year tutor, for example, might be given specific responsibility for Peter's supervision and pastoral care. At the same time his status in an anti-authority, potentially subversive group of disaffected pupils could be weakened by a change of class and by close supervision during the lunch hour and mid-morning and afternoon breaks.

Yet against the wider picture as proposed above, these measures are pretty inadequate. At best they constitute a limited but perhaps necessary starting point. Their limitation is that they are based on an analysis which fails to see beyond Peter as the problem. Peter, though, is the product of his school as well as of his family.

Being realistic, probably not very much can be done to make Peter's remaining time at school more satisfactory either for his teachers or for Peter himself than his previous years. This is not an argument for doing nothing. It merely acknowledges that the probable benefits will not equal the effort expended. Further, the greater the gap between the effort expended and the observed benefit, the greater will be the teachers' sense of frustration. If the gap is too wide, efforts to help Peter and perhaps Elaine, will be counter productive by increasing the anger which their teachers already feel towards them and towards other poor attenders.

Tackling the pupils' problems does nothing about the weaknesses and tension in the school system exposed by analysis of the problems they have presented. Tackling these requires firm and effective leadership and long-term planning which recognises the needs of staff as much as those of children. Something, for example, will have to be done about the problem year tutor. His behaviour must be modified, even if it cannot be radically altered. Alternatively, the head may need to find him some administrative responsibility to justify removing him from the year tutor post.

All head teachers face this sort of problem from time to time. Sometimes a head of department is resisting necessary curriculum changes, discouraging keen younger staff in the process. At other times senior pastoral staff and a year tutor or assistant heads hold attitudes, or wish to pursue policies, which are inconsistent with the head's aims for the school as a whole. Effective leadership requires recognition of such tensions, combined with a creative and flexible approach in seeking solutions.

The stigma associated with membership of the remedial department raises questions about the organisation of provision for academically backward pupils. Placing such pupils together in classes of their own, separate from the mainstream, gives them a special, but undesirable status. An additional point is that this policy often unintentionally encourages senior staff to place disruptive pupils in the remedial department. The ostensible reason is that the smaller class-size and sympathetic teachers will help the children to get over *their* problems. An equally plausible interpretation is that removing them from higher ability classes is dealing with the *teacher's* problems. Placing poor attenders in the remedial department is seen to have two advantages. Not only is the pupil placed in a small, sympathetic class, but the work of the higher status examination orientated classes will be unaffected by the intrusion of absentees who have missed previous work.

Following the 1981 Education Act, l.e.a.s are reviewing the organisation and philosophy of remedial teaching. Our intention here is simply to point out that decisions taken in good faith can rebound to the detriment of those they are intended to help. Placing Peter in the remedial department labelled him an academic failure, and led him to label himself in this way. The indifference noted by his primary school teacher developed into more openly disruptive behaviour and eventually into truancy.

Teachers at the school could ask two questions in considering future developments for children with special needs. First, can we prevent the social isolation of the remedial department? One possibility would be to place all pupils in mixed ability classes, or in two broad ability bands with mixed ability classes in each band. Teachers in the remedial department might either withdraw pupils for extra help from these mixed ability classes, or offer extra help *in* the ordinary class, working alongside the teacher. The second question concerns the effect which any reorganisation may have on other teachers and on other pupils throughout the school.

Whatever approach is selected there will be initial tensions. These tensions will affect teachers and pupils alike. Our analysis of Peter's and Elaine's poor attendance, however, suggests that the way their school caters for them has far-reaching effects. In deciding how to cater for children with special needs teachers unavoidably take decisions which affect not only the children concerned but also other children in the school.

At Peter and Elaine's school this is well illustrated by the lack of specialist help either for pupils or for their teachers in the final two compulsory school years. Lacking the knowledge or the resources to cater satisfactorily for a substantial minority, teachers and pupils found themselves in a vicious circle. The pupil's lack of ability caused the teacher to feel angry and frustrated. Failure to achieve something they considered worthwhile, combined with resentment at their teachers' anger encouraged increasingly disaffected behaviour from the pupils, which in turn led to further frustration for the teachers. In these circumstances, poor attendance might charitably be seen as a merciful solution for all concerned.

If the school is to continue organising the final two years in the same way, long-term planning will be necessary in two areas. First, staff will need in-service training in teaching a wide ability range. Without this, they will continue to teach at the average level for the class, thus boring the brightest and dullest pupils who then disrupt activities for the remainder. Second, they will need some form of support from specialist teachers in preparing materials to cater for the extremes in the ability range. This of course, brings us back to the re-organisation of the remedial department so that its teachers are enabled to respond to special needs outside the confines of a special class.

WIDER PRESSURES

Employment Prospects

For the first time in their careers teachers in the 1980s find themselves unable to justify education to their pupils in terms of future employment prospects. Nationally the unemployment rate for young people under eighteen rose from 11 per cent in October 1979 to 25 per cent in April 1982 (Social Trends, 1983). In Sheffield only 363 out of 5005 school leavers in the Summer of 1982 had jobs by November, or 7.25 per cent (Pratt, 1984). There is no serious argument that unemployment is highest amongst pupils with few or no formal qualifications. The evidence on the family backgrounds and intellectual abilities of samples of poor attenders suggests that many would leave school with few formal qualifications even if they attended regularly. For the foreseeable future teachers will be unable to claim with credibility that regular attendance will bring its rewards in work after school. Life after school for the overwhelming majority of their less able pupils will be unemployment interspersed with occasional spells on government training schemes.

Whether unemployment is making much difference to attendance figures in the last two years of compulsory schooling is debatable. Attendance at Sheffield schools was marginally higher in 1930 and 1938 than in earlier years, though apart from a drop in 1920 following the first world war the differences were slight (Galloway, 1980a). If history repeats itself, we shall see little evidence of a dramatic increase in absenteeism associated with high unemployment rates amongst school leavers.

At the risk of stating the obvious, moreover, poor attendance was also considered a problem in the halcyon days of the 1960s and early 1970s when the country enjoyed what today would be applauded as full employment. This does not deny that impending unemployment may constitute a powerful disincentive to regular attendance for some pupils. Nor does it deny the possibility that impending unemployment may actually cause an increase in absenteeism. That remains a matter for research. In many industrial areas in the north of England the dream of full employment for school leavers is overshadowed by the nightmare of virtually full unemployment. Yet attributing deteriorating attendance throughout the secondary school years to lack of employment prospects conveniently overlooks the existence of the problem before the current recession.

Quality and "Relevance" in Education?

The effects of the recession do nevertheless have important implications for ways in which schools justify what they have to offer. The evidence may not support the view that poor attendance is attributable to a feeling of hopelessness about the future. That, however, will not necessarily stop young people and their parents from justifying absence from school on the grounds that there are no long-term benefits in sight. Probable unemployment may thus provide a focus for disaffection even if it is not a cause.

Teachers consequently have to justify their wares in the light of more immediate and tangible benefits. They have to persuade reluctant or apathetic pupils that attendance is worthwhile for what it offers *now*, not for what it may offer in the future. This has in fact probably always been the case but is spotlighted by the long-term prospects for many pupils.

Explaining the benefits of education to fifteen- and sixteen-year-olds is no easy task. The task is doubly difficult when the explanation has to focus on *actual current* benefits, rather than *possible future* benefits. Any explanation in terms of the curriculum will arouse legitimate scepticism. Pupils could say: "So what use is maths (or technical drawing, or English or any other subject) to us now? And don't talk about the basic skills; if you haven't managed to teach us those in the last nine or ten years, what's going to be so special about the next one or two?"

Actual and potential absentees will not be persuaded to attend school because of the benefits they expect to derive from the curriculum. A curriculum which can arouse their interest is necessary to encourage regular attendance, but certainly not sufficient. In addition they will need to feel that attendance brings greater personal and social benefits than absence. These benefits are often described in a school's prospectus under the general heading: Aims of the School. The aims are generally based on current educational rhetoric. In Chapter 9 we consider the relationship between popularly stated aims and the experiences of pupils and their families.

CONCLUSIONS: MULTI-FACETED NATURE OF PERSISTENT ABSENCE

Why Attend?

Our own interviews with persistent absentees suggested that family stress was frequently a contributing factor in their poor attendance. Feelings of stress arising from home circumstances, however, were seldom, if ever, sufficient on their own to explain the pupil's absences. The increase in absenteeism towards the end of compulsory schooling cannot plausibly be attributed to home circumstances becoming more stressful at this time.

The interviews also identified sources of stress at school which contributed to many pupil's absence. Yet these too were seldom, if ever, sufficient on their own to explain the poor attendance. When pupils felt they were deriving little satisfaction from school, subsequent attendance would depend largely on other factors. One factor might be the strength of parental insistence on regular attendance. Another might be the strength of the pupil's own dislike of school. Perhaps the most frequent, though, was the absence of any positive incentive to attend in the face of competing attractions. These competing attractions varied from pupil to pupil. For some, membership of a peer group of similarly disaffected adolescents predominated. For others the opportunity to remain at home to help a parent or to look after younger brothers or sisters was more important. For many, well-founded concern about a parent's health provided a strong incentive to remain at home. When combined with a feeling that school no longer offered useful or satisfying experiences, threats from the school and from the local e.w.o. could not outweigh the benefits from staying away.

A Measure of Communication

Viewed in this way, attendance can be seen: (i) as a measure of agreement between a school, its pupils and their parents on the actual potential benefits from regular attendance; (ii) as a measure of the school's success in communicating its goals to parents and their pupils, and in enlisting their active cooperation in attaining these goals. In areas where attendance rates have always been high, teachers and the overwhelming majority of parents agree on the necessity for regular attendance and on the potential benefits. There may well be conflict between parents and teachers both on general aims and on teaching methods. The conflict, though, generally starts with parents questioning the school's aims and methods. Thus, communication is initiated by parents who accept as a basic premise the need for regular attendance.

In other areas, where there is a tradition of poor attendance among a substantial minority of pupils, this basic premise cannot be taken for granted. Consequently, communication has to be initiated by teachers. To put the situation in its starkest terms they have a choice. They can bemoan and bewail parental apathy and pupil intransigence, demanding action from e.w.o.s, social workers, educational psychologists and anyone else who will listen. Alternatively they can take a leaf from the commercial salesman's notebook, by getting out into the community, and, figuratively if not literally, selling the product. Taking the analogy a stage further, if a product is worthwhile it deserves energetic promotion. Unlike commercial salesmen, teachers whose schools serve disadvantaged areas do not face unemployment if they fail to sell their product. Instead, they face a lot of empty desks. If a soap powder salesman meets consumer resistance he has to find a way round the resistance. The same applies when teachers face consumer resistance in the form of apathetic or hostile parents from multiply disadvantaged homes with no tradition of regular attendance and low expectations of what education can offer their children. We must now turn to ways in which teachers can seek, in many schools with success, to make their product more attractive.

CHAPTER 9

Wider Implications for Teachers

INTRODUCTION

At first sight the conclusion from previous chapters is pessimistic: teachers cannot rely on educational psychologists, e.w.o.s or magistrates to achieve any substantial improvement in attendance levels. A handful of children may be helped by clinical treatments. A further handful may be coerced into return by legal action. Such successes may create a comforting illusion that everything possible is being done. The children concerned and their families may indeed benefit, but the illusion remains no less insubstantial for their progress. The problems remain: (i) that treatment is appropriate for no more than a tiny minority of all unauthorised absentees; (ii) that existing services can scarcely cater adequately even for this small minority, (iii) that legal action is generally ineffective in securing return to school; the superficially encouraging results associated with continuous adjournment look less impressive when the practical and ethical problems are considered.

In the present climate, calls for additional resources to counter the problem of poor attendance will be a waste of breath. Neither teachers nor politicians will enthusiastically support calls for more e.w.o.s, educational psychologists and social workers, particularly if resources for schools are likely to be cut to fund increases in the support services. Teachers can, moreover, argue that "more of the same" holds out little hope of progress. The heady optimism of the 1960s and early 1970s in the ability of social work and educational support services to tackle problems arising in and out of school has given way to a more sober appraisal of what they can realistically aim to achieve.

The question for teachers, then, is how they themselves can create an environment attractive and stimulating enough to retain the interest and loyalty of pupils who might otherwise drift away. The question for members of the l.e.a. support services is how they can use their knowledge and skills in partnership with teachers. Both for teachers and for the support services the focus is on the more effective use of existing resources. A starting point lies in analysis of reason for ineffective communication between members of different professions. In the last chapter we identified some of the obstacles to cooperation between e.w.o.s, social workers and teachers. We now need to go further, considering what teachers themselves can do.

THE AIMS OF SCHOOLING

A recurring theme throughout previous chapters has been that pupils stay away from school because they feel that they lack any worthwhile incentive to attend. Another way of putting this is that they stay away because the school fails to compete with other, more powerful attractions in the home or in the community. The general failure of legal action to improve attendance is entirely predictable in the light of research evidence that teachers have frequently never met the parents of poor attenders (e.g. Galloway *et al.*, 1981b). Returning to an unchanged situation, already associated with failure, is a recipe for further failure.

If potential absentees are to remain in school, teachers will need to find answers to two questions: (i) What do we hope pupils will gain from regular attendance? (ii) What can we do to ensure that these hopes are realised? An extension to the first question is: What is this school trying to achieve, not only for its pupils, but also for its teachers and for its local community? Discussion about school attendance cannot be distinguished from discussion of the school's overall aims, objectives and methods.

Broad aims can be criticised as abstract, unrealistic or inappropriate. Agreement on broad aims nevertheless provides a necessary framework for review of the school's objectives and methods. Objectives are more specific, indicating in more concrete terms what may be implied in each aim. One aim, for example, might be to develop in all pupils pride in the school. Objectives might be eliminating vandalism, keeping the buildings and grounds free of litter, achieving favourable publicity within the local press for sports and cultural events, displaying pupil's work throughout the school, or ensuring that all pupils wear school uniform.

These objectives could also be criticised. School uniform, for example, offers a convenient excuse for truancy amongst disaffected pupils. By refusing to wear the correct uniform they can signal their opposition to the school's values. Far from developing pride, it may facilitate the expression of disaffection. The same principles apply to the methods used to attain each objective. Carrying the uniform example a stage further, possible methods of encouragement are giving house points for correct uniform, spot checks in assembly or at registration, or detentions for repeated offenders. Once stated, these too are open to criticism and discussion.

The problem is that the day-to-day pressures of the job prevent this sort of logical planning and review. All too easily the methods can dictate the objectives, which in turn dictate the aims. Carried to its logical, and superficially absurd, conclusion, the practice of regular checks on uniform becomes the reason for enforcing uniform. The absurdity is less evident when seen from the pupils' perspective. For some pupils, particularly potentially poor attenders, the possibility of punishment is the only reason for wearing uniform. Some traditional aims no longer seem credible with the prospect of long-term unemployment facing many school leavers. Such aims as "preparation for work" can perhaps be redefined as "preparation for life after leaving school". Similarly, many school prospectuses emphasise such aims as "enabling each pupil to recognise his or her potential", "promoting positive attitudes towards work", "encouraging concern and respect for others".

Two aims less frequently stated in prospectuses are nevertheless implicit in those which do most frequently appear. One is "enhancing self concept". The other is "acquiring a sense of developing competence". Reid (1982) has noted the low self-concept of many persistent absentees. Their low educational attainments have been noted repeatedly. Clearly, low self-concept is a poor preparation for life after leaving school. Equally, pupils who believe that they are not acquiring new skills and/or new knowledge cannot realistically be expected to value their experiences in school. Yet children require more from school than routine acquisition of more information. The task needs to have some intrinsic interest. Further, it must offer a worthwhile but realistic challenge. Boredom is frequently given by persistent absentees as a reason for their poor attendance. For many such pupils, the experience of schooling has reduced rather than enhanced their self-esteem. Far from a sense of pride in developing new abilities (i.e. becoming more competent as they grow older), each day at school emphasises their failure to compete with other pupils.

If we accept enhancing self-concept and a sense of developing competence as valid aims, what objectives might follow from them? Low self-concept is often associated with chronic lack of success. Hence, one objective might be to give all pupils a sense of achievement within a well-organised and effectively taught curriculum.

Regarding improvement of self-concept as one of a school's most fundamental aims for its pupils would not be uncontroversial. It could be argued that pupils need to acquire a realistic concept of their own abilities. More seriously, some pupils are too satisfied with themselves, and need to be firmly encouraged to greater effort. Finally, some highly disruptive pupils already exert undue influence on their peers. Enhancing their self-image might make them even more anti-social.

The answers are fairly simple. First, it is the task of teachers to encourage pupils to take pride in their conscientious efforts irrespective of the absolute level of their achievements. For a backward pupil to produce laboriously a page of work may be as great an achievement as another pupil's prizewinning sixth form essay. Ascribing low status to the efforts of "non academic" pupils encourages a poor self-concept, and associated attendance and discipline problems. Second, some pupils do indeed need encouraging to greater effort; self-concept is based on achievement, and the apparently self-satisfied pupil needs this experience as much as anyone else. Finally, members of a school's anti-social subculture have generally joined this group after a long history of failure in their earlier years at school. Their anti-social activities may be seen as an attempt to achieve the status and recognition they failed to achieve on terms set by the school. In effect they are saying: "you've called us failures; well then, we'll be successful failures!" This was why Peter (see Chapter 8) was delighted by his year tutor's disapproval of his friendship with Elaine.

Hargreaves (1981, 1983) has argued that a major failure of comprehensive schools lies in their failure to give their pupils worthwhile social experiences. Personal identity, he points out, is established in a social context. The emphasis in educational rhetoric on individual achievements and individual needs has led teachers to under-value the importance of corporate identity, or a sense of belonging and contributing to a group. He writes:

> We fall into what I shall call the *fallacy of individualism*. This is the belief that if only schools can successfully educate every individual pupil in self-confidence, independence and autonomy, then society can with confidence be left to take care of itself. The good society will be automatically produced by the creation through education of good individuals (Hargreaves, 1983).

Denied a sense of belonging within the school's mainstream, some pupils assume an alternative identity as members of anti-social sub-groups. These are the pupils described so vividly by Willis (1977) (see Chapter 4). The low self-concept and poor educational progress of many persistent absentees suggests that they too lack a sense of social identity as contributing members of the school. Unlike Willis' and Corrigan's (1979) boys, they simply stop attending. Some develop alternative social networks through companionship with other poor attenders. Others, like Tyerman's (1958) truants have few friends, appearing lonely and unhappy. Others still, like some of the girl absentees described in Chapter 5, spend much of their time at home, effectively opting out of social relationships both at school and in the community.

THE CURRICULUM

The content and organisation of the curriculum is the subject of a large literature in its own right. The curriculum can either encourage or discourage regular attendance. Here we can only mention briefly aspects of probable importance in generating poor attendance.

The training of teachers and the subject based focus of secondary school curricula facilitates discord between aims and methods. Teachers are trained to teach specific subjects. Neither an emphasis on pastoral care in their training courses nor a requirement that they equip themselves to teach more than one subject negates this. The school's aims, in contrast, are stated in abstract terms. The primary school teacher's abusive cliché that he teaches children while his secondary colleagues teach subjects is offensive precisely because it contains a grain of truth.

Yet the primary teacher's taunt also offends secondary colleagues because they feel that enormous efforts have been made to provide a more "relevant" education for the euphemistically named "less able" pupils. The range of subject choices open to pupils entering their final two compulsory school years provides impressive evidence of these efforts. Many schools, moreover, can legitimately claim to have spent much time and effort providing courses for non-examination classes. Such courses range from "integrated" social studies to community service in the school's catchment area.

There are sound educational arguments for an integrated approach to social studies. These arguments apply as much to fourteen- to sixteen-year-olds working towards public examinations as to younger children. Equally sound educational arguments apply to community service. It is intrinsically desirable that children and adolescents should learn at school that they have something worthwhile to contribute to others in the community. Nor is there any inherent objection to many of the other activities frequently provided for "less able" pupils. The miscellany of topics subsumed under "life skills", for example, may range from filling in an income tax form to bathing a baby. The objection lies not in the topics as such, but rather in the unspoken assumptions, implicit in their relationship with the rest of the curriculum, about what is worthwhile in education.

In their earliest stages, when they were struggling to gain public acceptance, comprehensive schools claimed to offer grammar school education to everyone. A blinding glimpse of the obvious fairly soon convinced teachers and educational administrators that not everyone needed grammar school education. Hence, the curriculum for less able pupils was largely added to an existing grammar school curriculum. This applied even in those comprehensives which had not incorporated a former grammar school. Commendably, their teachers were determined to establish a reputation for high academic standards. A reputation for high standards required more than passes in the G.C.E. "O" level and "A" level examinations. It also required a high pass-rate in what parents regarded as traditional academic subjects. Almost inevitably, therefore, the social and academic divisions of grammar and secondary modern schools were reproduced with relatively minor variations in the new comprehensives.

The Certificate of Secondary Education was initially seen as an attempt to offer a worthwhile goal to pupils for whom G.C.E. was inappropriate. C.S.E. also aimed to offer a wider, more practical range of subjects with more flexible assessment procedures. In practice these hopes have not been realised. There is widespread doubt amongst pupils regarding the value of C.S.E.s, which are seen as inferior to "O" levels. This doubt is shared by many employers. Although a grade one pass at C.S.E. is the equivalent of an "O" level pass, it is not always recognised as such. More seriously, C.S.E. has come in many schools to reflect a watered down "O" level curriculum, offering what is seen as a second rate qualification to academically second rate pupils. Further, the increasingly academic bias of the C.S.E. curriculum has accentuated the divide between academic and non-academic subjects. Providing something "suitable" for the least academic pupils has remained a problem.

Teachers may recognise the problems associated with the C.S.E. examination. They less frequently recognise how the "non-academic" curriculum seems from their pupils' perspective. The question is not simply how "non-academic" pupils view what is provided for them, since their attitudes will necessarily be coloured by how their curriculum is regarded by the academic elite.

Hargreaves (1983) quotes a pupil on a community service course:

> I think the community service was just to get us out of school so that other kids could have a lesson, just to let other people look after us for a bit so other children could have the teachers.

Referring to this, a pupil on an examination course had said:

> I think it's worthwhile in their own way, because a lot of them aren't intelligent enough to take exams, some of them are, but not all of them . . . and they spend their time doing a worthwhile programme really. They can't learn in Maths and English, that sort of thing, but they learn about the community.

Hargreaves comments:

> The moral is clear: academic education is to be contrasted with "learning about the community" which is for pupils who are "thick" and who waste teachers' time and efforts. The hidden-curriculum message being transmitted to *both* groups of pupils is a disastrous one.

It would be naive to assume that the pupils who stay away from secondary schools towards the end of compulsory schooling are insensitive to this message. The implications for teachers are as clear as for pupils. Return to school, at best, offers a curriculum designed, in the pupils' words, for "thick kids", or in the teachers' words for "less able pupils". We cannot be surprised that pupils opt out of a situation in which they feel inferior.

The long-term implications for teachers concern both the curriculum and the public examination system. How to organise a curriculum catering for the needs of all pupils will remain a source of controversy. We can nevertheless start by identifying policies and practices which transmit the sort of message described above. This requires attention to the range of messages pupils may receive from the existing system rather than long-term theorising about possible future reform.

Rutter *et al.* (1979) appeared to regard curriculum content as relatively unproblematic. Closer study seems likely to show that this view is mistaken. Through the curriculum, teachers may enhance a pupil's feelings of self-worth, or undermine them. This is particularly relevant to working class pupils and pupils from ethnic minority groups, at least some of whom are "at risk" of poor attendance.

Ramsay *et al.* (1981) studied schools in a depressed, multi-cultural area of South Auckland, New Zealand. They identified eight characteristics distinguishing "successful" from "unsuccessful" schools. Referring specifically to the curriculum they observe:

> The difference took two forms. The "successful" schools ascertained what their community wished to emphasise in respect of ethnic culture maintenance. Programmes were adjusted accordingly, using community personnel where necessary. While the most obvious changes were in social studies, they also permeated other curriculum areas. We found, for example, elements of Maori and Pacific Island ethnicity discussed in both science and mathematics. The second difference related to the language pattern of the students. Teachers in the "successful" schools had virtually abandoned the available texts and were translating literature into codes which were consonant with the children's lived experiences (Ramsay, 1984).

It could be argued that the sort of differences Ramsay is noting reflect the school's hidden curriculum rather than the curriculum content. Certainly, they *do* reflect the hidden curriculum, but that ignores the interactive relationship between formal and hidden curricula. If the school's hidden curriculum emphasises respect for self and for others, with an associated pride in the pupil's cultural heritage, this will affect not only *what* is taught formally but also *how* it is taught. This may not require any new curriculum development, but rather a shift of emphasis in what is currently taught. Lessons on nutrition, for example, can include reference to the pupils' own countries or origin, for example in the Caribbean. Similarly, assembly can reflect ethnic and cultural diversity within a school.

In rejecting a suggestion that Asian children should contribute to morning assemblies one state school head teacher replied: "This is a Christian school; they are here because they want to be, not because we want them to be". Such blatant racism is hopefully rare. More subtle ways of derogating the value of working class culture are much less rare in a predominantly middle class teaching profession. Blatant racism merely illustrates the more widespread problem concerning the values teachers transmit to their pupils. When these values appear implicitly to undervalue them as individuals, or to under-value their family and cultural background, they help to create a climate in which absenteeism becomes a realistic alternative.

SPECIAL EDUCATIONAL NEEDS

We have noted repeatedly the high prevalence of educational backwardness in groups of poor attenders (see Chapters 3 and 5). A conventional response to pupils with special needs is to provide special, or remedial classes. Thus, almost all secondary schools have a remedial department which, since the 1981 Education Act is increasingly being extended or redefined as a department of special education. The 1981 Act formed the government's response to the Warnock Report (D.E.S., 1978) which accepted research indicating that about 16 per cent of pupils would need some form of special education at any one time, and up to 20 per cent at some stage in their school career. The Act also reflected a growing international trend towards catering for children with special needs in ordinary schools, rather than in special schools or units.

The distinction between a department of special education and a remedial department is not just semantic, at least in principle. The implication in the term remedial is that some fault or problem exists in the pupil which can be remedied by specialist teaching. For many pupils with special educational needs this is unrealistic and offensive. It is unrealistic, for example, to expect that "remedial" help will remedy the educational problems facing an intellectually backward pupil with a predictably low reading age. It is offensive, moreover, to imply that some remediable fault or problem exists in a pupil who is being well taught and who cannot sensibly be regarded as under-achieving.

The pupil clearly has special educational needs, which require some form of specialist teaching. The emphasis, though, is on provision of teaching appro-priate to the pupil's current ability and aptitude, rather than on remedying something which is hypothesised to have developed in the past. The signifi-cance of the distinction for actual or potential absentees is evident by considering how schools aim to meet special educational needs.

Both the amount and nature of provision varies widely from school to school. Some schools with one thousand pupils have a special education department staffed by four or five full-time teachers. Others manage to allocate only one teacher to the "department". The funds available for resources vary as widely. Some schools provide one or two full-time remedial or special classes in each year group. Others have no full-time classes, but withdraw pupils from ordinary lessons for special help in the basic skills.

Before considering other possibilities, it is worth asking how these may seem from the pupils' perspective. The whole concept of special education has recently come under critical scrutiny. Tomlinson (1982), for example, argues that it acts as a form of social control, effectively segregating "problem" pupils from the more academic majority. The fact that the separation is carried out ostensibly for the pupils' own benefit does not negate its underlying function. Special education, then, may be seen in the same light as the non-academic curriculum, as an inferior alternative which ensures that teachers spend their time on the pupils whose achievements really matter, namely those in the examination classes.

There is no easy answer to these criticisms. Resources in some classes supposedly offering special education are undoubtedly inferior to those available in the school's mainstream. Also, some school-based units have been set up explicitly to cater for poor attenders and other problem pupils outside the mainstream. The issue here is that generous provision, in staffing and in resources, offers no guarantee that pupils will find what is offered attractive. The danger is rather that older pupils may see it as a crude attempt to keep them occupied, if not happy, away from the school's mainstream. Whatever teachers intend, if this is the picture pupils see, high absentee rates will ensure that their special educational needs remain unmet. Generous provision is misplaced if the intended recipients reject the gift.

The Warnock Report's emphasis on catering for special educational needs in the ordinary school merely reflected an international trend. An unfortunate paradox which is only gradually becoming recognised is that the group of pupils benefiting least from integration are the groups which in theory have always been catered for in the ordinary school system. These are children with learning difficulties and/or behaviour problems. Separate special schools catering for children with moderate learning difficulties, formerly called the ESN(M), and the maladjusted offer more places than all other special schools combined. Nevertheless, separate special schools cater for no more than a small minority of pupils who could be labelled in these ways (Galloway and Goodwin, 1979). In most parts of Britain less than 2 per cent of pupils attend a formally recognised special school or special class, compared with the 20 per cent considered by Warnock to need some form of special educational treatment.

As yet, there is little evidence of a wide-spread attempt within secondary schools in Britain to explore ways of catering within ordinary classes for slow learning and behaviourally disturbing pupils. The Warnock report has alerted teachers to the needs of these pupils. The effect, however, may be to increase the amount of separate provision within the ordinary school. If confirmed by future research, this will inevitably legitimise the impression of many older pupils, including poor attenders, that they are different, and hence implicitly inferior, to their more academic peers. If this happens, there is a realistic possibility that increases in special educational provision will promote an increase in absenteeism rather than in attendance rates.

The danger is realistic, but not unavoidable. Goodwin (1979) has described the network of special educational support at Countesthorpe College in Britain. Galloway and Barrett (1982) have described New Zealand secondary schools where special education is based on ordinary classes. A common feature in these accounts is their emphases: (i) on support for the classroom teacher, and hence (ii) on supporting the child with special needs within an ordinary mixed ability class.

Making such a system work requires much more than an administrative decree from the head teacher. It requires a climate in which teachers throughout the school see it as their own responsibility to teach children with learning difficulties and children whose behaviour can be disturbing. Guidance and material help will be available from colleagues in the special education department. Material help can, for example, include provision of work cards to enable children with widely varying ability to work on a common theme. In an emergency there may even be provision for removing a child temporarily from the class.

Responsibility though, rests with class teachers. It implies an acceptance that children with special needs are their responsibility, and that the role of "experts" in the special education department is to help teachers, not to remove the children concerned into separate classes. In turn, this requires a climate throughout the school in which teachers can be flexible and imaginative in adapting the curriculum to meet their pupils needs. This stands in contrast to the more conventional view, inherent in the notion of remedial teaching, which implies that the remedial teacher's task is to adapt the pupils to the needs of the curriculum. In discussing the curriculum we acknowledged the influence of the school's hidden curriculum. Not surprisingly, we have returned to the same point in discussing provision for children with special educational needs.

PASTORAL CARE

Scope

The primary concern of pastoral care is with pupils' progress and adjustment at school (Galloway, 1981, 1983b). It is concerned with problems in the child's home background only to the extent that they affect progress in this respect. Hamblin (1978) has defined pastoral care as:

> that element of the teaching process which centres around the personality of the pupil and the forces in his environment which either facilitate or impede the development of intellectual and social skills, and foster or retard emotional stability ... (it) is also concerned with the modification of the learning environment, adapting it to meet the needs of individual pupils, so that every pupil has the maximum chance of success whatever his background or general ability.

The organisation of pastoral care in most secondary schools is hierarchical. Typically, assistant head teachers responsible for boys' and girls' welfare are answerable to the head. Year tutors, or less commonly heads of houses, are answerable to the assistant heads. In their turn, year tutors coordinate the work of form tutors. Head teachers would generally agree that the form tutor is the basic unit of pastoral care. Year tutors, responsible for up to three hundred pupils, cannot know everyone in their year. Hence, an effective network of form tutors is needed to ensure that all pupils are known reasonably well by at least one teacher.

Form Tutors

So much for the formal organisation of pastoral care. The practice is not always as tidy. Poor attenders can illustrate both the strengths and the weaknesses of a school's pastoral care. A convenient starting point is the role of form tutors. Murgatroyd (1975) and Lewis and Murgatroyd (1976) have found evidence that high truancy rates are associated with a school policy that absences should be investigated at middle management level, for example by year tutors. In schools with low truancy rates, on the other hand, absences were more frequently investigated by form tutors.

There is an obvious problem of cause and effect here. Perhaps the problem is only passed to year tutors when it becomes too extensive to be dealt with by form tutors. Murgatroyd argues, though, that the increase in posts with responsibility for pastoral care, associated with the reorganisation of secondary schools along comprehensive lines, may have reduced the traditional pastoral duties of form tutors.

Although head teachers agree on the importance of a form tutor's pastoral duties, relatively few schools have established a system which enables form tutors to carry out these duties. Studies in Sheffield and in New Zealand revealed five factors which reduced the form tutor's pastoral role (Galloway, 1983b): (i) form tutors changed every year; as soon as they had got to know one group of pupils well, they were confronted with another; (ii) they seldom taught all the children in their tutor groups; (iii) they saw their tutor groups for only five or ten minutes once or twice daily, this period only gave them sufficient time to complete the attendance register and make announcements; (iv) they felt that year tutors were paid to do pastoral care, and saw no reason for accepting the responsibility themselves; (v) the year tutor's job was defined by the head in terms of investigating and dealing with problems, rather than as leader of a pastoral team.

Galloway (1984) comments:

> Expecting form tutors to take their pastoral responsibilities seriously, while providing an organisational framework which makes them unable to do so, is hardly a way to enhance job satisfaction. Effective teaching requires that children should have realistic goals, and that they should feel that their efforts in attaining them are valued. Effective organisation, or leadership, requires the same for teachers.

Pastoral Care, Discipline and Educational Progress: False
Distinctions

Pastoral care can be seen as inherent in any successful teaching. Finlayson and Loughran (1978) compared pupils' attitudes at secondary schools with high and low delinquency rates in the north of England. In the schools with high delinquency rates pupils saw their teachers as being concerned about them as individuals. In this respect there was little difference in pupils' attitudes in the two groups of schools. The difference lay in how pupils saw their teachers as interacting with the class as a whole. In the high delinquency schools teachers were seen as authoritarian and arbitrary in their classroom practices. The implication is that elaborate pastoral care networks will do little to solve problems in the classroom, over which the pastoral specialists have little or no control. Yet when relationships between pupils and teachers are unsatisfactory in the classroom, pastoral care can do little except prop up an essentially unhealthy system.

It is in this sense that the best form of pastoral care lies in a carefully planned and well taught curriculum. At the risk of becoming banal it is worth saying that not all pupils can be motivated in the same way. Teachers need to know their pupils as individuals in order to tell what approach will succeed with each individual. The need for quick action to deal with misbehaviour is not in dispute. An instant reaction does not, however, prevent a more considered response later.

This indicates the absurdity of distinguishing between pastoral care, discipline and educational progress. Investigating the reasons for a pupil's absence, for example, may identify tensions with one or two particular teachers. Alternatively it may identify problems with one or two subjects. More frequently, especially in the age groups with the highest absence rates, occasional absences indicate lack of any sense of commitment to the school, or rather a strong commitment to competing attractions in the community or in the family. The school's response will vary according to the circumstances in each case. There is no sense at all, though, in regarding one set of problems as pastoral, another as disciplinary and a third as educational or scholastic. Concern about behaviour and educational progress is implied by pastoral care.

Unfortunately this is another case in which schools sometimes defeat their own objectives. In our studies in Sheffield and in New Zealand (Galloway *et al.*, 1982 and Galloway and Barrett, 1982, 1983) we found that some schools required teachers to make the spurious distinction between discipline and pastoral care. Teachers were expected to refer discipline problems to the head of department and pastoral problems to the year tutor. The teacher required to decide whether a problem should be considered pastoral or disciplinary was the subject teacher who might only see the pupil once a week. Consequently, the treatment a pupil received was arbitrary, depending largely on the person to whom he was referred, which in turn could depend on the whim of the teacher concerned. At its crudest level it meant that a child could be sent to the year tutor for behaving disruptively at the start of the week when the teacher was feeling tolerant and sympathetic, and to the head of department if the behaviour occurred at the end of the week when the teacher was feeling tired and impatient. In practical terms the choice could make the difference between counselling and caning.

This, though, raises two further issues, one concerning pastoral care for absentees, and the second the nature of support teachers offer each other. The arbitrary distinction between discipline and pastoral care in some of the schools we studied made a systematic approach virtually impossible. It weakened chains of communication throughout the school, thus enabling poor attenders, and others, to "play the system". The arbitrary justice gave pupils a legitimate sense of grievance, from which a short step enabled them to justify, in their own eyes, their erratic attendance. The inadequate system of communication between teachers then enabled them to skip lessons, or stay away altogether, without attracting too much attention.

Referral Policy

Referral policies within the school raise another point, of even more immediate importance to teachers. In some schools teachers were expected to refer problems upwards, to a year tutor or head of department, who could then investigate and deal with them. In the short run this was helpful, providing a safety valve for a teacher under stress. In the long run the results were less satisfactory. Teachers did not always discover what was done about the pupils they referred to their senior colleagues. When they did find out what action was taken, they did not always agree with it. More seriously, the fact of referral to a senior colleague carried an implication that the teacher could not deal with the problem himself, being too young, too inexperienced or, simply, too incompetent. From here it was all too easy to conclude that pastoral care should be "done" by the senior staff paid for the purpose. This policy not only reduced the class teacher's commitment to pastoral care, it also ensured that problems such as poor attendance were regarded as someone else's responsibility. Yet the sense of boredom and/or failure which often contributed to pupils' absences initially arose from experiences in the class-room. Anything which discouraged classroom teachers from recognising and tackling these would be predictably ineffective as a way of encouraging better attendance, and in the long run demoralising for teachers themselves.

This was not the pattern in all schools. From the fourteen schools studied in Sheffield and New Zealand, Galloway (1983b) identified four in which pastoral care had contributed to exceptionally low rates of problem behaviour. Three of these schools had a highly developed form tutor system, in which the year tutor played an active coordinating and supporting role.

Form tutors were expected to know the pupils in their tutor group. They were also expected to be involved in discussions about the management of any pupil who was presenting problems. This meant that if another teacher was having attendance or discipline problems from a child, the first person with whom to discuss these was the form tutor. It also meant that senior staff had to direct their colleagues to the form tutor if they were approached directly. In an emergency, of course, senior staff could, and did, act unilaterally. Because serious incidents seldom occurred they did not threaten the general principle that matters be discussed initially with the pupil's form tutor.

Emphasising the form tutor's pastoral responsibilities had two further consequences. First, it contributed to a climate of opinion throughout each of the schools that teachers should deal with their own classroom problems. The form tutor might be able to provide helpful background information on a pupil, but responsibility would rest with the teacher concerned. Second, it enabled year tutors and senior staff to see their task essentially in terms of supporting their colleagues, rather than in terms of investigating and dealing with problems referred to them.

The year tutor, therefore, became the coordinator of a team of form tutors, with a responsibility for his colleagues' pastoral activities. Similarly, year tutors and other senior staff were available to discuss possible solutions with a teacher who was having discipline problems. Yet responsibility continued to rest with the teacher. In the short term this undoubtedly increased feelings of stress: problems could not be shunted on to someone else. In the long term the result was generally more positive. Just as much as their pupils, teachers require a sense of self respect and a feeling that they are acquiring new skills. Passing a problem to a colleague does nothing to enhance self-respect, nor to develop new skills. Help or advice from a colleague which enables a teacher to deal with the matter himself is both more constructive and more rewarding.

Here again we return to the school's overall climate. A senior teacher at one of the four schools remarked that having problems, in or out of the classroom, was no matter for shame. The only cause for shame was failing to seek help in dealing with them. This contrasted starkly with the sense of overwhelming exhaustion and failure experienced by teachers in other schools where the support network, for pupils as well as for teachers was inadequate. One teacher said:

> Quite honestly, I tend not to refer kids (for disruptive behaviour) if I can help it. It involves one in more hassle than it's worth. There's no trust in the relationships involved (i.e. between the teacher speaking and his senior colleagues). A number of kids have been in the special groups or out of school altogether for swearing at the deputy—but if it is one of us it happens to, nothing is done. When I informed the head of a boy being rude to the school nurse, nothing

was done. When the head saw a similar incident several months later, the boy was excluded at once (Galloway *et al.*, 1982).

This teacher was being interviewed about pupils' behaviour. The issues he raised apply equally to their attendance. Teachers who feel exhausted, lacking support from senior colleagues, cannot sensibly be expected to summon the energy or the will to follow up cases of erratic attendance, let alone to modify classroom practice in the light of their investigations. Change is stressful, requiring an atmosphere of trust. Many absentees find it much easier to stay away from school than to attend. In some schools many teachers find it much easier to accept the prevailing apathy, seeing attendance as someone else's problem, than to explore solutions. It is not like this in all schools. Indeed, the improving attendance figures at some schools may constitute an accurate barometer of teachers' morale.

Parental Involvement

Parents who themselves have unhappy memories of their school days will listen sympathetically to their children's complaints. If these parents feel unwelcome or undervalued when they visit their children's schools, they are unlikely to make intensive efforts to discover the teacher's version of events. If, moreover, the parents are in poor health or living in multiply disadvantaged circumstances, condoning their children's absence may be the course of least resistance. More positively, it may indicate sympathy with their children's complaints.

In one of the classic studies of educational sociology Jackson and Marsden (1966) describe the experience of working class boys who won a grammar school place by passing the eleven plus exam. The feature concerning us here is that their parents felt uncomfortable when they visited the grammar school, and consequently soon stopped attending even for the formal parents evenings. The teachers did not set out to make parents feel unwelcome. Yet the way they organised contact with parents ensured the absence of the parents they might most have needed to see.

Parents who maintain little or no contact with their children's school tend to be labelled uncooperative. It is ironic that the parents are discouraged by the reception they have received from the teachers who label them uncooperative. It would be over-optimistic to assume that the communication failure noted by Jackson and Marsden has been overcome by the introduction of a comprehensive school system. Contact between parents and teachers in Sheffield was frequently non-existent before the l.e.a. took legal action for non-attendance. The e.w.o. acting as a go-between is scarcely a satisfactory way to encourage trust and informal communication.

In a recent episode of the B.B.C. television programme *Grange Hill*, a parent heard on the school's open day that her child had been attending irregularly for several weeks. Having heard nothing about this before, the mother was furious with her son, to the teacher's rather obvious satisfaction. The mother's anger should perhaps have been directed at the teacher for gross professional neglect in failing to alert her of the situation at a much earlier stage. It is not, however, at all unusual for parents to learn of their children's poor attendance several weeks after it started. Every eductional psychologist, and possibly every e.w.o., can remember parents who complain, quite legitimately: "Why didn't the school tell me about this earlier? The first I knew was when they referred him to you!"

If all this seems unduly critical of teachers in some schools it has to be recognised that they face a daunting task. Keeping track of pupils registered absent is difficult enough. The complexity of the secondary school time-table, with its range of subject combinations makes the task of checking on absences from occasional lessons even more difficult. Bearing in mind that classes of fifteen-year-olds on Friday afternoons in some inner city schools will have less than 50 per cent attendance, the scale of the problem becomes clearer still. The choice, nevertheless lies between strenuous efforts to elicit parental support over attendance and weary acceptance that such efforts will not repay the time or energy expended.

The response from parents depends largely on the nature of their contacts with the school. Teachers cannot expect parental cooperation if the parents themselves see little benefit in regular attendance. The Warnock Report on special education (D.E.S., 1978) talked about parents as partners. This concept is as valid in ordinary schools as in special schools. Education takes place in the home as well as in the school. Parents and teachers need to learn from each other.

A striking feature of the four schools offering outstanding pastoral care described by Galloway (1983b) was their success in establishing close informal liaison with parents. This had three central characteristics. First, a concerted effort was made to keep parents informed about their children's progress and achievements, so that contact was not only made when problems occurred. Second, contacts were frequently informal. The head of a school in New Zealand pointed out that a formal typed letter could intimidate some parents, particularly from ethnic minority groups. To overcome this, each pupil in the school kept a log book, which teachers would complete at the end of each week, briefly noting progress or problems. The log book would be taken home at the end of the week, and contained space for parents' comments and queries. Finally, contact with parents aimed explicitly to seek their advice in dealing with any problem which had occurred.

In talking to parents of absentees it is striking that many feel that discussions with teachers consists of listening to a lot of complaints which they are then expected to solve. Once again, we have to note that this is in no way inevitable. Some schools in disadvantaged areas have had conspicuous success in winning cooperation from their pupils' parents. Doing so requires an atmosphere of respect for parents' ability to contribute to the school's efforts and a willingness to adapt teaching organisation and methods in the light of parents' suggestions.

Few training courses for teachers pay much attention to the question of parent–teacher contact. Not surprisingly, it has been reported as an important source of stress for teachers (Galloway *et al.*, 1983). An important task for senior staff is providing the guidance and support to enable their colleagues to establish mutually satisfactory contact with parents.

OVERVIEW

While it is clear that schools exert a significant influence on their pupils' attendance, there is as yet little agreement as to how this influence is exerted. Hence, much of the chapter has been speculative, relying partly on interviews with pupils, partly on observations in schools and partly on research which focused primarily on responses to disruptive behaviour. Many poor attenders are disruptive in school, but not all. Many disruptive pupils have a record of poor attendance, but not all. There is a need for research which looks in detail at pupils' experiences in school, with particular reference to those experiences which contribute to regular, or irregular, attendance.

There is less doubt, though, that analysis of absentees' experiences at school identifies stresses and weaknesses in the curriculum, in provision for children with special educational needs and in pastoral care. A more contentious way of putting this is that poor attendance reflects weaknesses in school organisation. This claim is not negated by the fact that poor attendance also reflects parental attitudes and social circumstances. Teachers have little or no influence on the social circumstances of their pupils parents. In contrast, they have an important influence both on their pupils' attitudes towards education and on those of their parents.

We have argued that experiences at school play a central role in the origin of absenteeism, especially towards the end of compulsory schooling. These experiences, moreover, are not associated only with peripheral issues, such as a clash with one particular teacher, though they are important. The basic assumptions of the curriculum, special education and pastoral care are also relevant. When parents have high expectations of education, they will insist on their children's regular attendance. If they have low expectations, or if they are living in chronically stressful conditions, they may see little point in regular attendance, or lack the energy to face a showdown with a reluctant teenager who claims that school is "boring". It nevertheless remains true that a school's attendance rate reflects its success in gaining the active cooperation of pupils and of their parents. The challenge for teachers lies in combining long term planning to raise the quality of education and its value in the eyes of the "clients", with more immediate procedures which ensure not only that individual pupils return to school, but also that they benefit from returning.

CHAPTER 10

Conclusion: Back to the School?

INTRODUCTION

The ambiguity of the chapter title is deliberate. The longer a pupil remains out of school the greater the difficulty in persuading him to return. The longer he remains out of school, moreover, the greater the obstacles to ensuring that return to school is associated with something more positive than boredom, educational failure and/or disruptive behaviour. Even if e.w.o.s, educational psychologists or the courts could get absentees back to school, there is no guarantee that their efforts would be appreciated, either by pupils or by teachers. To repeat a theme throughout the last two chapters, returning to an unchanged situation is a recipe for further failure.

Yet the question in the title is also a question for teachers. Should responsibility for attendance rest, after all, with teachers? Are teachers justified in attributing absenteeism to family backgrounds which they perhaps regard as deprived or depraved? Do they have a justification for expecting external agencies to investigate and deal with attendance problems? Or should poor attendance be regarded essentially as an educational problem, remaining the responsibility of teachers, even though they may be able to call on assistance from external agencies?

This chapter concludes that teachers should expect support from external agencies, but that they cannot realistically expect these agencies to solve problems for them. Even in the small minority of cases for which individual or family therapy is appropriate, successful return to school requires active cooperation from teachers. Assessment indicates the need both for short term palliative measures to facilitate successful return to school, and for long term planning to deal with the underlying tensions. The chapter reviews some of the possibilities, concluding on a note of cautious optimism that teachers can substantially improve overall attendance by combining attention to individual needs with long term planning which raises the quality of education throughout the school as a whole.

SUPPORT SERVICES

Each school has its hidden curriculum as well as its formal, time-tabled curriculum. In just the same way, referring a child to one of the support or treatment services can have a hidden agenda as well as the stated reason for referral. Ostensibly, referral is generally motivated primarily by a desire to help the child and his family. The hidden agenda, particularly in referral to educational psychologists, is not infrequently a hope that the child be referred to a special class or unit. Even when this is not the unstated intention, we saw in Chapter 8 how members of the support services can be socialised into describing the situation in terms of the child's or the family's problems. Put crudely, an e.w.o. or educational psychologist who suggests that the school is at fault is likely to find his position in some staffrooms untenable, if not to be out on his ear. The problem is that the schools whose high absentee rates reflect an unhealthy climate are generally the least receptive to implicit criticism.

This cycle is not unbreakable. A starting point is for teachers to accept that they themselves have needs. Having accepted that, problem behaviour, including poor attendance, can be redefined in terms which acknowledge their own needs besides those of their pupils. Teachers can derive little job satisfaction when as many as half the pupils have stayed away. They can derive no satisfaction from a class of bored pupils, even if a combination of truancy patrols and legal action has coerced the majority into regular attendance. Teachers who claim that their only desire is to help the child are ignoring their own needs, and thereby blinding themselves to a critical part of the solution.

In the Sheffield and New Zealand studies of school based provision for disruptive pupils, a feature of the most successful schools was their acceptance of responsibility in solving, or helping to solve, the problem. This involved a subtle shift of emphasis in defining the problem which the teachers themselves did not always recognise, let alone articulate. Briefly, it involved seeing children not as learning problems, behaviour problems or attendance problems, but as a *teaching* problem. Thus, in contacts with external agencies there was less hope that the children would be brought back to school or referred elsewhere, and more of an expectation that the agencies would suggest what teachers themselves could do.

This model implies an active role both for teachers and for the external agencies. It is illustrated by the case of Albert, described by Galloway (1980c).

Albert was referred at the age of fifteen with a long history of truancy and delinquency. His offences were sometimes committed on his own, sometimes in company. He was of low average intelligence, severely retarded educationally and had few friends. His parents were concerned about him, but his mother suffered from depression and his father worked long hours. His mother reported that her depression had started after the death from acute leukaemia of

Albert's older sister, to whom he had been very close. This happened two months after he started secondary education. Perhaps understandably his parents were relieved, rather than concerned, that he showed no grief. In a family interview Albert astonished his parents by bursting into tears when asked if he had been close to his sister.

A provisional formulation saw Albert's *initial* truancy as a response to unresolved grief and associated anxiety about his mother's health. They were offered separate interviews using a modified version of the approach described by Ramsay (1977) for treating grief reaction. However, it was felt that Albert's *current* truancy was maintained by secondary factors, mainly his social isolation and his educational retardation. This highlighted two problems in his school's provision for pupil welfare: (i) that class teachers were encouraged to pass all "welfare" problems to the head of year (the teacher responsible for each age group) whose time was mainly spent investigating cases of disruptive behaviour; (ii) the school currently had no remedial teaching facilities for fifteen and sixteen-year-olds. Arrangements were made to tackle the immediate problem by drawing up an individual time-table in cooperation with Albert. . . . The broader issues were discussed in a series of meetings with senior staff, when future policy was under consideration.

Albert's story illustrates three points. First, treatment may be desirable, but on its own will not necessarily promote the chances of successful return to school. Indeed, in offering Albert treatment the psychologist had no expectation that this would solve, or even reduce the current problems of delinquency and truancy. Second, the treatment could perfectly well have been carried out by someone with no knowledge of Albert's school. Yet if that person had also been responsible for the initial assessment he might well have missed half the picture, and would have been in no position to work with teachers in tackling the educational aspects identified in assessment. The point is simply that the focus of therapy was not truancy but the unresolved grief and associated features of relationships within the family. The educational issues still had to be tackled. Third, the educational issues needed tackling at two levels. The danger for teachers and for the psychologist was that palliative measures to facilitate Albert's return would be unsuccessful and would obscure the need for a more fundamental review of policy and practice within the school.

LEGAL ACTION

It will by now be clear that merely returning a persistent absentee to school solves neither the pupil's nor the teacher's problems. Probably a more valid analysis is that return to an unchanged situation at school will be followed by a resumption of the problems associated with the pupil's initial absence. Yet as long as education remains free and compulsory legal sanctions will remain, as a way of enforcing parental obligations or of protecting the interests of children. The danger is that their availability encourages their indiscriminate or arbitrary use in a way that does little to promote cooperation from parents and is actively opposed to the child's interests.

Probably the most depressing evidence from the Sheffield research described in earlier chapters was that prosecution of parents was so seldom seen as part of a wider programme to meet the child's educational needs. The philosophy behind parent prosecutions seemed in many cases to be the same as that behind the Leeds juvenile court repeated adjournment procedure: getting the pupil back to school is seen as a valid goal in itself; once back, the simple fact of regular attendance will ensure that his educational needs are met. The only virtue of this philosophy lies in its simplicity: for pupils, parents, teachers, e.w.o.s and magistrates alike, legal action is assumed to provide the only incentive to return.

The naivety of the philosophy is exposed by its failure. In the Sheffield studies legal action was seldom effective. In Leeds their apparent successes concealed the disproportionate number of pupils committed to expensive and potentially damaging placement in custodial care. The most superficial assessment of persistent absentees shows: (a) that their school experiences have been less than favourable; (b) that they frequently have special educational needs requiring skilled teaching.

Return to school, therefore, requires detailed planning. In itself it provides no adequate justification for legal action. Prosecutions for their potential deterrent value—"pour encourager les autres"—are ethically dubious. Prosecutions could therefore seem ethically legitimate only when combined with a carefully thought out plan aiming to deal with inadequacies or tensions in the school itself. Even when seen as part of a wider plan, prosecution will often be of little value, unless something can be done to give parents a positive reason for insisting on their child's attendance. Prosecution merely gives them a negative reason for not condoning absences. Unless teachers themselves can do something to win more active cooperation, little progress is likely.

Juvenile court proceedings raise somewhat different questions. Here, too, successful return is improbable without careful planning to cater for the pupil educationally. Placing the pupil on supervision to a local authority social worker seldom results in active cooperation between social workers and teachers. The social worker may be able to help the family deal with its more pressing problems. This is a valid end in itself, but should be seen as logically distinct from the question of school attendance.

The alternative to supervision is a care order. This raises the possibility of using juvenile court action primarily as a way of removing the child from a harmful home background, with resumed school attendance seen as a secondary objective. The problem here, as social workers know too well, is that placing a child in care may replace an unsatisfactory situation with another even more unsatisfactory one. The apparent confidence of Leeds juvenile court magistrates that sending a poor attender into care is preferable to allowing him to remain at home lacks, as yet, any basis in evidence. Juvenile court action, then, becomes a reasonable proposition only when two questions can be answered with confidence. The first concerns the criteria for deciding whether to consider the possibility of care proceedings. It is not clear that non-attendance alone constitutes adequate grounds. The second concerns the quality of provision the local authority can make in each particular case. Teachers are not in a position to answer either question, though they may often have information relevant to the decision-making process.

THE HALF WAY HOUSE FALLACY

One of the few growth areas in British education in the last ten years has been special units or centres for problem pupils. Some have been established by the l.e.a. to cater for pupils from several schools. Others have been set up by individual schools, to cater for their own pupils. The initial aims both of on-site and of off-site units sound eminently reasonable. A few have catered specifically for poor attenders. A larger number have catered principally for disruptive pupils, many of whom have had a record of absenteeism. They generally aim to admit pupils who cannot cope with pressures in the school's mainstream or who cannot be tolerated in the mainstream, hoping that after a period in the unit they will return to the mainstream, attending regularly, without disrupting classes.

In practice, few off-site units have achieved the aim of successful return to school, though there have been exceptions (e.g. Lane, 1977; Dain, 1977). More frequently they develop, or degenerate, into long-term alternatives to ordinary schools, with pupils remaining on roll until they reach school-leaving age. The reasons lie partly in the way off-site units are established, partly in the preferences of the teachers responsible for them and partly in their curriculum and organisation. There may be a parallel here with the very poor results following home tuition with psychotherapy with school refusers (Blagg and Yule, 1984).

Typically, off-site units cater for pupils whose previous schools already regarded them as beyond redemption, having tried all other possibilities. Thus, they started with a strong bias against the pupil's return. The unit teachers often sense this bias. Describing units set up by the New Zealand Education Department, Galloway and Barrett (1982) comment that the teachers, like the pupils, could be seen as refugees from the ordinary school system. In other words, the teachers recognised the stress and/or lack of satisfaction the pupils had experienced at school. They sympathised, and had decidedly mixed feelings about urging pupils to return to the schools which had already rejected them, or which, for legitimate reasons they had rejected. Finally, the regime in many off-site units is so radically different from that in ordinary schools that it is hard to see how attending the unit could act as preparation for return to school.

Plenty of descriptions of off-site units have been published (e.g. Galway,

1979; White and Brockington, 1978; Rowan, 1976; Pick, 1974; Taylor *et al.*, 1979). These descriptions, however, have not generally incorporated any systematic evaluation, though Galloway and Barrett (1983) noted that fewer than 33 per cent of pupils leaving units in New Zealand entered regular employment. A report by the inspectorate in England was discretely critical of buildings, equipment and the curriculum (H.M.I., 1978). The general impression from the literature is that attendance may well improve substantially while the pupil attends the unit, but successful return to school is achieved only in rare instances. Further, the number of places available in off-site units for poor attenders remains small. Even if they achieved 100 per cent success in returning pupils to the mainstream, with regular attendance subsequently, they would still be of little more than token value in dealing with the wider problem.

Somewhat similar objections apply to units established by individual schools. The Pack Report on truancy and indiscipline in Scotland encouraged such units without providing any adequate research evidence in their support (Scottish Education Department, 1977). Galloway *et al.* (1982) showed that basing units in seven Sheffield secondary schools did nothing to reduce the number of pupils suspended for indiscipline or transferred to special schools.

In one school, fifteen of the twenty-six pupils on the unit's role had attended an average of 12 per cent of possible attendances in the twelve weeks before their admission. When time-tabled to attend the unit for at least half the week their mean attendance improved to 31 per cent. Although most pupils showed some improvement, only two reached 75 per cent attendance, and neither of these pupils maintained this level for more than a term. In another school three pupils improved from an average of 24 per cent attendance in the twelve weeks before admission to 74 per cent when time-tabled to attend the group for at least half the week. In the twelve weeks following discharge to attend ordinary lessons for at least half the week, attendance fell only slightly to 69 per cent. An only slightly less encouraging pattern was evident in one other school.

As with off-site units, descriptive accounts of school-based projects are readily available (e.g. Labon, 1973, 1974; N. Jones, 1971, 1973, 1974; Holman and Libretto, 1979). Again, though, systematic evaluation is lacking. The picture overall suggests that attendance and behaviour of some pupils improves while attending a unit. Vacc (1968), for example, noted improvement while children were attending a special group; but they failed to maintain this improvement when they returned to ordinary classes (Vacc, 1972).

A possible reason was suggested by Galloway *et al.* (1982). They noted that although the curriculum was in theory integrated closely with that in the mainstream in all units, this was extremely difficult to arrange in practice. Of the seven units studied, only one had succeeded in this aim. It appeared that subject teachers did not relish the task of providing work for pupils who had not cooperated in ordinary classes. Consequently, responsibility for the curriculum rested principally with the unit teachers, with the result that it bore little relationship to what was happening in the school's mainstream. Predictably, this made return to ordinary classes difficult to arrange, and led some units to act as a long term alternative to ordinary classes. The effect of this development in one school was grafitti scribbled on walls announcing that "Unit Rules OK". Thus, membership of the unit conferred a social identity and deviant status on the pupils selected to attend it.

Problems of this sort are not insuperable. They do, however, illustrate the argument that the activities in school-based units cannot be seen in isolation from everything that happens in the mainstream. Their success as a "half-way house" back to ordinary lessons will depend partly on the level of cooperation with teachers in the mainstream, and partly in the quality of experiences offered to pupils in the mainstream. Once again, therefore, we return to the school.

A COORDINATED APPROACH BASED ON THE SCHOOL

A. Jones (1980) identifies the central issue in the plethora of attempted solutions to the problem of poor attendance.

> School counsellors, sanctuaries, sinbins, special units, social workers, nurture groups, withdrawal groups, off-site centres, on-site units: all of this special provision *can* work splendidly, and in many cases is still needed, but these extras can confuse and undermine the *main* body of the school if it is not functioning properly. In other words, the hard centre core of the institution must be in good order if it is to benefit from its splendid accessions.

It is this "hard centre core" which is too often ignored or underestimated in responses to poor attenders, whether the responses take the form of police truancy patrols, repeated adjournments in the juvenile court, social work support or special units. Provision of "extras" can indeed, as Jones suggests, confuse and undermine the main body of the school. Yet the extras can also obscure the tensions and weaknesses in the main body. All too easily strenuous, and expensive, efforts to solve a problem create an illusion that everything possible is being done.

Creating a climate conducive to regular attendance requires "constant if not eternal vigilance" (Boyson, 1974). However, it also requires more than this. Boyson is unfortunately not clear whether to blame subversive administrators, neglectful parents or lazy teachers for truancy. The approach in his own school involved frequent spot-checks for pupils who skipped lessons and phone calls to parents whenever any pupil was absent without explanation.

All this is necessary, and can be seen as caring. After all, if teachers fail to take absences seriously, pupils can legitimately conclude that they consider regular attendance unimportant. It is not, however, sufficient. Pressure on absentees to attend regularly is seldom successful unless these pupils recognise attendance as intrinsically worthwhile.

In considering what makes attendance worthwhile, it is worth drawing an analogy between pupils and teachers. At least in Sheffield, teachers have a higher average attendance than their pupils or than workers in most industrial concerns. Motivation to attend regularly presumably lies partly in what professional posts offer. Factors such as pay, job security, status in society and at school, may all be relevant. Motivation also lies partly in what teaching offers. Here factors such as relationships with colleagues, satisfaction at pupil's progress and enjoyment of work with children and adolescents may be relevant. Yet all these points overlook the importance of working as a contributing member of a team of staff. We argued earlier that teaching can be a lonely activity, with little support from colleagues. When this is the case feuding staffroom cliques offer an inadequate outlet to the need for active membership of a peer group.

The parallel with pupils is clear. A network of welfare, counselling and social work services may uncover sources of stress for the individual and for his family. Occasionally it is even possible to help families resolve or alleviate the problems facing them. Yet as A. Jones (1980) observed:

> attempting to improve attendance by *individual* efforts was to throw workers into a bottomless pit. The demand on the extra resources was infinite, and however much extra was done, it was still not enough. (My underlining)

Nor will elaborate special educational provision be adequate on its own. Indeed, nothing that the school gives its pupils will do much to encourage regular attendance unless the pupils feel that they are themselves contributing something worthwhile.

This is not a hopeless challenge. Jones reported an improvement over three years in average September attendances at her London comprehensive school from 77 per cent to 88 per cent. The improvement coincided with a wide-ranging review of the school's procedures. The review affected all pupils, not just the absentees. Other studies too have demonstrated the impact of a school's policies and practices on its pupils' attendance (see Chapter 4). Disadvantaged and stressful family circumstances will doubtless continue to be associated with poor attendance. They do not, however, provide any direct causal link. Poor attendance remains an educational problem. If the problem is to be reduced nationally, as it already has been in a number of schools, teachers will play the major part.

CONCLUDING COMMENTS

Absence from school is a source of interest to pretty well every group with a professional interest in children and young people. Chronic absenteeism by a large number of pupils may be both a symptom and a cause of low morale in teachers. Even an isolated case can raise disturbing questions about what the school itself has to offer.

The time of educational welfare officers is still largely spent on attendance problems. Educational psychologists are frequently asked for advice about these pupils. Social workers are expected to return them to school, after other professionals have failed, when the juvenile court imposes a supervision order. Diagnosis and treatment is sought from family doctors, paediatricians and child psychologists. School governors expect reports on attendance, and occasionally wish to become more actively involved, either in deciding what action should be taken over particular individuals, or in pressing the l.e.a. for extra resources. The l.e.a. administration and the elected councillors on the education committee have to decide what resources should be made available to schools and to the support services. Magistrates in both juvenile and adult courts are required to uphold the law relating to non-attendance.

The ways in which school attendance has been investigated reflect the varied interests and priorities of those involved. Research has been carried out by teachers, psychologists, sociologists, doctors and social workers. Many research projects have provided useful insights into limited aspects of the problem. Yet both the sheer quantity of research and the range of methodologies that have been used merely underline the complexity of this topic. There is no *one* way of understanding absenteeism from school.

This book has argued that teachers should themselves take more direct responsibility for school attendance, not through coercive measures but through provision of positive incentives to regular attendance. This argument does not deny the need for treatment from specialists such as psychologists or psychiatrists in a few cases. Nor, emphatically, does it negate the need for investigation of possible educational difficulties or family problems. The cooperation of agencies outside the school may well be essential here. The view that schools should themselves take more direct responsibility for school attendance does, however, have implications for the relationships between teachers and the support or treatment services. It also has implications for the relationships between teachers and all the other interest groups concerned about education, not least parents.

The point is that any improvement in overall school attendance rates depends on increased school effectiveness. In other words we must emphasise the centrality of the school as a community which attracts, or fails to attract, the interest and commitment of its members. The fact that some pupils have positive incentives *not* to attend only underlines the need for the school to provide stronger, more positive incentives.

The effective school is one in which all pupils know not only that their attendance is expected, and that their absence will instantly be recognised, but also that they themselves can contribute something worthwhile, and which is recognised as worthwhile by teachers and by other pupils. Such a school is a demanding, yet supportive and satisfying place, both for pupils and for teachers. The curriculum presents a realistic challenge, seen as having relevance both to immediate interests and future needs. Teachers do not see themselves as struggling to compensate for inadequate home backgrounds, but are moving beyond the rhetoric of parents as partners to find ways of enlisting parental co-operation.

These views have implications for everyone involved in education. For school governors and elected councillors on the education committee the implication is that they should be stimulating and supporting school based development programmes, rather than frittering away their time in the quasi legal field of coercion. There is no adequate evidence that summoning parents and children for an interview with school governors or elected councillors constitutes an effective way of improving subsequent attendance.

At best the interviews act as a very crude filtering process which could be carried out just as well by e.w.o.s. Nor is there any legal necessity for these procedures. The 1944 Education Act requires Education Committee approval for legal action, but the committee can legitimately delegate to its officers responsibility for day to day decisions, retaining only a general watching brief. This does indeed happen in many l.e.a.s, without any objection to its legality being raised. The education of poor attenders might be better served if governors and councillors were to interest themselves more actively in the resources and in the quality of teaching available to pupils whose poor attendance or disruptive behaviour suggest disaffection from school. So, incidentally, might the cause of community involvement in education.

For the support and treatment services, the implication is that they should be working in active partnership with teachers. The aim is not simply to return poor attenders to school. The aim is to return them to a school which is better able to cater for them, and to enlist a commitment to more regular attendance in the future. The support services, however, are constrained by D.E.S. and l.e.a. policy.

Unfortunately the D.E.S. has failed to provide the guidelines which might produce clear and consistent policies on school attendance at l.e.a. level. There is no consistency between l.e.a.s, for example, in the qualifications that should be expected of e.w.o.s, nor even in the salary scale appropriate to the service. There may be an ill-defined agreement on the need for joint planning with teachers when arranging a persistent absentee's return to school. Yet there appears to be no consensus on how this need should be reflected in the professional training of e.w.o.s. Indeed, some l.e.a.s place such a low priority on training for e.w.o.s as, apparently, to regard it as an unnecessary luxury. While the scope and role of the service remains a matter for discussion, the present arrangements, varying haphazardly from authority to authority, cannot sensibly be expected to promote a coherent policy towards school attendance.

There is no blue-print for an effective school. If such a blue-print existed, there would be no need for this book, and most of the professionals involved in the school attendance industry could divert their energy to something else. The search for simple solutions to such a complex problem as absenteeism is a displacement activity, serving mainly to reduce anxiety about the problem while doing little or nothing to solve it.

In saying this we are not denying the value of treatment by psychologists, psychiatrists or social workers for a very small minority of absentees. Nor are we denying the possible usefulness of special schools, groups or units for an equally small minority, though research evidence for their effectiveness is lacking. We are not even denying that legal procedures may be necessary and helpful in very rare instances, especially when used as part of a broader plan to cater for the pupil's needs at school. Our point is not that all of these procedures can cater for no more than a tiny minority of all pupils who miss at least 25 per cent of their schooling illegally in any one term. Nor is it a crucial issue here that all the procedures are least effective with pupils aged fourteen or older, amongst whom the problem is most prevalent. The point is simply that none of these procedures will produce a substantial improvement in attendance rates unless combined with a rigorous review of the school's own policies, organisation and curriculum.

Increasing school effectiveness is not an unrealistic goal. Improvement in attendance rates and reduction in incidents of disruptive behaviour are merely two aspects of increased effectiveness. Research has shown that many schools have responded to this challenge, producing impressive evidence of high standards in behaviour, attendance and academic results. With a clear lead from the D.E.S., H.M.I. and their own l.e.a., many other schools might do likewise.

Bibliography

Anon (1955) War on Absentees. *Education*, **105**, 425.

Anon (1973) Truancy: What the Official Figures Don't Show. *Where*, **83**, 228–229.

Baldwin, J. (1972) Delinquent Schools in Tower Hamlets I: A Critique. *British Journal of Criminology*, **12**, 399–401.

Barker, R. (1944) (Ed.) *The Education Act, 1944: Supplement to Owen's Education Acts Manual*, 23rd Edition. London: Chas. Knight.

Baum, T. (1979) Surveys of Absenteeism: A Question of Timing, *Educational Research*, **20**, 226–230.

Beaumont, G. R. (1976) A Comparison of the Effects of Behavioural Counselling and Teacher Support on the Attendance of Truants. Unpublished Diploma in School Counselling Dissertation: University College, Swansea.

Berg, I. (1970) A Follow-Up Study of School Phobic Adolescents Admitted to an In-Patient Unit. *Journal of Child Psychology and Psychiatry*, **11**, 37–47.

Berg, I. (1980) Absence from School and the Law. In Hersov, L. and Berg, I. (Eds.). *Out of School: Modern Perspectives in Truancy and School Refusal*. Chichester: Wiley.

Berg, I., Marks, I., McGuire, R. and Linsedge, M. (1974) School Phobia and Agoraphobia. *Psychological Medicine*, **4**, 428–434.

Berg, I., Hullin, R., McGuire, R. and Tyrer, S. (1977) Truancy and the Courts: Research Note. *Journal of Child Psychology and Psychiatry*, **18**, 359–365.

Berg, I., Butler, A., Hullin, R., Smith, R. and Tyrer, S. (1978a) Features of Children Taken to Juvenile Court for Failure to Attend School. *Psychological Medicine*, **8**, 447–453.

Berg, I., Consterdine, M., Hullin, R. and McGuire, R. (1978b) The Effect of Two Randomly Allocated Court Procedures on Truancy. *British Journal of Criminology*, **18**, 232–244.

Blagg, N. (1977) A Detailed Strategy for the Rapid Treatment of School Phobics. *Bulletin of the British Association of Behavioural Psychotherapy*, **5**, 70–75.

Blagg, N. R. and Yule, W. (1984) The behavioural treatment of school refusal: a comparative study. *Behaviour Research and Therapy*, **22**, 119–127.

Bowlby, J. (1973) *Attachment and Loss, Vol. 2: Separation, Anxiety and Anger*. London: Hogarth Press.

Boxall, M. (1973) Nurture Groups. *Concern*, **13**, 9–11.

Boyson, R. (1974) The Need for Realism. In Turner, B. (Ed.). *Truancy*. London: Ward Lock Educational.

Brandon, R. (1974) Local Authority Experiment: Liverpool. In Turner, B. (Ed.). *Truancy*. London: Ward Lock Educational.

Bransby, E. R. (1951) A Study of Absence from School. *The Medical Officer*, **86**, 223–230, 237–240.

Brewer, C., Morris, T., Morgan, P. and North, M. (1981) *Criminal Welfare on Trial*. London: Social Affairs Unit.

Broadwin, I. T. (1932) A Contribution to the Study of Truancy. *American Journal of Orthopsychiatry*, **2**, 253–259.

Brooks, D. B. (1974) Contingency Contracts with Truants. *Personnel Guidance Journal*, **52**, 315–320.

Burt, C. (1925) *The Young Delinquent*. London: University of London Press.

Cain, J. (1974) *A Study of the Effect of Counselling on Pupils Displaying an Irregular Pattern of School*

Attendance. Unpublished Diploma in School Counselling Dissertation: University College, Swansea.

Cannan, C. (1970) Schools for Delinquency. *New Society,* **16,** 1004 (3rd December).

Carroll, H. C. M. (1977a) Pupil Attendance in Three Comprehensive Schools: A Study of the Pupils and their Families. In Carroll, H. C. M. (Ed.). *Absenteeism in South Wales: Studies of Pupils, their Homes and their Secondary Schools.* Swansea: University College, Swansea, Faculty of Education.

Carroll, H. C. M. (1977b) The Problem of Absenteeism: Research Studies Past and Present. In Carroll, H. C. M. (Ed.). *Absenteeism in South Wales: Studies of Pupils, their Homes and their Secondary Schools.* Swansea: University College, Swansea, Faculty of Education.

Caven, N. and Harbison, J. (1978) *Persistent School Non-Attendance: The Northern Ireland Situation and the Links Between Non-Attendance and some School and Socio-Economic Factors.* Paper read at conference of the Northern Ireland Branch of the British Psychological Society.

Chadwick, O. (1976) Personal Communication.

Chartered Institute of Public Finance and Accountancy Statistical Information Service (1981) *Personal Social Services Statistics 1981–82 Estimates.* London: CIPFA.

Chazan, M. (1962) School Phobia. *British Journal of Educational Psychology,* **32,** 209–217.

Children and Young Persons Act (1969) *Great Britain Statutes.* Chapter 54. London: HMSO.

Cicourel, A. V. and Kitsuse, J. I. (1968) The Social Organisation of the High School and Deviant Adolescent Careers. In Rubington, E. and Weinberg, M. (Eds.). *Deviance: The Interactionist Perspective.* New York: Macmillan.

Cline, T. (1980) More Help for Schools: A Critical Look at Child Guidance. *Therapeutic Education,* **8,** (i), 3–11.

Clyne, M. B. (1966) *Absent: School Refusal as an Example of Disturbed Family Relationships.* London: Tavistock.

Coleman, J. S. *et al.* (1966) *Equality of Educational Opportunity.* Washington: U.S. Government Printing Office.

Coolidge, J. C., Hahn, C. B. and Peck, A. L. (1957) School Phobia: Neurotic Crisis or Way of Life. *American Journal of Orthopsychiatry,* **27,** 296–306.

Cooper, M. G. (1966a) School Refusal. *Educational Research,* **8,** 115–127.

Cooper, M. G. (1966b) School Refusal: An Inquiry into the Part Played by School and Home. *Educational Research,* **8,** 223–229.

Cornish, D. B. and Clarke, R. V. G. (1975) *Residential Treatment and its Effects on Delinquency.* London: HMSO.

Corrigan, P. (1979) *Schooling the Smash Street Kids.* London: Macmillan.

Cox, K. M. and Lavelle, M. (1982) *Staff Development Through Teacher Interaction: A School-Based Case Study.* Sheffield: Sheffield City Polytechnic, Department of Educational Management.

Cross, J. (1983) Absence Makes the Heart Grow Harder. *Times Educational Supplement,* 11th February, 23.

Dain, P. (1977) Disruptive Children and the Key Centre. *Remedial Education,* **12,** (iv), 163–167.

Davidson, S. (1960) School Phobia as a Manifestation of Family Disturbance: Its Structure and Treatment. *Journal of Child Psychology and Psychiatry,* **1,** 270–287.

Dayton, N. A. (1928) Mental Deficiency and Other Factors that Influence School Attendance. *Mental Hygiene,* **12,** 794–800.

Department of Education and Science (1967) *Children and their Primary Schools* (The Plowden Report). London: HMSO.

Department of Education and Science (1974) *Press Notice: Results of School Absence Survey.* London: DES.

Department of Education and Science (1978) *Special Educational Needs* (The Warnock Report). London: HMSO.

Department of Education and Science (1984) *The Education Welfare Service: An HMI Inquiry in Eight Areas.* London: HMSO.

Department of Health and Social Security (1968) *Report of the Committee on Local Authority and Allied Personal Social Services* (The Seebohm Report). London: HMSO.

Department of Health and Social Security (1976) *Not for the Future: Report of the Committee on the Child Health Services* (The Court Report). Vols I and II. London: HMSO.

Douglas, J. W. B. and Ross, J. (1965) The Effects of Absence on Primary School Performance. British Journal of Educational Psychology, 35, 18–40.

Eaton, M. J. and Houghton, D. M. (1974) The Attitudes of Persistent Teenage Absentees and Regular Attenders Towards School and Home. Irish Journal of Psychology, 2, 159–175.

Education Act (1944) 7 and 8 George VI, Chapter 31. London: HMSO.

Education Act (1981) Chapter 60. London: HMSO.

Eisenberg, L. (1958) School Phobia: A Study in the Communication of Anxiety. American Journal of Psychiatry, 114, 712–718.

Elementary Education Act (1870) 33 and 34 Victoria, Chapter 75. London: HMSO.

Elementary Education Act (1876) 39 and 40 Victoria, Chapter 79. London: HMSO.

Estes, H. R., Haylett, C. and Johnson, A. (1956) Separation Anxiety. American Journal of Psychotherapy, 10, 682–695.

Evans, E. G. S. (1965) Truancy and School Avoidance: A Review of the Literature. London Educational Review, 4, 63–71.

Eysenck, S. B. G. (1965) Manual of the Junior Eysenck Personality Inventory. University London Press.

Eysenck, H. J. and Rachman, S. (1965) The Application of Learning Theory to Child Psychiatry. In Howells, J. G. (Ed.). Modern Perspectives in Child Psychiatry. Edinburgh: Oliver and Boyd.

Farrington, D. (1972) Delinquency Begins at Home. New Society, 21, 495–497 (14th September).

Ferguson, T. (1952) The Young Delinquent in his Social Setting. London: University of London Press.

Finlayson, D. S. and Loughran, J. L. (1976) Pupils' Perceptions in High and Low Delinquency Schools. Educational Research, 18, 138–144.

Fitzherbert, K. (1977a) Unwillingly to School. New Society, 17th February, 332–334.

Fitzherbert, K. (1977b) Child Care Services and the Teacher. London: Maurice Temple Smith.

Fogelman, K. (1976) Britain's Sixteen Year Olds. London: National Children's Bureau.

Fogelman, K. (1978) School Attendance, Attainment and Behaviour. British Journal of Educational Psychology, 48, 148–158.

Fogelman, K. and Richardson, K. (1974) School Attendance: Some Results from the National Child Development Study. In Turner, B. (Ed.). Truancy. London: Ward Lock Educational.

Galloway, D. M. (1967a) Size of School, Socio-Economic Hardship, Suspension Rates and Persistent Unjustified Absence from School. British Journal of Educational Psychology, 46, 40–47.

Galloway, D. M. (1976b) Persistent Unjustified Absence from School. Trends in Education, 1976/4, 22–27.

Galloway, D. (1980a) A Study of Persistent Absence from School in Sheffield: Prevalence and Associated Educational, Psychological and Social Factors. Unpublished Ph.D. Thesis. Sheffield City Polytechnic.

Galloway, D. (1980b) Exclusion and Suspension from School. Trends in Education, (ii), 33–38.

Galloway, D. (1980c) Problems of Assessment and Management of Persistent Absenteeism from Schools. In Hersov, L. and Berg, I. (Eds.). Out of School: Modern Perspectives in Truancy and School Refusal. Chichester: Wiley.

Galloway, D. (1981) Teaching and Counselling: Pastoral Care in Primary and Secondary Schools. London: Longman.

Galloway, D. (1982a) Persistent Absence from School. Educational Research, 24, 188–196.

Galloway, D. (1982b) A Study of Persistent Absentees from School and their Families. British Journal of Educational Psychology, 52, 317–330.

Galloway, D. (1983a) Research Note: Truants and Other Absentees. Journal of Child Psychology and Psychiatry, 24, 607–611.

Galloway, D. (1983b) Disruptive Pupils and Effective Pastoral Care. School Organisation, 3, 245–254.

Galloway, D. (1984) Pastoral Care and School Effectiveness. In Reynolds, D. and Gray, J. (Eds.). School Effectiveness. Lewes: Falmer Press.

Galloway, D. and Miller, A. (1978) The Use of Graded In Vivo Flooding in the Extinction of Children's Phobias. Behavioural Psychotherapy, 6, 7–10.

Galloway, D. and Goodwin, C. (1979) Educating Slow-Learning and Maladjusted Children: Integration or Segregation? London: Longman.

Galloway, D., Ball, C. and Seyd, R. (1981a) Administrative and Legal Procedures Available to Local Education Authorities in Cases of Poor School Attendance. Durham and Newcastle Research Review, 9, 201–209.

Galloway, D., Ball, C. and Seyd, R. (1981b) The Selection of Parents and Children for Legal Action in Connection with Poor School Attendance. *British Journal of Social Work*, 11, 445–461.

Galloway, D., Ball, C. and Seyd, R. (1981c) School Attendance Following Legal or Administrative Action for Unauthorised Absence. *Educational Review*, 33, 53–65.

Galloway, D., Ball, C. and Seyd, R. (1981d) Finding a Way Back for Reluctant Children. *Social Work Today*, 12, xxxiii, 15–17.

Galloway, D., Ball, C., Blomfield, D. and Seyd, R. (1982) *Schools and Disruptive Pupils*. London: Longman.

Galloway, D. and Barrett, C. (1982) *Unmanageable Children? A Study of Recent Provision for Disruptive Pupils in the New Zealand Education System*. Report on Research Carried Out Under Contract to the New Zealand Education Department. Wellington: Victoria University of Wellington.

Galloway, D. and Barrett, C. (1983) Disruptive Pupils: A Result of Teacher Stress as Well as a Cause? *New Zealand Post Primary Teachers Association Journal*. Term 2, 40–44.

Galloway, D., Martin, R. and Wilcox, B. (1984) Persistant Absence from School and Exclusion from School: The Predictive Power of School and Community Variables. *British Educational Research Journal* (accepted for publication).

Galway, J. (1979) What Pupils Think of Special Units. *Comprehensive Education*, 39, No. 375, 18–20.

Gath, D., Cooper, B. and Gattoni, F. E. G. (1972) Child Guidance and Delinquency in a London Borough: Preliminary Communication. *Psychological Medicine*, 2, 185–191.

Gath, D., Cooper, B., Gattoni, F. and Rockett, D. (1977) *Child Guidance and Delinquency in a London Borough*. Oxford: Oxford University Press.

Gillham, B. (1981) (Ed.). *Problem Behaviour in the Secondary School: A Systems Approach*. London: Croom Helm.

Gittelman-Klein, R. and Klein, D. F. (1971) Controlled Imipramine Treatment of School Phobia. *Archives of General Psychiatry*, 25, 204–207.

Goodwin, C. (1979) Innovations for ESN(M) Children in the English Education System. In Galloway, D. and Goodwin, C. *Educating Slow-Learning and Maladjusted Children: Integration or Segregation*. London: Longman.

Gorrell-Barnes, G. (1973) Work with Nurture-Group Parents. *Concern*, 13, 13–16.

Gray, G., Smith, A. and Rutter, M. (1980) School Attendance and the First Year of Employment. In Hersov, L. and Berg, I. (Eds.). *Out of School: Modern Perspectives in Truancy and School Refusal*. Chichester: Wiley.

Greenbaum, R. S. (1964) Treatment of School Phobia: Theory and Practice. *American Journal of Psychotherapy*, 18, 616–633.

Gutfreund, R. (1975) Resolving the Problem. *Youth in Society*, May/June, 12–15.

Hamblin, D. H. (1977) Caring and Control: The Treatment of Absenteeism. In Carroll, H. C. M. (Ed.). *Absenteeism in South Wales: Studies of Pupils, their Homes and their Secondary Schools*. Swansea: University College, Swansea, Faculty of Education.

Hamblin, D. (1978) *The Teacher and Pastoral Care*. Oxford: Blackwell.

Hampe, E., Miller, L., Barrett, C. and Noble, H. (1973) Intelligence and School Phobia. *Journal of School Psychology*, 11, 66–70.

Harbison, J. and Caven, N. (1977) Persistent School Absenteeism in Northern Ireland. Belfast: Statistics and Economics Unit, Department of Finance (Northern Ireland).

Hargreaves, D. H. (1967) *Social Relationships in a Secondary School*. London: Routledge and Kegan Paul.

Hargreaves, D. (1980) A Sociological Critique of Individualism in Education. *British Journal of Educational Studies*, 28, 187–198.

Hargreaves, D. (1983) *The Challenge of the Comprehensive School: Culture, Curriculum, Community*. London: Routledge and Kegan Paul.

Hargreaves, D., Hester, S. and Mellor, F. J. (1975) *Deviance in Classrooms*. London: Routledge and Kegan Paul.

Her Majesty's Inspectorate of Schools (1978) *Behavioural Units*. London: Department of Education and Science.

Her Majesty's Inspectorate of Schools (1980) *Community Homes with Education*. London: HMSO.

Hersov, L. (1960a) Persistent Non-Attendance at School. *Journal of Child Psychology and Psychiatry*, 1, 130–136.

Hersov, L. (1960b) Refusal to go to School. *Journal of Child Psychology and Psychiatry*, **1**, 137–145.

Hersov, L. (1977) School Refusal. In Rutter, M. and Hersov, L. (Eds.). *Child Psychiatry: Modern Approaches*. Oxford: Blackwell.

Hill, B. (1971) Worried About Truancy. *Times Educational Supplement*, 2nd July, 5.

Hoback, J. R. (1976) The Problem of Attendance. *Bulletin of National Association of Secondary School Principals*, **60**, 20–29.

Holman, P. and Libretto, G. (1979) The On-Site Unit. *Comprehensive Education*, **39**, No. 375, 10–12.

Home Office (1978) *Juveniles: Cooperation Between the Police and Other Agencies*. Circular 211/1978. London: Home Office.

Home Office (1980) *Juveniles: Cooperation Between the Police and Other Agencies*. Circular 83/1980. London: Home Office.

Horn, P. (1977) The Employment of Children in Victorian Oxfordshire. *Midland History*, **4**, (i), 61–71.

Jackson, D. (1978) *A Comparative Study of the Perceptions of their School of Frequent Absentees and Regular Attenders*. Unpublished Master of Education Thesis. University of Sheffield.

Jackson, B. and Marsden, D. (1966) *Education and the Working Class*. Harmondsworth: Penguin.

Johnson, A. M., Falstein, E. I., Szurek, S. A. and Svendsen, M. (1941) School Phobia. *American Journal of Orthopsychiatry*, **11**, 702–711.

Jones, A. (1980) The School's View of Persistent Non-Attendance. In Hersov, L. and Berg, I. (Eds.). *Out of School: Modern Perspectives in Truancy and School Refusal*. Chichester: Wiley.

Jones, D. (1974) The Truant. *Concern*, **14**, 12–24.

Jones, N. (1971) The Brislington Project at Bristol. *Special Education*, **60**, (ii), 23–26.

Jones, N. (1973) Special Adjustment Units in Comprehensive Schools, I: Needs and Resources, II: Structure and Function. *Therapeutic Education*, **1**, (ii), 23–31.

Jones, N. (1974) Special Adjustment Units in Comprehensive Schools, III: Selection of Children. *Therapeutic Education*, **2**, (ii), 21–62.

Kahn, J. H. and Nursten, J. P. (1968) *Unwillingly to School*. Oxford: Pergamon.

Karweit, N. L. (1973) Rainy Days and Mondays: An Analysis of Factors Related to Absence from School. Report No. 162. Baltimore: John Hopkins University, Centre for the Study of Social Organisation of Schools.

Kennedy, W. A. (1965) School Phobia: Rapid Treatment of Fifty Cases. *Journal of Abnormal Psychology*, **70**, 285–289.

Kennedy, W. A. (1971) A Behaviouristic Community—Orientated Approach to School Phobia and Other Disorders. In Richard, H. C. (Ed.). *Behavioural Intervention in Human Problems*. Oxford: Pergamon.

Kenny, D. (1981) *I. T. Review of Practices and Policies in the Central London Boroughs*. London: Central Policy Unit, Greater London Council.

Klein, E. (1945) The Reluctance to go to School. *The Psychoanalytic Study of the Child*, **1**, 263–279.

Labon, D. (1973) Helping Maladjusted Children in Primary Schools. *Therapeutic Education*, **1**, (ii), 14–22.

Labon, D. (1974) Some Effects of School-Based Therapy. *Association of Educational Psychologists Journal*, **3**, (vi), 28–34.

Lane, D. A. (1977) Aspects of the Use of Behaviour Modification in Secondary Schools. *Bulletin of the British Association for Behavioural Psychotherapy*, **5**, 76–79.

Law, B. (1973) An Alternative to Truancy. *British Journal of Guidance and Counselling*, **1**, 91–96.

Lemert, E. M. (1967) *Human Deviance: Social Problems and Social Control*. Englewood Cliffs: Prentice-Hall.

Leventhal, T. and Sills, M. (1964) Self-Image in School Phobia. *American Journal of Orthopsychiatry*, **34**, 685–695.

Levitt, E. E. (1957) Results of Psychotherapy with Children: An Evaluation. *Journal of Consulting Psychology*, **21**, 189–196.

Levitt, E. E, (1963) Psychotherapy with Children: A Further Evaluation. *Behaviour Research and Therapy*, **1**, 45–51.

Lewis, G. and Murgatroyd, S. J. (1976) The Professionalisation of Counselling in Education and its Legal Implications. *British Journal of Guidance and Counselling*, **4**, (i), 2–15.

Lindsay, G. A. (1980) The Infant Rating Scale. *British Journal of Educational Psychology*, **50**, 97–104.

Local Government Training Board (1972) *The Role and Training of Education Welfare Officers: Report of the Working Party*. Luton: Local Government Training Board.

Lockley, A. (1984) Child care: note for guidence for solicitors acting on behalf of children and parents. *The Law Society's Gazette*, **81**, 1566–1571.

Loxley, F. D. (1974) Beyond Child Guidance. Occasional Papers. British Psychological Society, Division of Educational and Child Psychology, 283–288.

Mawby, R. I. (1977) Truancy: Data from a Self-Report Survey. *Durham and Newcastle Research Review*, **8**, (xxxix), 21–34.

May, D. (1975) Truancy, School Absenteeism and Delinquency. *Scottish Educational Studies*, **7**, 97–107.

Metge, J. and Kinloch, P. (1978) *Talking Past Each Other: Problems of Cross-Cultural Communication*. Wellington: Victoria University of Wellington Press.

Miller, L. C., Barratt, C. L. and Hampe, E. (1974) Phobias of Childhood in a Pre-Scientific Era. In Davies, A. (Ed.). *Child Personality and Psychopathology: Current Topics*, Vol. 1. New York: Wiley, 89–134.

Mitchell, S. (1972) The Absentees. *Education in the North*, **9**, 22–28.

Mitchell, S. and Rosa, P. (1981) Boyhood Behaviour Problems as Precursors of Criminality: A Fifteen Year Follow-Up. *Journal of Child Psychology and Psychiatry*, **22**, 19–33.

Mitchell, S. and Shepherd, M. (1967) The Child Who Dislikes Going to School. *British Journal of Educational Psychology*, **37**, 32–40.

Moore, T. (1966) Difficulties of the Ordinary Child in Adjusting to Primary School. *Journal of Child Psychology and Psychiatry*, **7**, 17–38.

Morgan, R. R. (1975) An Exploratory Study of Three Procedures to Encourage School Attendance. *Psychology in the School*, **12**, 209–215.

Murgatroyd, S. J. (1975) The Psychologist, the Sociologist and the Truant. *New Psychology*, **1**, (ii), 3–18.

National Association of Chief Education Welfare Officers (1974) *These we Serve: The Report of a Working Party Set up to Enquire into the Causes of Absence from School*. Bedford: National Association of Chief Educational Welfare Officers.

Newell, P. (1983) *ACE Special Education Handbook*. London: Advisory Centre for Education.

Pallister, R. (1969) The Determinants of Elementary School Attendance About 1850. *Durham and Newcastle Research Review*, **5**, 384–398.

Phillipson, C. M. (1971) Juvenile Delinquency and the School. In Carson, W. G. and Wiles, P. (Eds.). *Crime and Delinquency in Britain: Sociological Readings*. London: Martin Robertson.

Pick, M. (1974) School for Truants. *The Guardian*, 19th February.

Power, M. J., Alderson, M. R., Phillipson, C. M., Schoenberg, E. and Morris, J. M. (1967) Delinquent Schools. *New Society*, **10**, 264, 542–543.

Power, M. J., Benn, R. T. and Morris, J. M. (1972) Neighbourhood, School and Juveniles Before the Courts. *British Journal of Crminology*, **12**, 111–132.

Pratt, J. (1983) Folklore and Fact in Truancy Research. *British Journal of Criminology*, **23**, 336–353.

Pratt, J. (1984) Truancy, Decision-Making and Normalisation: Towards a New Perspective. *British Journal of Law and Society* (in press).

Radical Statistics Education Group (1982) *Reading Between the Numbers: A Critical Guide to Educational Research*. London: BSSRS Publications.

Ramprakash, D. (1983) (Ed.) *Social Trends*, No. 13. London: HMSO.

Ramsay, P. (1983) Fresh Perspectives on the School Transformation—Reproduction Debate: A Response to Anyon from the Antipodes. Curriculum Inquiry, **13**, 295–320.

Raven, J. C. (1960) *Guide to the Standard Progressive Matrices*. London: H. K. Lewis.

Reid, K. (1982) The Self-Concept and Persistent Absenteeism. *British Journal of Educational Psychology*, **52**, 179–187.

Reynolds, D. (1976) When Pupils and Teachers Refuse a Truce: The Secondary School and the Creation of Delinquency. In Mungham, G. and Pearson, G. (Eds.). *Working Class Youth Culture*. London: Routledge and Kegan Paul.

Reynolds, D. (1978) Truants Under Suspended Sentence. *Community Care,* 31st May, 20–22.

Reynolds, D. and Grey, J. (1984) *Research on School Effectiveness.* Lewes: Falmer Press.

Reynolds, D. and Murgatroyd, S. (1974) Being Absent from School. *British Journal of Law and Society,* **1,** 78–80.

Reynolds, D. and Murgatroyd, S. (1977) The Sociology of Schooling and the Absent Pupil: The School as a Factor in the Generation of Truancy. In Carroll, H. C. M. (Ed.). *Absenteeism in South Wales: Studies of Pupils, their Homes and their Secondary Schools.* Swansea: University College, Swansea, Faculty of Education.

Reynolds, D., Jones, S., St. Leger, S. and Murgatroyd, S. (1980) School Factors and Truancy. In Hersov, L. and Berg, I. (Eds.). *Out of School: Modern Perspective in Truancy and School Refusal.* Chichester: Wiley.

Rines, W. B. (1973) Behaviour Therapy Before Institutionalization. *Psychotherapy: Theory, Research and Practice,* **10,** 281–283.

Robins, L. N. (1966) *Deviant Children Grown Up.* Baltimore: Williams and Wilkins.

Robins, L. and Ratcliffe, K. (1980) The Long-Term Outcome of Truancy. In Hersov, L. and Berg, I. (Eds.). *Out of School: Modern Perspectives in Truancy and School Refusal.* Chichester: Wiley.

Rodriguez, A., Rodriguez, M. and Eisenberg, L. (1959) The Outcome of School Phobia: A Follow Up Study Based on 41 Cases. *American Journal of Psychiatry,* **116,** 540–544.

Rose, G. and Marshall, T. F. (1974) *Counselling and School Social Work.* Chichester: Wiley.

Ross, A. O. (1972) Behaviour Therapy. In Wolman, B. B. (Ed.). *Manual of Child Psychopathology.* New York: McGraw Hill.

Rowan, P. (1976) Short-Term Sanctuary. *Times Educational Supplement,* 2nd April, 21–24.

Rubenstein, D. (1969) *School Attendance in London, 1870–1904: A Social History.* Hull: University of Hull.

Rutter, M. (1965) Classification and Categorisation in Child Psychiatry. *Journal of Child Psychology and Psychiatry,* **6,** 71–83.

Rutter, M. (1966) *Children of Sick Parents: An Environmental and Psychiatric Study.* Institute of Psychiatry, Maudsley Monographs, No. 16. London: Oxford University Press.

Rutter, M. (1967) A Children's Behaviour Questionnaire for Completion by Teachers: Preliminary Findings. *Journal of Child Psychology and Psychiatry,* **8,** 1–11.

Rutter, M. (1978) Family, Area and School Influences in the Genesis of Conduct Disorders. In Hersov, L. A., Berger, M. and Schaffer, D. (Eds.). *Aggression and Antisocial Behaviour in Childhood and Adolescence.* Oxford: Pergamon.

Rutter, M. (1981) Stress, Coping and Development: Some Issues and Some Questions. *Journal of Child Psychology and Psychiatry,* **22,** 323–356.

Rutter, M. and Graham, P. (1968) The Reliability and Validity of the Psychiatric Assessment of the Child: Interview with the Child. *British Journal of Psychiatry,* **114,** 563–579.

Rutter, M., Tizard, J. and Whitmore, K. (1970) (Eds.) *Education, Health and Behaviour.* London: Longman.

Rutter, M., Yule, B., Quinton, D., Rowlands, O., Yule, W. and Berger, M. (1975) Attainment and Adjustment in Two Geographical Areas, III: Some Factors Accounting for Area Differences. *British Journal of Psychiatry,* **126,** 520–533.

Rutter, M., Graham, P., Chadwick, O. F. D. and Yule, W. (1976) Adolescent Turmoil: Fact or Fiction. *Journal of Child Psychology and Psychiatry,* **17,** 35–56.

Rutter, M. and Quinton, D. (1977) Psychiatric Disorder—Ecological Factors and Concepts of Causation. In McGurk, H. (Ed.). *Ecological Factors in Human Development.* Amsterdam: North Holland.

Rutter, M., Maughan, B., Mortimore, P., Ouston, J. and Smith, A. (1979) *Fifteen Thousand Hours: Secondary Schools and their Effects on Pupils.* London: Open Books.

Saltmarsh, M. (1973) Misalliance? Or a Working Partnership? Social Work in the School Setting. *Social Work Today,* **4,** 161–163.

Sandon, E, (1938) The Comparative Effect on School Progress of (a) Many Short, (b) One Long Absence(s) in a Secondary School. *British Journal of Educational Psychology,* **8,** 172–177.

Sassi, L. C. F. (1973) *The Effect of Counselling on School Truants.* Unpublished Diploma in School Counselling Dissertation. University College, Swansea.

Scherman, A. and Grover, V. M. (1962) Treatment of Children's Behavior Disorders: A Method of Re-Education. *Medical Proceedings,* **8,** 151–154.

Scottish Education Department (1977) *Truancy and Indiscipline in Schools in Scotland* (The Pack Report). London: HMSO.

Sheffield Education Committee (1907) Report for 1906–1907. Sheffield: Sheffield Education Committee.

Sheffield Education Committee (1938) Report for Year Ending 31st March, 1938. Sheffield: Sheffield Education Committee.

Shepherd, M., Oppenheim, B. and Mitchell, S. (1971) *Childhood Behaviour and Mental Health.* London: University of London Press.

Skynner, R. (1974) School Phobia: A Reappraisal. *British Journal of Medical Psychology*, **47**, 1–16.

Stott, D. H. (1971) *The Bristol Social Adjustment Guides.* 2nd Edition. London: University of London Press.

Talbot, M. (1957) Panic in School Phobia. *American Journal of Orthopsychiatry*, **27**, 286–295.

Taylor, M., Miller, J. and Oliveira, M. (1979) The Off-Site Unit. *Comprehensive Education*, **39**, No. 375, 13–17.

Tennent, T. G. (1970) The Use of Section 40 of the Education Act by the London Juvenile Court. *British Journal of Criminology*, **9**, 175–180.

Tennent, T. G. (1971) School Non-Attendance and Delinquency. *Educational Research*, **13**, 185–190.

Tibbenham, A. (1977) Housing and Truancy. *New Society*, **39**, 753, 501–502.

Tizard, J. (1973) Maladjusted Children and the Child Guidance Service. *London Educational Review*, **2**, 22–37.

Tomlinson, S. (1982) *A Sociology of Special Education.* London: Routledge and Kegan Paul.

Trigg, J. E. (1973) Focus on the Absent Minority. *Special Education*, **62**, (ii), 24–28.

Tumelty, A. (1976) *A Study of the Effectiveness of Peer Counselling of School Truants.* Unpublished Diploma in School Counselling Dissertation. University College, Swansea.

Tutt, N. S. (1974) Care or Custody. London: Darton, Longman and Todd.

Tutt, N. S. (1981) Treatment under attack. In Gillham, B. (Ed.) *Problem Behaviour in the Secondary School: A Systems Approach.* London: Croom Helm.

Tyerman, M. J. (1958) A Research into Truancy. *British Journal of Educational Psychology*, **28**, 217–225.

Tyerman, M. J. (1968) *Truancy.* London: University London Press.

Tyrer, P. and Tyrer, S. (1974) School Refusal, Truancy and Neurotic Illness. *Psychological Medicine*, **4**, 416–421.

Vacc, N. A. (1968) A Study of Emotionally Disturbed Children in Regular and Special Classes. *Exceptional Children*, **35**, 197–204.

Vacc, N. A. (1972) Long Term Effects of Special Class Intervention for Emotionally Disturbed Children. *Exceptional Children*, **39**, September, 15–22.

Waldfogel, S., Coolidge, J. C. and Hahn, P. B. (1957) The Development, Meaning and Management of School Phobia. *American Journal of Orthopsychiatry*, **27**, 754–776.

Wechsler, D. (1974) *Wechsler Intelligence Scales for Children—Revised.* Windsor: NFER.

Wedge, P. and Prosser, H. (1973) *Born to Fail?* London: Arrow Books.

Weinberger, G., Leventhal, T. and Beckman, G. (1973) The Management of a Chronic School Phobia Through the Use of Consultation with School Personnel. *Psychology in the Schools*, **10**, 83–88.

Werthman, C. (1963) Delinquents in Schools: A Test for the Legitimacy of Authority. *Berkely Journal of Sociology*, **8**, 39–60.

West, D. J. and Farrington, D. (1973) *Who Becomes Delinquent?* London: Heinemann.

White, R. and Brockington, D. (1978) *In and Out of School: The ROSLA Community Education Project.* London: Routledge and Kegan Paul.

Willis, P. (1977) *Learning to Labour: How Working Class Kids Get Working Class Jobs.* Farnborough: Saxon House.

Yule, W. (1977) Behavioural Treatment of Children and Adolescents with Conduct Disorders. In Hersov, L., Berger, M. and Shaffer, D. (Eds.). *Aggression and Anti-Social Behaviour in Childhood and Adolescence.* Oxford: Pergamon.

Yule, W., Hersov, L. and Treseder, J. (1980) Behavioural Treatments of School Refusal. In Hersov, L. and Berg, I. (Eds.). *Out of School: Modern Perspectives in Truancy and School Refusal.* Chichester: Wiley.

Sheffield School and Home Project
Summary of Completed Research Programme*
by David Galloway

Introduction

In 1977 the Department of Education and Science made funds available to the University of Sheffield Division of Education for research on persistent unauthorised absence from school and on severely disruptive behaviour in school. The research programme took place in Sheffield local education authority in 1978 and 1979. The research team was based in the l.e.a.'s psychological service and was led by David Galloway, then a senior educational psychologist. He was assisted by one full-time and two part-time research officers (Tina Ball, Diana Blomfield and Ros Seyd). The research was coordinated by an advisory committee under the chairmanship of Professor John Roach, of the University of Sheffield.

The research programme contained three separate projects:

(i) A study of persistent unauthorised absence from school and related issues.

(ii) A study of exclusion and suspension from school on disciplinary grounds, and related issues.

(iii) A study of special groups for problem pupils in ordinary secondary schools, and related issues.

The link between persistent absentees and excluded pupils lay in the fact that both groups require an administrative response from the l.e.a. In the first case,

*Submitted to Department of Education and Science on completion of the research, and later published in the Association of Educational Psychologists Journal, vol 5, no. 6, pp. 39–47.

the l.e.a. has to decide whether: (a) to continue informal attempts to secure the pupil's return to school, or (b) to take legal action, either against the parents in the Magistrate's Court, or on behalf of the child in the Juvenile Court. In the case of exclusion the l.e.a. must decide what alternative form of education can be provided, and what specialist investigations are needed in order to reach a decision. The project on special groups for problem pupils was related to the rest of the research programme in the sense that special groups were seen as a way of catering within the ordinary school for pupils who might otherwise have become persistent absentees, or been at risk of suspension on disciplinary grounds.

Persistent Absence from School

(a) *Prevalence*

Research on school attendance in Sheffield started in 1974 when an l.e.a. working party on problem children commissioned a survey of persistent absentees in the previous Autumn term. In this, as in subsequent surveys, a persistent absentee was defined as a pupil who had missed at least 50 per cent of his schooling during the survey period. Two results attracted particular attention at the time:

(i) a school's size bore no relationship to its persistent absentee rate;
(ii) absentee rates remained stable throughout the primary school years, but rose steadily thereafter with a very sharp peak in the final year of compulsory education.

The pilot project was carried out in the year of the raising of the school leaving age to sixteen. It was predicted that the increase in final year absentee rates would become less marked as the raising of the leaving age became more widely accepted. We also wished to investigate the possibility of marked changes in absentee rates in individual schools over the three years of the study. Similar surveys were therefore carried out in 1975, 1976 and 1977. In each case head teachers provided information about all pupils who had missed at least half their schooling in the previous Autumn term. Education welfare officers subsequently stated which of eight categories accounted for the majority of each pupil's absence.

The results confirmed that persistent absentee rates remained static throughout the primary school years, at roughly 0.5 per cent of the total on roll. In contrast, they rose sharply in the second and third years of secondary schooling. In the fourth year the increase was less marked, but the final year of compulsory education saw an extremely sharp rise. By this age, 4 per cent of pupils were persistently absent. Overall, roughly 900 pupils were recorded as persistent absentees in each annual survey. At the time, Sheffield had about 105,000 children of school age.

In secondary schools education welfare officers regarded illness as the principal reason for less than 25 per cent of persistent absence. Truancy, defined as absence without parental knowledge or consent, was the principal explanation for less than 20 per cent. Truancy was considered extremely rare amongst persistent absentees from primary schools. Conversely, these pupils' absences were more often attributed to illness. The evidence suggests not only: (i) that absence is a great deal more common in secondary schools, but also (ii) that absence from secondary schools is less likely to have a legally acceptable explanation. According to education welfare officers' ratings, the majority of persistently absent pupils were at home with their parents' knowledge, though not always with their active consent.

Statistical analysis of the results showed no important association between a secondary school's size and its absentee rates. On the other hand, there was a close relationship between persistent absenteeism and poverty in the catchment area, as measured by the proportion of pupils receiving free school meals. By knowing the latter, it is possible to predict the number of persistent absentees with a high level of reliability. It is not, however, possible to predict who the absentees will be. At schools with high absentee rates, pupils authorised to receive free meals do not appear more likely to be persistently absent than other pupils.

In an important minority of schools, absentee rates varied substantially over the three years. This indicated that factors operating within the school could also exert an influence on attendance. The evidence suggested that the school's influence is greatest in socially disadvantaged areas where the likelihood of absence is greatest in the first place. Moreover, in these areas reduction in absentee rates was normally associated with obvious developments in the school. Conversely, an increase in absentee rates was usually associated with equally obvious stresses within the school.

(b) *Persistent Absentees and their Families*

The city-wide surveys provided no evidence about the educational, family and personality characteristics of persistent absentees, nor did it provide any information on the nature of possible contributory factors at school. The next stage of the research was therefore to carry out a detailed study of all unauthorised absentees from one secondary school and its feeding primary schools. The area selected for study contained many social problems and few owner-occupied houses. For comparison purposes two other groups were also included. One consisted of pupils who had been referred to the psychological service on account of their poor school attendance, and the second of good attenders selected from the same class as the secondary school absentees. Information was collected from the pupils, their parents and their schools.

The results showed clearly that persistent absentees from primary schools were living under severely and multiply disadvantaged circumstances. The same applied, though somewhat less consistently, to secondary school absentees and to absentees who had been referred to the psychological service. Both parents were unemployed in over 50 per cent of the families in the three absentee samples, but in only 9 per cent of the good attenders' families.

Problems at school were seldom reported by parents of primary school absentees as contributory reasons for absence. The general picture with these pupils was not one of serious hostility between home and school, but rather one of massive social and medical problems within the home. These seemed to have the effect of reducing regular school attendance to a rather low position in the family's scale of priorities. Many of the same problems were also evident in the families of secondary school absentees, but with this age-group school influences became increasingly important. Clashes with individual teachers, difficulties with particular subjects in the curriculum, and difficulty in social adjustment at school were reported both by pupils and by parents. Pupils referred to the psychological service tended to have a more serious history of anti-social behaviour at home and of inadequacy in social relationships at school.

An important observation was that many absentees resisted pressure to attend school at least in part because of anxiety about their parents' health. Information obtained from their parents showed that this anxiety was often realistic. On a health questionnaire which investigates stress-related symptoms, the mothers of all three absentee samples obtained similar scores to women in another part of England who had been diagnosed at out-patients' clinic as suffering from psychiatric disorder. In this respect our results were consistent with what was already known about the high rates of depression and related symptoms in inner city areas. Our results were also consistent with what was already known about the effect of poor parental health, and particularly poor mental health, on children's development.

The outlook for subsequent school attendance was poor for all three groups of absentees. Primary school absentees were the only group to show any consistent improvement, from an average of 38 per cent in the Autumn term of 1975 to 59 per cent in the Summer of 1977.

(c)   *The Local Education Authority's Response*

The poor subsequent attendance of many pupils raises two questions about l.e.a. policy: First: how does the l.e.a. decide what action to take? Second: what is the effect of intervention on subsequent attendance?

Two statutory procedures are available in cases of poor school attendance:

(i) Parents may be prosecuted in the Magistrates Court under Section 40 of the 1944 Education Act: (ii) Children may be brought before the Juvenile Court, under Section 1 of the 1969 Children's and Young Persons' Act, so that poor school attendance may be used as evidence in care proceedings. In addition, Sheffield Education Committee has for many years contained a School Attendance Section consisting of councillors and co-opted members of the teachers' associations. The functions of the School Attendance Section have been described in a number of ways, of which the two most frequently mentioned are: (i) to provide a final attempt to prevent the necessity for legal action, by impressing on parents the seriousness of their child's absence from school, and (ii) to provide an advisory service for members of the education social work service.

Education welfare officers were interviewed about their reasons for recommending a particular course of action, or for continuing to work with the family informally, without recourse to formal intervention. In addition, we recorded the subsequent attendance of all pupils aged fourteen or under who had been the subjects of formal intervention in one school year, and of a group of unauthorised absentees, with equally poor attendance, against whom no formal intervention had been taken.

The results suggested that education welfare officers did not all share the same views about the usefulness of formal intervention. Consequently they differed in the circumstances in which they advocated it. In spite of these differences, however, it was clear that the majority of education welfare officers did from time to time have clients who appeared before the School Attendance Section. Moreover, recommendations made by the Section were generally followed, even when they differed from those of the officer concerned. The evidence suggests that this body has a considerable influence on subsequent action by the l.e.a.

Persistent absentees against whom no formal action had so far been taken were more likely to have a history of unnecessarily prolonged illness, and less likely to have committed offences, than pupils against whom the l.e.a. had taken action. Pupils brought before the Juvenile Court were more likely to have a history of truancy, and to be regarded as beyond their parents' control. In general, e.w.o.s reported that they had been able to establish satisfactory relationships more easily with parents than with pupils. Similarly, they appeared a great deal more knowledgeable about stresses the child experienced at home than about possible difficulties at school. Nearly half the e.w.o.s said the parents had never visited their child's school.

The subsequent attendance of pupils brought before the School Attendance Section, the Magistrates Court and the Juvenile Court showed a marginal improvement immediately after action was taken. The group with the highest average attendance before formal intervention was the School Attendance Section. These pupils improved on average, from 46 per cent before intervention to 58 per cent for the remainder of the term. No further improvement was noted in the following two years. Results for the Magistrates Court and Juvenile Court samples were even less satisfactory. In contrast, the pupils against whom no formal intervention was taken improved from an average of 34 per cent in the Autumn term 1976, when they were identified as persistent unauthorised absentees, to 60 per cent in the Autumn term 1978. One would like to think this reflected the efforts of their teachers and education welfare officers.

By combining the four samples, we were able to consider the effect on subsequent attendance of a change of school. An ordinary, age-related transfer from primary to secondary school was not associated with better subsequent attendance. In contrast, transfer to a special school led to a spectacular improvement, from an average 15 per cent before transfer to 68 per cent afterwards. A special arranged transfer, from one ordinary school to another, was also associated with improved attendance, from 37 per cent to 62 per cent.

(d) *Implications*

The following policy implications emerge from our programme of research on poor school attendance:

(i) Four years after the raising of the school leaving age, persistent absentee rates in fifth year pupils remained as high as in the first year. While accepting the existence of family and community influences, one must also ask whether the results reflect older pupils' perceptions regarding the benefits of education.

(ii) The majority of unauthorised absentees remained at home with their parents' knowledge. On this evidence searching for truants in the streets and the supermarkets will not solve the problem of persistent un-authorised absence.

(iii) The majority of unauthorised absentees come from families with many and severe financial, social and medical problems. Unless approached with skill and understanding, as well as firmness, such families may quickly come to regard compulsory education as yet another burden imposed by—to them—faceless authority.

(iv) In view of what is known about the children and their families, it is predictable that legal proceedings should be unsuccessful in the majority of cases. It is theoretically possible that such proceedings may be useful "*pour encourager les autres*" but we were not able to investigate this aspect of the question.

(v) It would not be realistic to take legal action at an early stage in the child's absence, in the hope that this would prevent serious problems from developing. Because of pressure on Magistrates, there were frequent, and sometimes lengthy, delays in hearing the cases of the 80 parents and 60 pupils who were brought before the Courts in one year of our study. There is evidence that at least 4000 pupils in Sheffield miss over 25 per cent of their education without an adequate reason. Those who advocate prosecution at an early stage should recognise that this will involve Magistrates in a lot of additional hearings.

(vi)   Persistent absence from school generally results from a complex interaction between family, social and educational problems. All of these need to be recognised in planning the child's return to school. A fruitful role for the e.w.o. may be in establishing a cooperative relationship between parents and teachers. This is a difficult and challenging task, both for e.w.o.s and for teachers, but without it successful action is unlikely.

(vii) Children are sometimes expected to return to schools which are unable to cater for them. This is particularly evident in the final two years of compulsory education. For quite justifiable reasons, many secondary schools concentrate their remedial teaching resources in the younger age-groups. A majority of persistent absentees is severely retarded educationally, perhaps because of previous absences. Nevertheless, older pupils can hardly be expected to view with enthusiasm return to a school which has no remedial teaching facilities, and at which, in consequence, they can only expect to experience educational failure. The implications are: (a) that professionals must set realistic objectives, both for themselves and for their clients, and (b) that these objectives must be set in the light of information about existing resources.

Exclusion and Suspension from School

(a)   *Prevalence and Reasons*

We recorded the number of pupils indefinitely suspended or temporarily excluded* from school in the four years 1975–1979. Only pupils whose exclusion lasted at least three weeks were included in this survey. The results showed a moderate increase in exclusions in the second and third years of the survey. In the fourth year, however, the number of excluded pupils showed a marked drop. Even in the peak year of 1977–1978 less than 50 pupils were indefinitely suspended, with only 39 in 1978–1979. Altogether, less than 100

---

* In Sheffield the term "suspension" implies that the pupil will not be readmitted, at least in the foreseeable future. The term "exclusion" is used when the pupil is sent home temporarily, pending discussion with his parents or assurances about his future behaviour. For the sake of brevity, "exclusion" is used here to include both temporary exclusion and indefinite suspension, unless otherwise stated.

pupils were involved in 1977–1978 and less than 70 in the subsequent twelve months. These figures do not suggest any uncontrollable increase in the size of the problem. It is clear that the number of excluded pupils in 1975–1976 was substantially exceeded in each of the following three years. However, part of the reason for this may have been that the l.e.a.'s procedures were becoming increasingly well known by head-teachers, and consequently that more head-teachers were willing to use them.

The number of pupils involved constituted an extremely small proportion of the total on roll. Exclusions from primary schools never exceeded .01 per cent of the total on roll, while in secondary schools the peak age was the final year of compulsory education, with around .3 per cent in each year of study. More boys were excluded than girls. With boys there was a consistent age-related increase, though the peak in the final year was not as sharp as the peak in persistent absentee rates. With girls there were minimal differences in exclusion rates in the final three years of compulsory education, though the incidence was consistently higher than in the primary school years.

Exclusion seldom resulted from a single, isolated incident, however serious. Rather it reflected a gradual build-up of tension. The precipitating incident sometimes seemed relatively trivial—the proverbial straw that snapped the camel's back. There was a seasonal variation, with more pupils excluded in November, February and March than in other months. Physical violence to teachers was seldom the reason for exclusion. Abusive, threatening or insolent behaviour towards a teacher was the most frequent precipitating incident, followed by bullying, unspecified bad behaviour and disobedience. Truancy was frequently a contributing factor, but seldom the only reason. A substantial minority of pupils was excluded for refusal to accept punishment (usually corporal punishment). In such cases the pupil was normally readmitted, when his or her parents supported the school's decision.

Of the 266 excluded or suspended pupils in the four years of the study, just over 70 were readmitted to their original schools. Fifty had reached school leaving age before the l.e.a. was able to arrange alternative education. Apart from these, the most frequent outcomes were that the pupil transferred to another ordinary school, was placed on home tuition, or was transferred to a special school. Only twenty pupils were placed in the l.e.a.'s centre for disruptive adolescents. The majority of pupils admitted to this centre were admitted because final breakdown was imminent, not because it had already occurred. Of the 266 pupils, 29 per cent were out of school for at least eight weeks before alternative education could be arranged.

(b) *Suspended Pupils and their Families*

The retrospective study described above provided no information about the pupils' educational background, nor about social and psychological factors associated with severely disruptive behaviour. To investigate those areas, we interviewed the parents of pupils who had been suspended indefinitely or excluded for at least a month from 1 May 1978—30 April 1979.

Where possible, we also interviewed the pupils themselves. Interviews with parents showed that suspension from school is not associated with the sort of multiple deprivation which characterises the families of persistent absentees. Only 51 per cent of families lived in the older, less satisfactory forms of council accommodation, and 30 per cent owned their own homes. The parents of 40 per cent of pupils had separated or divorced, but relatively few had died. In both respects, suspended pupils differed little from the comparison group of good attenders in the study of persistent absentees.

As a group the children appeared in good health, but over two-thirds had a history of serious illness, or accidents requiring hospital treatment. This did not apply to their siblings. It was also interesting that over a quarter had a history of illnesses or accidents which might possibly be associated with subsequent minimal neuro-pathology. Poor health was fairly common in the children's parents. Just under half the mothers reported some form of chronic illness, though this was incapacitating in very few cases. Nearly as many had either received medication for minor psychiatric symptoms, or reported symptoms associated with anxiety or depression.

Suspended pupils appeared a particularly vulnerable group in other ways. They were more likely than their siblings to have been in care. Over two-thirds were severely backward educationally. As a group they were highly delinquent, with two-thirds of the boys and a surprising 87 per cent of the girls known to the police. Parents of 78 per cent of the pupils reported truancy, but parents of half the group also admitted that they had occasionally tolerated their children's absence on days when they could have attended.

(c)   *The School's Contribution*

Excluded children were not distributed evenly amongst the city's secondary schools. Schools varied widely in the number of pupils they excluded. Moreover, the differences were consistent from year to year. With only one or two exceptions, the number of temporary exclusions was closely related to the number of indefinite suspensions. Over the four year period six schools reported no exclusions. In the study of suspended pupils and their families, half the secondary school pupils had attended five of the l.e.a.'s 39 secondary schools.

The obvious question which arose from the uneven distribution amongst schools was whether exclusion and suspension were associated with exceptionally disadvantaged catchment areas. The findings were clear. Unlike persistent absenteeism, exclusion was not strongly associated with socio-economic disadvantage. On average, schools with disadvantaged catchment areas excluded neither more nor fewer pupils than schools serving privileged catchment areas.

Since a school's exclusion rate did not appear to be related in any obvious way to problems in its catchment area, we looked for possible explanations in the schools' social, academic and disciplinary organisation. There was some evidence that schools which had incorporated a former selective school on secondary re-organisation tended to exclude more pupils than schools which had not, though this was by no means an invariable relationship. There was also some evidence that schools with high exclusion and suspension rates tended to refer more pupils for special education in schools for the ESN(M) or maladjusted, with no major overlap between exclusion and special educational referrals.

On the other hand, it appeared that policy on ability grouping, and on the organisation of remedial provision was in no way related to exclusion rates. Nor did it seem that some schools preferred to exclude or suspend pupils rather than resort to other sanctions such as corporal punishment. There were wide variations between schools in the use of corporal punishment as reported by pupils, but these were not related to exclusion rates.

Our evidence suggested that exclusion rates reflected each school's own idiosyncratic policy or practice. They did not seem to reflect difficulties in the catchment area, nor any consistent patterns of school organisation or ethos. It is important, however, to emphasise that although policy on exclusion appeared to be idiosyncratic, this does not necessarily imply that it was arbitrary. It is perhaps worth pointing out that places in some of the schools with high exclusion rates were much sought after in the parental option scheme for secondary school places.

(d) *Implications*

The following implications emerge from our study of exclusion and suspension on disciplinary grounds.

(i) Few primary school pupils were excluded from school. To some extent this may be due to the fact that special school places were more readily available for this age-group. It may not be too much of an over-statement to say that difficult primary school pupils are labelled maladjusted and transferred to special schools, while difficult secondary school pupils are liable to be excluded as disruptive.

(ii) Whether a pupil is excluded from school depends at least as much on which school he happens to attend as on any tensions within his family, or any constitutional factors in the pupil himself.

(iii) It is clear that suspended pupils constitute an exceptionally "high risk" group on educational, temperamental and constitutional grounds. They are likely to present problems at any school, but the evidence suggests that these problems only lead to suspension in a minority of schools.

(iv) It is nevertheless important for the l.e.a. to provide suitable assessment and support services in order to cater adequately for excluded pupils. The proportion who would benefit from individual treatment by a psychologist or psychiatrist is very small indeed. It follows that the function of assessment and support services should be to provide schools with practical assistance in catering for these pupils. In cases of formal suspension these services should advise the l.e.a. on the child's educational needs, and on the circumstances in which these needs may best be met.

Special Groups for Disturbing Pupils

(a) *Origins*

By the time of our research seven secondary schools had established special groups. Each group was established by the head-teacher, to cater primarily for the school's own pupils. In most cases the l.e.a. provided limited financial assistance and in four schools it assisted with staffing. All the groups were based on the school's campus, though in three cases in "terrapins"— relocatable buildings.

The groups were not established in response to any common set of problems. The host schools varied in size, catchment area and internal policy on such matters as ability grouping and the organisation of discipline and pastoral care. Because they were established in response to different perceived needs, they had different objectives. One group catered exclusively for younger pupils. Another catered exclusively for older pupils, and three others catered mainly, though not exclusively, for this age-group. The remaining two admitted pupils of all ages, depending on the school's, and pupils, needs at the time. At first five of the groups aimed to cater primarily for deviant, disruptive pupils, who were upsetting the normal life of the school. One aimed to cater for pupils with a wide range of problems, and one for pupils who were not outwardly disruptive, but seemed unable to cope with the social demands of ordinary school life. Three groups started with something of the deterrent philosophy of the "short sharp shock".

Since they opened, the groups had evolved in interesting ways. All of the five groups established primarily for deviant, disruptive pupils had either modified or extended their original objectives. Most still catered for these pupils, but found themselves also able to cater for pupils with a wider range of problems than was at first envisaged. An example in one group was a child with a broken leg, who needed a single base as he could not move around the school.

(b) *Staffing, Organisation and Curriculum*

The number of teachers working in each group ranged from one to eight. In the latter case, the teachers spent part of their time in the group and the remainder in the school's mainstream. By noting the number of hours each teacher worked in the group, it was possible to calculate the number of "full-time equivalent" teachers responsible for it. In each case this ranged between one and two. Three groups had one and a half full-time equivalent teachers. The teacher:pupil ratio was astonishingly favourable, varying between 1:1.6 and 1:5.3. These calculations were based on a week's observation in the group. Even after allowing for pupils who were absent, the teacher:pupil ratio in almost all the groups was more favourable than in special schools for maladjusted pupils.

The seven groups catered for between 7 and 26 pupils in the Autumn term 1978. There was an equally wide variation in the time pupils spent in the groups. In one group they spent an average of 2.7 weeks in the group before returning full-time to ordinary lessons; in another they spent an average of 18.5 weeks.

The number of teachers working in the group had implications for the curriculum. To state the obvious, one teacher cannot easily cover the full range of a secondary school curriculum. It was noteworthy that the amount of time spent in English or Maths ranged from 15 per cent in one group to 48 per cent in another. Similarly, the time spent on other academic work ranged between 12 per cent and 59 per cent. These differences did not seem to depend on whether the pupils were attending full-time or part-time. In principle, all teachers responsible for groups were able to arrange for their subject teacher colleagues to set work for pupils to complete in the group. This was seen as a way of ensuring that the pupil would keep abreast of his original curriculum, thus facilitating his return to ordinary lessons. In practice, some group teachers experienced considerable difficulties in obtaining work from their colleagues. We only saw this happen successfully in one group, though two other teachers told us they could obtain work from colleagues when they needed it.

A striking point about the pupil's work in the groups was their high level of concentration and generally good behaviour. Pupils were rated as "on task" (i.e. concentrating on what the teacher had told them to do) for less than 70 per cent of the time in only one of the seven groups. The favourable teacher–pupil ratio and the formality of some of the groups probably explains this observation. However it is also likely that some pupils welcomed the control and individual attention they received in the groups.

Teachers in the mainstream of each school were asked about their own experience of pupils who had been admitted to a group. Again, we found wide variations from school to school. At one school, only 21 per cent of teachers interviewed believed that the group benefited the pupils who attended it. At another school, 92 per cent believed this to be the case. This latter school had a carefully phased and closely supervised policy for early return to ordinary lessons. This was the school in which pupils spent, on average, less than three weeks in the group full-time, and followed their ordinary timetable while attending it. Subject teachers at this school may perhaps have felt more closely involved in their pupils' progress than at some other schools.

(c)   *Alternatives and Limitations*

As part of the research programme, we interviewed teachers and pupils in three schools in which the head made absolutely clear that he had no wish to establish a special group. The head of one of these schools had previously seen a special group in operation. The experience had convinced him that he did not want one in his school. The principal reason was that pupils in the group developed an identity which was inconsistent with what the rest of the teachers in the school were trying to achieve. The identity was not anti-school so much as pro-group, but this had an adverse effect by tempting other pupils to opt out of the mainstream as well.

Another head-teacher, in a school with a developing tradition of mixed ability teaching, regarded the conforming majority as the strongest pro-school pressure group. By placing children in a special group he felt he would remove the containing influence of this pressure group. Other head-teachers had dismissed this as naïve, wishful thinking, yet the school concerned achieved a significantly greater reduction in its persistent absentee rates between 1974 and 1976 than any other school in Sheffield. The head of the third school developed this theme: "in my experience, as soon as you identify children as problems in this way, they live down to your expectations. It's collecting all of your troubles into one area. In simplistic terms, I'd rather divide than conquer."

The schools with groups had, of course, thought about these problems. Some had in fact occurred. Two points need to be made here. The first is that the dangers inherent in establishing a special group can be overcome; yet the amount of time, energy and resources needed to overcome them and hence to operate the group successfully, should not be underestimated. The second is that some schools appear to have established a curriculum, and discipline and pastoral care system, in which special groups seem unnecessary and/or inappropriate.

The special groups in Sheffield were not established as a formal explicit way of helping schools to reduce the number of pupils excluded. Nor were they established as a way of helping teachers to phase out corporal punishment. It is worth pointing out, however, that they have been set up with these objectives in other l.e.a.s, notably the Inner London Education Authority. Moreover, it was clear that some senior members of Sheffield l.e.a. hoped that encouraging a school to establish a special group might assist that school in containing its disruptive pupils, and thus reduce the number of pupils excluded.

We compared the number of excluded pupils in the two years before six of the groups were set up with the number excluded in the first two years of their existence. (The seventh group was established before the l.e.a. started to keep systematic records on excluded pupils. The school in which this group was based virtually never excluded pupils.) The results showed clearly that opening a special group had no effect on the number of pupils excluded or suspended for disciplinary reasons. It was also clear from interviews with teachers that few, if any, of the schools saw admission to the group as an alternative to corporal punishment, though admission might be considered when other sanctions, including corporal punishment, had failed.

(d) *Implications*

The following implications for school and l.e.a. policy may be drawn from our results.

(i) Establishing a special group with the deterrent philosophy of the "short sharp shock" may create difficulties, for at least two reasons: (a) teachers are generally not prepared to adopt a consistently punitive role, nor are they prepared to adopt an essentially passive custodial role; if the groups are to be staffed by teachers, they must have wider educational or therapeutic objectives which satisfy teachers; (b) disruptive pupils sometimes enjoy the success which they achieve in a formal atmosphere with plenty of hard work; some pupils may enjoy what is intended to deter them.

(ii) Special groups are not a cheap alternative to special schools. Although running costs in the Sheffield groups were low, staffing costs were high.

(iii) Rapid return to ordinary lessons is a frequently stated ideal, but in practice can be difficult to achieve. It is most likely to be achieved when the work of the group is closely integrated with that of the school's mainstream, but this requires a great deal of time and effort on the part of the teacher in charge of the group.

(iv) On our evidence, it would be unwise for policy-makers to hope that, by assisting schools to set up special groups, they will thereby reduce the number of pupils excluded. It would be equally unwise to regard special groups as a form of assistance that might enable schools to phase out corporal punishment. These were not the stated objectives of the Sheffield groups. Special groups *might* be useful in reducing exclusions and in phasing out corporal punishment if these were their explicit objectives. Nevertheless, observation and interviews, both in the groups and in the mainstream of the schools concerned, gives us no confidence that this is a realistic possibility.

(v) Special groups can complement an effective discipline and pastoral care system, but cannot create one. They cannot be expected to solve problems which arise within the mainstream of the school. Behaviour which results either in corporal punishment or in exclusion is an example of such problems. Tackling such problems involves the school as a whole. Special groups are most effective when their aims are clear—and limited.

Concluding Comments

The research programme covered a wide field. Inevitably, some areas were investigated more adequately than others. School attendance and disruptive behaviour are sensitive issues, in which teachers, parents, members of the l.e.a. support services, senior officers of the l.e.a., and elected members of the Educational Committee have different—and often conflicting—interests. Satisfying all of these interests is a forlorn hope.

In planning and carrying out the research programme, the team was guided by two broad aims. First, we wished to provide a body of systematic evidence about controversial educational issues. Second, we wished to promote informed debate about these issues. This summary of our work has consciously acknowledged the distinction between these two aims. In describing each project, I have tried to draw attention to the most important results. These results will certainly be challenged, but they provide as factual a summary as possible of the evidence we obtained. In contrast, the "Implications" section which concludes the report on each project constitutes a conscious attempt to promote debate about the results. It is fully recognised that other people may draw quite different conclusions from the same material. My hope is not that my own tentative conclusions will be accepted, but rather that they will stimulate informed critical discussion about the topics we investigated.

Index

As this book deals with "absenteeism" and "schools" on almost every page, there are no index entries for these terms; readers should consult more specific terms such as "truancy" or "teachers". The detailed Contents table shows the arrangement of broader aspects.
References are given for all authors cited in the text.

Aberdeen, truancy in 34, 40
Absence notes 4
Absentees *see* Children
Academic progress of children 4–5, 65, 85, 91, 128–135 *passim*, 141–4
Acts of Parliament *see under* Children's ... Act *and* Education Act
Adjournment procedure, Leeds Juvenile Court 114–121, 160
Administrative measures against absentees 95–106
Adolescents
case history of 128–35
higher absenteeism of 11, 14–5, 18, 37, 50, 53–4, 109, 127
psychiatric disorders 66
Adult life of former absentees 84, 85
Ages of absent children 11, 14–5, 18, 37, 50, 53–4, 109, 116, 127
Agoraphobia 71
and school refusal 84
Aims of schooling 95, 140–2
Anxiety *see* Fears
Attainment, academic *see* Academic progress
Attendance
obligation to ensure 5–8, 95, 106
regular 50, 58, 60, 62, 65, 68, 138
resumed *see* Return to school
Attendance rates *see* Prevalence of absenteeism
Attendance registers 2, 8, 36, 88
Attitudes to absenteeism
children's 42–3, 55, 68–9, 93, 128–37 *passim*, 181
parents' 20, 35, 37, 68–9, 72–3, 75, 93, 98, 132, 153, 155, 181
teachers' 9, 24, 27, 42, 95, 100, 108, 125, 129, 152–3, 161

Backwardness *see* Retardation
Baldwin, J. 50
Ball, T. 176
Barker, R. 7
Barrett, C. 123
Beaumont, G. R. 85
Behaviour disorders
multiple 64
in school refusal 25–6
truancy-related 23
Behavioural treatments 81–3, 85, 86
Belfast 41
Benefits of schooling
seen by pupils 17, 73–5, 128–37 *passim*, 141–2, 181
seen by teachers 74, 129, 136–8
Berg, I. 25, 56, 80, 83, 84, 115, 116, 118, 119
Bias and selectivity
in diagnosis and research 23, 29, 31, 34–5, 44–5, 76
in prosecution 111–2, 117
in referral 34, 56
Blagg, N. 81, 83, 161
Blame for absenteeism *see* Responsibility
Boredom of pupils 62, 141, 155
Bowlby, J. 79, 80
Boxall, M. 87
Boys' absenteeism, compared to girls' 11, 17, 30–1, 116, 183
Boyson, R. 163
Brandon, R. 88
Bransby, E. R. 9
Brewer, C. 116
Bristol Social Adjustment Guide 10
Broadwin, I. T. 25, 26
Brockington, D. 162
Brooks, D. B. 84

Bullying at school   24, 37, 62
Burt, C.   23, 49

Cain, J.   85
Caning of pupils   73, 130
Cannan, C.   52
Care, commital to   96, 109–11, 118, 120,
   160
Carroll, H. C. M.   4, 27, 49
Case conferences, teachers' and other
   professionals'   124–6
Case studies and histories
   adolescents   128–35
   behavioural treatment   81–2
   integrated support treatment   158–9
   working class boys   42–3
Catchment areas of schools   39, 41, 45–8,
   52–3, 57, 68, 88, 178
Causes of absenteeism *see under* Diagnostic
   categories; Explanations *and*
   Responsibility
Caven, N.   9, 14, 41
Certificate of Qualification in Social
   Work   4, 101
Chadwick, O.   61, 66
Changing schools *see* Transfer
Chazan, M.   21, 25, 26, 27, 78, 80, 81, 86
Child guidance clinics, treatment by   56,
   77–9, 87, 89
Children
   adolescents *see* Adolescents
   ages of   11, 14–5, 18, 37, 50, 53–4, 109,
      116, 127
   attitudes to absence   42–3, 55, 68–9, 93,
      128–37, 181
   attitudes to schooling   17, 55, 73–5,
      128–37, 141–2, 150, 180
   case histories of   42–3, 128–35, 158–9
   committed to care   96, 109–11, 118, 120,
      160
   delinquent   48–52, 91–2, 150
   disruptive   48–52, 123, 134, 141, 155,
      183–4, 186–90
   ESN(M)   67, 147, 185
   excluded from school   7, 52, 162, 182–6
   fears *see* Fears
   home behaviour   91, 179
   illness   6, 8–10, 15, 26, 27–30, 57, 60, 62,
      64, 66, 79, 84, 178
   interviews with   64–6
   relations with parents   *see* Parent-child
      relationship
   school refusers   *see* School refusal
   sex differences in absenteeism   11, 17,
      30–1, 116, 183

teacher-pupil relationship   39, 42, 44, 95,
   129–35, 150–1
truants   *see* Truancy
Children and Young Persons Act 1933   117
Children's and Young Person's Act 1969   6,
   87, 110, 126, 180
Cicourel, A. V.   44
Clarke, R. V. G.   120
Class, social, as factor   5, 12, 40, 42, 46, 68,
   90, 145
Cline, T.   78
Clinical treatments   20, 56, ch. 6
Clyne, M. B.   82
Coleman, J. S., report by   38
Committees *see* Cooperation *and* Truancy
Communication, professionals' *see*
   Cooperation
Community based treatment   87–9
Community influences   12, 23, 37, 38–42
Community service, pupils'   143
Comprehensive schools, compared with
   grammar schools   52, 143, 153
Compulsory education
   legal obligations   5–8, 95, 101, 106
   necessity acknowledged   *preface*, 55, 120
   origins of   1, 43
Condoning of absenteeism, by parents   20,
   35, 37, 68–9, 72–3, 75, 93, 98, 132, 153,
   155, 181
Conduct disorders   23
Contigency contracts, with truants   84
Coolidge, J. C.   82, 83
Cooper, M. G.   21, 23, 24, 26, 27
Cooperation
   by committees of councillors and welfare
      professionals   101–6
   education welfare officers, with
      teachers   88, 122–5, 158–9
   parents, with teachers   138, 140, 153–6
   psychologists, with teachers   77, 87–8,
      125–6, 139, 158–9
   social workers, with teachers   99–101,
      126–7
Cornish, D. B.   120
Corrigan, P.   42, 43, 54, 142
Costs
   fines against parents   108
   residential places for pupils   118
   secondary education   3
   welfare services   4
Councillors, local, involvement with
   absenteeism   101–6
Counselling in schools   84–5, 88, 131
Countesthorpe College   147
Court Committee on Child Health Services,
   report of   87
Courts of law   *see* Juvenile *and* Magistrates'

Cox, K. M. 77
Crime
  adult, of former truants 85
  juvenile 33, 49, 50–1, 91–2
Curriculum 13, 53, 62, 65, 129–37 *passim*,
  142–5, 148
  "hidden" 39, 145, 148, 158
  relevance of 136–7, 142–5, 148
  in residential schools 120

Dain, P. 161
Davidson, S. 21, 80, 83, 86
Delinquency 48–52, 91–2
  and pastoral care 150
Dependency, parent-child 25, 69–70, 92, 93
Depressive illness 71–2, 86
  in school refusal 25–6
Diagnostic categories
  in clinical treatment Ch. 6
  criticism of 32–7
  definitions 21–2
  physically ill pupils 8–10, 57
  in Sheffield survey 29–32
Disadvantage, social (*see also* Poverty) 12,
  18, 22–3, 41–2, 71, 75, 87, 89–90, 93,
  117, 178
Discipline and punishment, school · 24, 27,
  37, 52, 130, 132, 150–1, 182–6
Disruptive children 48–52, 123, 134, 141,
  155, 183–4, 186–90
Doctors
  certificates 6, 28
  visits to schools 78

Eaton, M. J. 14
Education, benefit of *see* Benefit
Education Act 1870 1
Education Act 1876 1
Education Act 1918 1
Education Act 1944 6–7, 21, 166, 180
Education Act 1981 77, 126, 134, 146
Education authorities, local *see* Local
  education authorities
Education in schools *see* Schooling
Educational failure (*see also*
  Retardation) 4–5, 62, 65, 85, 91,
  128–35 *passim*, 141–4
Educational psychologists
  categorising of absentees 20–7 *passim*
  clinical treatment of absentees Ch. 6
  conformism with teachers' judgements
  125–6, 158
  qualifications and roles 77–9
  support services for teachers 77, 87–8,
  139, 158–9

Educational retardation 4–5, 7, 22, 119,
  145–7
Educational welfare officers
  categorising of absentees 9, 15–6, 29–37
  passim
  and clinical treatments 79
  conforming with teachers' judgements
  124–5
Educational welfare officers
  cooperation with councillors 101–6
  cooperation with teachers 88, 122–5,
  158–9
  prosecution of parents 104, 107, 112
  qualifications and training 4, 88
Educational welfare services 4, 29, 35,
  77–8, 88–9, 102
Effectiveness of treatments *see*
  Ineffectiveness
Eisenberg, L. 25, 26, 79
Employment *see* Unemployment
ESN(M) and maladjusted children 67, 147,
  185
Estes, H. R. 25
Ethnic minorities 85, 145
Evans, E. G. S. 21
Evidence about absenteeism
  incompleteness noted 14, 21, 29, 34–5,
  53, 55, 84–7, 112, 167
  sufficiency claimed 122
Examinations, CSE and GCE 66, 128,
  143–4
Exclusion and suspension from school 7, 52,
  162, 182–6
Explanations for absenteeism
  child and family centres 20–8, 37–8,
  53–4, 79
  conflict between 3, 7, 8, 11, 17, 33, 41–2,
  67–8, 76, 80, 86
  illness of pupils 8–10
  psychological *see* 'child and family' *above*
  sociological 7, 39, 42–3
  "Tom Sawyer" theory, rebutted 66
Eysenck, H. J. 80
Eysenck Personality Inventory, Junior 45

Families (*see also* Parents *and* Social
  disadvantage)
  and absenteeism 18, 40, 55, 89, 178–9,
  183–4
  relationships *see* Parent-child relationships
  school refusers' 24–6
  size of 12, 40, 59
  stress 63, 71–2, 93, 111, 119, 129, 137
  suspended pupils' 183–4
  truants' 22–5
Farrington, D. 50

Fears of absentees
  bullying   24, 35, 62
  educational failure   62, 65
  parents' illness   61, 65, 70–1, 129
  teachers   24, 62, 65, 72–4
Ferguson, T.   49
Final school years of pupils   11, 14–5, 18,
  54, 104, 109, 177
Financial disadvantage   40–1, 55, 57, 90,
  108
Fines, imposed on parents   108
Finlayson, D. S.   150
Fitzherbert, K.   88, 122
Fogelman, K.   10, 13, 40
Free school meals   40–1, 55, 178

Galloway, D.   14, 15, 29, 31, 34, 40, 41, 46,
  47, 48, 49, 52, 58, 81, 89, 101, 102, 109,
  111, 112, 119, 123, 126, 136, 140, 147,
  148, 149, 158, 161, 162
Gath, D.   52, 56
Geographical area affecting absenteeism
  12–3
Gillham, B.   77
Girls' absenteeism, compared to boys'   11,
  17, 30–1, 116, 183
Glasgow, prosecutions in   49
Goodwin, C.   147
Gorrell-Barnes, G.   87
Graham, P.   35, 66
Grammar schools   27, 52, 143, 153
Grange Hill, television serial   154
Gray, G.   85
Greenbaum, R. S.   80
Groups, peer, influence on pupils   17, 42–3,
  132, 137, 141
Grover, V. M.   81

Hamblin, D.   39, 148
Hampe, E.   26
Harbison, J.   9, 14, 41
Hargreaves, D.   25, 44, 54, 142, 144
Head-teachers (*see also* Teachers)   15, 48, 79,
  101, 125, 134, 149, 154, 188
Health problems *see* Illness
Health Questionnaire results, in
  Sheffield   61, 66, 91
Her Majesty's Inspectorate of Schools
  (HMI)   120, 124, 162
Hersov, L.   20–1, 23, 24, 26, 49, 59, 76, 79,
  80, 83
"Hidden curriculum"   39, 145, 148, 158
"Hidden truancy"   2, 13, 42, 48, 163
History of absenteeism   1–2, 22
Hoback, J. R.   85

Holman, P.   162
Home background, absentees *see* Families;
  Parents *and* Social Disadvantage
Home behaviour of absentees   91, 179
Home Office, The   101
Horn, P.   22
Hospital based treatment   78, 80, 83, 87
Houghton, D. M.   14

Illness
  children's reason for absence   6, 8–10, 15,
    27–30, 57, 60, 62, 178
  parents'   60–1, 65, 70–2, 91, 129
  psychiatric, in children   64, 66, 79, 84
  "somatic disguise" of school refusers   26
Incidence of absenteeism   *see* Prevalence
Individualism, anti-social effect of   142
Ineffectiveness of measures against
  absenteeism   39, 83–4, 87, 94, 96, 98,
    113–4, 116, 123, 138–40, 159–60, 160,
    164
Information   *see* Evidence
Inner city absenteeism (*see also named
  cities*)   1, 18, 87, 154
Inner London Education Authority   1, 13,
  46–7, 50, 189
Integrated treatment   *see under* Cooperation
Integration of deviant pupils in ordinary
  schools   147
Intelligence
  school refusers'   26
  truants'   23–4
Interactive learning model, rejected   95
Interactive nature of truancy   92
Intermediate treatment units   98–9
Interpretation   *see* Attitudes, Diagnostic
  categories *and* Explanations
Interviews
  by the Sheffield School Attendance
    Section   101–14, 166
  with children   64–6
  with education welfare officers   107,
    111–2, 180
  with families   90–2
  with parents   58–62
Isle of Wight   61

Jackson, B.   153
Jackson, D.   13
Johnson, A. M.   25, 79
Jones, A.   47, 88, 163, 164
Jones, D.   24
Jones, N.   87, 162
Junior Eysenck Personality Inventory   45
Junior schools   *see* Primary schools

Juvenile Courts   6–7, 23, 36, 49–51, 56, 96,
    109–111, 114–21, 160, 180–2

Kahn, J. H.   26, 78, 79
Karweit, N. L.   13
Kennedy, W. A.   82, 83, 84
Kinloch, P.   124
Kitsuse, J. I.   44
Klein, E.   26, 80

Labelling, negative   44–5
Labon, D.   87, 162
Lane, D. A.   161
Lavelle, M.   77
Law, B.   85
Leaving age, school, raising of   15, 17, 177
Leeds Juvenile court procedures   56, 110,
    114–21, 160
Legal obligation to attend school   5–8, 95,
    106
Legal sanctions   *see* Prosecution
Lemert, E. M.   44
Lessons missed in school   2, 13, 42, 48, 163
Leventhal, T.   26
Levitt, E. E.   84, 86
Lewis, G.   149
Libretto, G.   162
Lindsay, G. A.   77
Local education authorities
    administrative and legal measures
        taken   95–121, 179–82
    educational welfare services provided   78,
        88–9
    legal obligations   5–8, 101, 106
Local Government Training Board   88, 102
Lockley, A.   117
London
    Inner London Education Authority   1, 13,
        46–7, 50, 189
    schools in   1, 47, 50, 85, 123
Loughran, J. L.   150
Low income   17, 40–1, 55, 57, 90, 108
Loxley, F. D.   87

Magistrates' courts   36, 96, 106–8, 180–2
Maladjusted and ESN(M) children   67, 147,
    185
Marsden, D.   153
Marshall, T. F.   85
Mawby, R. I.   11
May, D.   4, 12, 14, 21, 34, 40, 49, 50
Medical problems   *see* Illness
Mental deficiency, and truancy   24
Metge, J.   124

Middle schools, in Sheffield   17
Miller, A.   81
Mitchell, S.   11–2, 40, 86
Moore, T.   28, 33
Morgan, R. R.   85
Multiple disadvantage   *see* Social
    disadvantage *and* Poverty
Murgatroyd, S. J.   1, 9, 13, 21, 23, 45, 46,
    149

National Association of Chief Education
    Welfare Officers   9, 12, 14
National Child Development Study   10–1,
    13, 40
Negative labelling   44–5
Neurotic disorders
    school refusal   21, 25–6, 82, 86
    truancy   23, 33
New Zealand   123, 124, 145, 147, 149,
    150–1, 154, 158, 161, 162
Newell, O.   126
Northern Ireland   9, 21, 41
Nursten, J. P.   26, 78, 79

Objections to prosecutions   117–20
Ordinary schools, integration of deviant
    pupils in   147
Outcomes of clinical treatment   83–4

Pack report 1977,   162
Pallister, R.   1
Parent-child relationships
    dependency   25, 69–70, 92, 93
    school refusers'   24, 26, 79–80, 91–3
    truants'   22—25, 91–3
Parents
    attitudes to absenteeism   1, 20, 35, 37,
        68–9, 72–3, 75, 93, 98, 132, 153, 155,
        181
    cooperation with teachers   138, 140,
        153–6, 166
    fined   108
    illness   60–1, 65, 70–2, 91, 129
    interviewed   58–62
    legal obligations   5–8, 95, 106
    prosecution   *see* Prosecution
    warnings to, by Sheffield l.e.a.   104–6
    withholding children from school   22, 28,
        55
Pastoral care   131, 148–52
Patterns of absence   13
Peer groups, influence on pupils   17, 42–3,
    132, 137, 141
Perceptions of absenteeism   *see* Attitudes

Persistent absenteeism
  distinguished from occasional 14–7
  multiple causes of 137–8
  in Sheffield secondary schools 47–8
Phillipson, C. M. 50
Pick, M. 162
Plowden report 1967 9, 38
Police involvment in absenteeism 49, 50,
  97–8
Poverty 17, 40–1, 55, 57, 90, 108
Power, M. J. 50
Pratt, J. 110, 117, 118, 124
Prevalence of absenteeism
  age-related *see* Age
  community factors 12, 23, 37, 38–42
  history of 1–2
  in Northern Ireland 14
  persistent 14–7
  school refusal as part of all absence 12,
    55, 76, 84
  in Sheffield 9–19, 21, 29–31, 177–8
  at times of day, week, month and
    year 13–4
  truancy as part of all absence 12, 55, 76,
    84
  unauthorised absence 9–19, 21
  in urban areas 1, 18, 154
  variation between schools 14, 15, 39,
    45–8, 50, 52, 68, 145, 155, 177
  in Wales 13, 18, 45, 52
Prevention of absenteeism (*see also*
  Treatment) 123
  legal and administrative attempts 97–101
  school based initiatives Ch. 9, Ch. 10
Primary schools
  compared with secondary 16, 30, 54, 55,
    57, 59, 62, 67, 103, 143
  in Sheffield 16–7, 57–8, 71, 73
Professionals, communication between *see*
  Cooperation
Prosecution 6–7, 14, 37, 49, 96, 106–11,
  159–61
  ineffectiveness of 96, 113, 116, 121, 140,
    160
  objections to 117–20
  selectivity of 111–2, 117
Prosser, H. 12, 41
Psychiatric illness
  in children 64, 66, 79, 84
  in parents 61, 70–2, 91
Psychiatrists
  categorising of absentees 20–8
  clinical treatment of absentees Ch. 6
Psychologists, educational *see* Educational
  psychologists
Psychotherapy 77, 79–80, 161
Puberty, higher absenteeism after 37

Punishment and discipline in schools 24, 27,
  37, 52, 73, 130, 132, 150–1, 182–6
Punishment doubled, on prosecuted
  parents 107–8
Pupils *see* Children

Questionaires (*see also* Interviews)
  on health 61, 66, 91
Quinton, D. 52

Rachman, S. 80
Racism, instance of 145
Rainy days, effect on attendance 13
Raising of the school leaving age 15, 17,
  177
Ralphs report 1972 88
Ramsay, P. 39, 145
Ratcliffe, K. 85
Rates of attendance *see* Prevalence of
  absenteeism
Raven's Standard Progressive Matrices 45,
  46
Reading backwardness 65–6, 91, 132–3, 146
Referral
  to psychiatrists and psychologists 14, 25,
    34, 56, 60, 66–7, 76–94 *passim*, 105, 158
  within pastoral care 151–2
Registers of attendance 2, 8, 36, 88
Regular attendance 50, 58, 60, 62, 65, 68,
  138
Reid, K. 141
Reliability of diagnostic categories 33–6
Remedial teaching 65–6, 133–5, 146, 148
Research findings *see* Evidence
Residential schooling 98, 120
Responsibility for absenteeism, ascribed
  to children and families 20–8, 37–8,
    53–4, 88, 94–5, 100, 104–5
  to teachers and schools 1, 24, 27, 39, 42,
    62, 65, 121–3, 138–9, 155, 158, 163–7
    passim
Retardation
  educational 4–5, 7, 22, 119, 145–7
  reading 65–6, 91, 132–3, 146
Return to school 39, 66–7, 80, 81, 83, 84,
  92, 112–6, 160, 162
  insufficient in itself 119, 121, 126, 157,
    159–60
Reynolds, D. 1, 9, 13, 21, 29, 45, 46, 47, 52,
  116
Richardson, K. 12, 40
Rines, W. B. 82
Roach, J. 176
Robins, L. 85, 86
Rodriguez, A. 80, 83

Rosa, P. 86
Rose, G. 85
Ross, A. O. 86
Rowan, P. 162
Rubenstein, D. 1
Rutter, M. 10, 23, 35, 42, 46, 47, 48, 52, 54, 61, 63, 64, 66, 123, 145

Saltmarsh, M. 88
Sandon, E. 13
Sassi, L. C. F. 85
Scherman, A. 81
School Attendance Section, Sheffield 101–14 *passim*, 124, 180
School effectiveness 165–7
School influences
  on persistent absenteeism 14–5, 38–9, 45–8, 61–2, 72–5, 155–6, 184–5
  on school refusal 27, 80
  on truancy 24, 149
School leaving age, raising of 15, 17, 177
School meals, free 40–1, 55, 178
School refusal
  clinical treatment of 79–84
  definitions of 21, 25–7, 32–3, 37
  family relationships 25–6
  prognosis good 33, 39, 83–4, 87, 92
  small proportion of all absence 12, 55, 76, 84
School uniform 140–1
Schooling
  aims of 95, 140–2
  benefits of *see* Benefits
  children's attitudes to 17, 55, 73–5, 128–37 *passim*, 141–2, 150, 181
Scotland 11–2, 34, 40, 49, 162
Secondary modern schools 52
Secondary schools
  adolescents' absenteeism in *see* Adolescents
  compared with primary schools 16, 30, 54, 55, 57, 59, 62, 67, 142–3
Seebohm report 1968, 87
Selectivity and bias
  in diagnosis and research 23, 29, 31, 34–5, 44–5, 76
  in prosecutions 111–2, 117
  in referrals 34, 56
Self concept of children 141–2, 145
Separation anxiety 25, 82, 91
Sex differences in absenteeism 11, 17, 30–1, 116, 183
Sheffield research study, described *preface*, 14–9, 29–32, 57–75, 101–14, 176–90
Shepherd, M. 12
Sills, M. 26
Skynner, R. 81

Social class as a factor 5, 12, 40, 42, 46, 68, 90, 145
Social disadvantage 12, 18, 22–3, 42–3, 71, 75, 87, 88–90, 93, 117, 178 (*see also* Poverty)
Social education teams 88–9
Social learning theory 81
Social workers 4, 36, 77, 87, 88, 91, 93, 99–101, 109, 116, 126–8
"Somatic disguise" 26, 32
Special educational needs 89, 145–8
Special groups, in Sheffield 123, 177, 186–90
Special units 98–9, 161–3
Stott, D. H. 10
Streaming in schools 27, 44–5
Stress
  of children at school 20, 62, 72–4, 111, 137
  in families 63, 71–2, 93, 111, 119, 129, 137
  felt by teachers 95, 152, 155
Subjects, taught *see* Curriculum
Subsequent attendance *see* Return to school
Supervision orders 109, 126
Support services for teachers 158–9
Suspension and exclusion from school 7, 52, 162, 182–6

Talbot, M. 81
Taylor, M. 162
Teacher-pupil relationship 39, 42, 44, 95, 129–35 *passim*, 150–1
Teachers (*see also* Headteachers)
  attitudes to absenteeism 9, 24, 27, 42, 95, 100, 108, 125, 129–35, 152–3, 161
  cooperation with education welfare officers 88, 122–5, 158–9
  cooperation with parents 138, 140, 153–6, 166
  cooperation with psychologists 77, 87, 125–6, 139, 158–9
  cooperation with social workers 99–101, 126–7
  cooperation with each other on curriculum 123
  feared by absentees 24, 62, 65, 72–4
  labelling of pupils 44–5
  morale 94, 123, 135, 152, 164
  need to revive pupils' interest in school 138, Ch. 9, Ch. 10
  past inability to prevent absenteeism 24, 42, 65, 121–3, 158, 163–7
  stress felt by 95, 152–3, 155
  training of 95, 128, 142–3, 155
Teenager *see* Adolescents

Tennent, T. G.   49, 50, 110
Terminology   *see* Diagnostic categories *and*
   Explanations
Therapy   *see under* Treatments
Tibbenham, A.   12
Tizard, J.   87
Tomlinson, S.   146
Tower Hamlets, London   50
Training of teachers   95, 128, 142–3, 155
Transfer between schools
   and school refusal   25
   in Sheffield study   114–5
   primary to secondary   17, 132, 181
   to special schools   114, 161–2
Treatments of absenteeism
   administrative   Ch. 7
   behavioural   81–3, 85, 86
   clinical   32–3, 56, Ch. 6
   ineffectiveness of   39, 83–4, 87, 94, 96, 98,
      113–4, 116, 123, 138–40, 159–60, 162,
      164
   legal   Ch. 7
   psychiatric and psychological   32–3, 56,
      Ch. 6
Trigg, J. E.   13
Truancy
   and crime in adult life   85
   and delinquency   48–52, 91–3
   clinical treatment   84, 89–91
   compared with other kinds of absence
      84–6, 89–93
   definitions of   21, 22–5, 32–3, 37, 89–93
   evidence lacking about,   21, 29, 34–5,
      84–7
   interactive nature of   92
   school influences on   149
   small proportion of all absenteeism   12,
      35, 55, 76
Truancy committees (*see also* School
   Attendance Section)   99–101
Tumelty, A.   85
Tutors, pastoral care   148–52

Tutt, N. S.   120
Tyerman, M. J.   4, 14, 21–4, 28, 33, 40, 41,
   49, 55, 109, 142
Tyrer, P.   84

Unemployment
   parents'   60, 94, 119
   prospects for pupils   66, 74, 85, 99, 129,
      135–6, 162
Uniform, school   140–1
Units, special   98–9, 161–63
Urban absenteeism (*see also named cities*)   1,
   18, 87, 154
U.S.A., former truants in   85
University of Sheffield, Division of
   Education   176

Vacc, N. A.   162
Validity of diagnostic categories   34–6
Variation between schools' attendance
   rates   14, 15, 39, 45–8, 50, 52, 68, 145,
   155, 177
Vauxhall Manor School, London   47

Waldfogel, S.   25
Wales   13, 18, 41, 45, 52, 109
Warnock report 1978,   146, 147, 154
Weather's effect on absence   13
Wechsler's Intelligence Scale for
   Children   65
Wedge, P.   12, 41
Weinberger, G.   81
Werthman, C.   44
West, D. J.   50
White, R.   162
Willis, P.   42, 43, 44, 54, 55, 142
Withholding of children from school   22, 28,
   55
Working class boys, study of   42–3

Yule, W.   81, 82, 83, 86, 161